Microsoft® Office

Outlook® 2007

Introductory Concepts and Techniques

Gary B. Shelly

Thomas J. Cashman

Jeffrey J. Webb

COURSE TECHNOLOGY
CENGAGE Learning™

Australia • Brazil • Japan • Korea • Mexico • Singapore • Spain • United Kingdom • United States

COURSE TECHNOLOGY
CENGAGE Learning™

Microsoft Office Outlook 2007
Introductory Concepts and Techniques
Gary B. Shelly, Thomas J. Cashman, Jeffrey J. Webb

Executive Editor: Alexandra Arnold

Product Manager: Heather Hawkins

Associate Product Manager: Klenda Martinez

Editorial Assistant: Jon Farnham

Senior Marketing Manager: Joy Stark-Vancs

Marketing Coordinator: Julie Schuster

Print Buyer: Julio Esperas

Director of Production: Patty Stephan

Production Editor: Matt Hutchinson

Developmental Editor: Amanda Brodkin

Proofreader: John Bosco

Indexer: Rich Carlson

QA Manuscript Reviewers: John Freitas, Serge Palladino, Chris Scriver, Danielle Shaw, Marianne Snow, Teresa Storch

Art Director: Bruce Bond

Cover and Text Design: Joel Sadagursky

Cover Photo: Jon Chomitz

Compositor: GEX Publishing Services

Printer: Banta Menasha

> For product information and technology assistance, contact us at
> **Cengage Learning Customer & Sales Support, 1-800-354-9706**
> For permission to use material from this text or product, submit all requests online at **cengage.com/permissions**
> Further permissions questions can be emailed to
> **permissionrequest@cengage.com**

ISBN-13: 978-1-4188-5978-7

ISBN-10: 1-4188-5978-8

Course Technology
25 Thomson Place
Boston, Massachusetts 02210
USA

Cengage Learning is a leading provider of customized learning solutions with office locations around the globe, including Singapore, the United Kingdom, Australia, Mexico, Brazil, and Japan. Locate your local office at:
international.cengage.com/region

Cengage Learning products are represented in Canada by Nelson Education, Ltd.

For your lifelong learning solutions, visit **course.cengage.com**

Purchase any of our products at your local college store or at our preferred online store
www.ichapters.com

Printed in the United States of America
7 8 9 10 10

Microsoft® Office
Outlook® 2007
Introductory Concepts and Techniques

Contents

Appendices

Preface

The Shelly Cashman Series® offers the finest textbooks in computer education. We are proud of the fact that our series of Microsoft Office 4.3, Microsoft Office 95, Microsoft Office 97, Microsoft Office 2000, Microsoft Office XP, and Microsoft Office 2003 textbooks have been the most widely used books in education. With each new edition of our Office books, we have made significant improvements based on the software and comments made by instructors and students.

Microsoft Office 2007 contains more changes in the user interface and feature set than all other previous versions combined. Recognizing that the new features and functionality of Microsoft Office 2007 would impact the way that students are taught skills, the Shelly Cashman Series development team carefully reviewed our pedagogy and analyzed its effectiveness in teaching today's Office student. An extensive customer survey produced results confirming what the series is best known for: its step-by-step, screen-by-screen instructions, its project-oriented approach, and the quality of its content.

We learned, though, that students entering computer courses today are different than students taking these classes just a few years ago. Students today read less, but need to retain more. They need not only to be able to perform skills, but to retain those skills and know how to apply them to different settings. Today's students need to be continually engaged and challenged to retain what they're learning.

As a result, we've renewed our commitment to focusing on the user and how they learn best. This commitment is reflected in every change we've made to our Office 2007 books.

Objectives of This Textbook

Microsoft Office Outlook 2007: Introductory Concepts and Techniques is intended for a three- to four-week period in a short course on Outlook 2007, or in a course that teaches Outlook in conjunction with other applications or computer concepts. No experience with a computer is assumed, and no mathematics beyond the high school freshman level is required. The objectives of this book are:

- To offer a brief presentation of Microsoft Office Outlook 2007

- To expose students to practical examples of the computer as a useful tool

- To acquaint students with the proper procedures to create messages suitable for professional purposes and personal use

- To help students discover the underlying functionality of Outlook 2007 so they can become more productive

- To develop an exercise-oriented approach that allows learning by doing

The Shelly Cashman Approach

Features of the Shelly Cashman Series Microsoft Office Outlook 2007 book includes:

- **Project Orientation** Each chapter in the book presents a project with a practical problem and complete solution in an easy-to-understand approach.

- **Plan Ahead Boxes** The project orientation is enhanced by the inclusion of Plan Ahead boxes. These new features prepare students to create successful projects by encouraging them to think strategically about what they are trying to accomplish before they begin working.

- **Step-by-Step, Screen-by-Screen Instructions** Each of the tasks required to complete a project is clearly identified throughout the chapter. Now, the step-by-step instructions provide a context beyond point-and-click. Each step explains why students are performing a task, or the result of performing a certain action. Found on the screens accompanying each step, call-outs give students the information they need to know when they need to know it. Now, we've used color to distinguish the content in the call-outs. The Explanatory call-outs (in black) summarize what is happening on the screen and the Navigational call-outs (in red) show students where to click.

- **Q&A** Found within many of the step-by-step sequences, Q&As raise the kinds of questions students may ask when working through a step sequence and provide answers about what they are doing, why they are doing it, and how that task might be approached differently.

- **Experimental Steps** These new steps, within our step-by-step instructions, encourage students to explore, experiment, and take advantage of the features of the Office 2007 new user interface. These steps are not necessary to complete the projects, but are designed to increase the confidence with the software and build problem-solving skills.

- **Thoroughly Tested Projects** Unparalleled quality is ensured because every screen in the book is produced by the author only after performing a step, and then each project must pass Course Technology's Quality Assurance program.

- **Other Ways Boxes and Quick Reference Summary** The Other Ways boxes displayed at the end of most of the step-by-step sequences specify the other ways to do the task completed in the steps. Thus, the steps and the Other Ways box make a comprehensive reference unit. A Quick Reference Summary at the end of the book contains all of the tasks presented in the chapters, and all ways identified of accomplishing the tasks.

- **BTW** These marginal annotations provide background information, tips, and answers to common questions that complement the topics covered, adding depth and perspective to the learning process.

- **Integration of the World Wide Web** The World Wide Web is integrated into the Outlook 2007 learning experience by (1) BTW annotations that send students to Web sites for up-to-date information and alternative approaches to tasks; (2) a Microsoft Business Certification Program Web page so students can prepare for the certification examinations; (3) a Quick Reference Summary Web page that summarizes the ways to complete tasks (mouse, Ribbon, shortcut menu, and keyboard); and (4) the Learn It Online section at the end of each chapter, which has chapter reinforcement exercises, learning games, and other types of student activities.

- **End-of-Chapter Student Activities** Extensive student activities at the end of each chapter provide the student with plenty of opportunities to reinforce the materials learned in the chapter through hands-on assignments. Several new types of activities have been added that challenge the student in new ways to expand their knowledge, and to apply their new skills to a project with personal relevance.

Q&A

What is a maximized window?

A maximized window fills the entire screen. When you maximize a window, the Maximize button changes to a Restore Down button.

Other Ways

1. Click Italic button on Mini toolbar
2. Right-click selected text, click Font on shortcut menu, click Font tab, click Italic in Font style list, click OK button
3. Click Font Dialog Box Launcher, click Font tab, click Italic in Font style list, click OK button
4. Press CTRL+I

BTW

Minimizing the Ribbon
If you want to minimize the Ribbon, right-click the Ribbon and then click Minimize the Ribbon on the shortcut menu, double-click the active tab, or press CTRL+F1. To restore a minimized Ribbon, right-click the Ribbon and then click Minimize the Ribbon on the shortcut menu, double-click any top-level tab, or press CTRL+F1. To use commands on a minimized Ribbon, click the top-level tab.

Organization of This Textbook

Microsoft Office Outlook 2007: Introductory Concepts and Techniques consists of two chapters on Microsoft Office Outlook 2007, seven appendices, and a Quick Reference Summary.

End-of-Chapter Student Activities

A notable strength of the Shelly Cashman Series Microsoft Office Outlook 2007 book is the extensive student activities at the end of each chapter. Well-structured student activities can

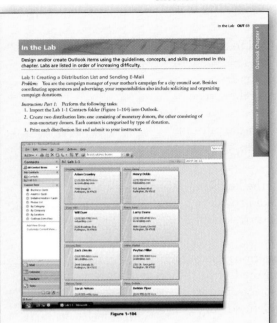

make the difference between students merely participating in a class and students retaining the information they learn. The activities in the Shelly Cashman Series Office books include the following.

CHAPTER SUMMARY A concluding paragraph, followed by a listing of the tasks completed within a chapter together with the pages on which the step-by-step, screen-by-screen explanations appear.

LEARN IT ONLINE Every chapter features a Learn It Online section that comprises six exercises. These exercises include True/False, Multiple Choice, Short Answer, Flash Cards, Practice Test, and Learning Games.

APPLY YOUR KNOWLEDGE This exercise usually requires students to open and manipulate a file from the Data Files that parallels the activities learned in the chapter. To obtain a copy of the Data Files for Students, follow the instructions on the inside back cover of this text.

EXTEND YOUR KNOWLEDGE This exercise allows students to extend and expand on the skills learned within the chapter.

MAKE IT RIGHT This exercise requires students to analyze a document, identify errors and issues, and correct those errors and issues using skills learned in the chapter.

IN THE LAB Three all new in-depth assignments per chapter require students to utilize the chapter concepts and techniques to solve problems on a computer.

CASES AND PLACES Five unique real-world case-study situations, including Make It Personal, an open-ended project that relates to student's personal lives, and one small-group activity.

Instructor Resources CD-ROM

The Shelly Cashman Series is dedicated to providing you with all of the tools you need to make your class a success. Information about all supplementary materials is available through your Course Technology representative or by calling one of the following telephone numbers: Colleges, Universities, and Continuing Ed departments, 1-800-648-7450; High Schools, 1-800-824-5179; and Career Colleges, Business, Government, Library and Resellers, 1-800-477-3692.

The Instructor Resources CD-ROM for this textbook include both teaching and testing aids. The contents of each item on the Instructor Resources CD-ROM (ISBN 1-4239-1226-8) are described on the following pages.

INSTRUCTOR'S MANUAL The Instructor's Manual consists of Microsoft Word files, which include chapter objectives, lecture notes, teaching tips, classroom activities, lab activities, quick quizzes, figures and boxed elements summarized in the chapters, and a glossary page. The new format of the Instructor's Manual will allow you to map through every chapter easily.

LECTURE SUCCESS SYSTEM The Lecture Success System consists of intermediate files that correspond to certain figures in the book, allowing you to step through the creation of a project in a chapter during a lecture without entering large amounts of data.

SYLLABUS Sample syllabi, which can be customized easily to a course, are included. The syllabi cover policies, class and lab assignments and exams, and procedural information.

FIGURE FILES Illustrations for every figure in the textbook are available in electronic form. Use this ancillary to present a slide show in lecture or to print transparencies for use in lecture with an overhead projector. If you have a personal computer and LCD device, this ancillary can be an effective tool for presenting lectures.

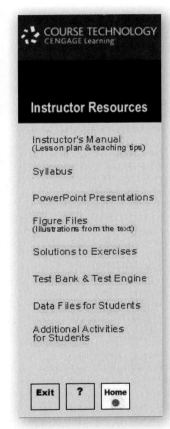

POWERPOINT PRESENTATIONS PowerPoint Presentations is a multimedia lecture presentation system that provides slides for each chapter. Presentations are based on chapter objectives. Use this presentation system to present well-organized lectures that are both interesting and knowledge based. PowerPoint Presentations provides consistent coverage at schools that use multiple lecturers.

SOLUTIONS TO EXERCISES Solutions are included for the end-of-chapter exercises, as well as the Chapter Reinforcement exercises. Rubrics and annotated solution files, as described below, are also included.

RUBRICS AND ANNOTATED SOLUTION FILES The grading rubrics provide a customizable framework for assigning point values to the laboratory exercises. Annotated solution files that correspond to the grading rubrics make it easy for you to compare students' results with the correct solutions whether you receive their homework as hard copy or via e-mail.

TEST BANK & TEST ENGINE In the ExamView test bank, you will find our standard question types (40 multiple-choice, 25 true/false, 20 completion) and new objective-based question types (5 modified multiple-choice, 5 modified true/false and 10 matching). Critical Thinking questions are also included (3 essays and 2 cases with 2 questions each) totaling the test bank to 112 questions for every chapter with page number references, and when appropriate, figure references. A version of the test bank you can print also is included. The test bank comes with a copy of the test engine, ExamView, the ultimate tool for your objective-based testing needs. ExamView is a state-of-the-art test builder that is easy to use. ExamView enables you to create paper-, LAN-, or Web-based tests from test banks designed specifically for your Course Technology textbook. Utilize the ultra-efficient QuickTest Wizard to create tests in less than five minutes by taking advantage of Course Technology's question banks, or customize your own exams from scratch.

LAB TESTS/TEST OUT The Lab Tests/Test Out exercises parallel the In the Lab assignments and are supplied for the purpose of testing students in the laboratory on the material covered in the chapter or testing students out of the course.

DATA FILES FOR STUDENTS All the files that are required by students to complete the exercises are included. You can distribute the files on the Instructor Resources CD-ROM to your students over a network, or you can have them follow the instructions on the inside back cover of this book to obtain a copy of the Data Files for Students.

ADDITIONAL ACTIVITIES FOR STUDENTS These additional activities consist of Chapter Reinforcement Exercises, which are true/false, multiple-choice, and short answer questions that help students gain confidence in the material learned.

Assessment & Training Solutions

SAM 2007

SAM 2007 helps bridge the gap between the classroom and the real world by allowing students to train and test on important computer skills in an active, hands-on environment.

SAM 2007's easy-to-use system includes powerful interactive exams, training or projects on critical applications such as Word, Excel, Access, PowerPoint, Outlook, Windows, the Internet, and much more. SAM simulates the application environment, allowing students to demonstrate their knowledge and think through the skills by performing real-world tasks.

Designed to be used with the Shelly Cashman series, SAM 2007 includes built-in page references so students can print helpful study guides that match the Shelly Cashman series textbooks used in class. Powerful administrative options allow instructors to schedule exams and assignments, secure tests, and run reports with almost limitless flexibility.

Student Edition Labs

Our Web-based interactive labs help students master hundreds of computer concepts, including input and output devices, file management and desktop applications, computer ethics, virus protection, and much more. Featuring up-to-the-minute content, eye-popping graphics, and rich animation, the highly interactive Student Edition Labs offer students an alternative way to learn through dynamic observation, step-by-step practice, and challenging review questions.

Online Content

Blackboard is the leading distance learning solution provider and class-management platform today. Course Technology has partnered with Blackboard to bring you premium online content. Instructors: Content for use with *Microsoft Office Outlook 2007: Introductory Concepts and Techniques* is available in a Blackboard Course Cartridge and may include topic reviews, case projects, review questions, test banks, practice tests, custom syllabi, and more.

Course Technology also has solutions for several other learning management systems. Please visit http://www.course.com today to see what's available for this title.

Workbook for Microsoft Office 2007: Introductory Concepts and Techniques

This highly popular supplement (ISBN 1-4188-4335-0) includes a variety of activities that help students recall, review, and master the concepts presented in Chapter One of Outlook 2007. The Workbook complements the end-of-chapter material with an outline; a self-test consisting of true/false, multiple-choice, short answer, and matching questions; and activities calculated to help students develop a deeper understanding of the information presented.

CourseCasts Learning on the Go. Always Available...Always Relevant.

Want to keep up with the latest technology trends relevant to you? Visit our site to find a library of podcasts, CourseCasts, featuring a "CourseCast of the Week," and download them to your portable media player at http://coursecasts.course.com.

Our fast-paced world is driven by technology. You know because you are an active participant — always on the go, always keeping up with technological trends, and always learning new ways to embrace technology to power your life.

Ken Baldauf, a faculty member of the Florida State University (FSU) Computer Science Department, is responsible for teaching technology classes to thousands of FSU students each year. He knows what you know; he knows what you want to learn. He is also an expert in the latest technology and will sort through and aggregate the most pertinent news and information so you can spend your time enjoying technology, rather than trying to figure it out.

Visit us at http://coursecasts.course.com to learn on the go!

CourseNotes

Course Technology's CourseNotes are six-panel quick reference cards that reinforce the most important and widely used features of a software application in a visual and user-friendly format. CourseNotes will serve as a great reference tool during and after the student completes the course. CourseNotes for Microsoft Office 2007, Word 2007, Excel 2007, Access 2007, PowerPoint 2007, Windows Vista, and more are available now!

To the Student . . .   Getting the Most Out of Your Book

Welcome to *Microsoft Office Outlook 2007: Introductory Concepts and Techniques*. You can save yourself a lot of time and gain a better understanding of the Office 2007 programs if you spend a few minutes reviewing the figures and callouts in this section.

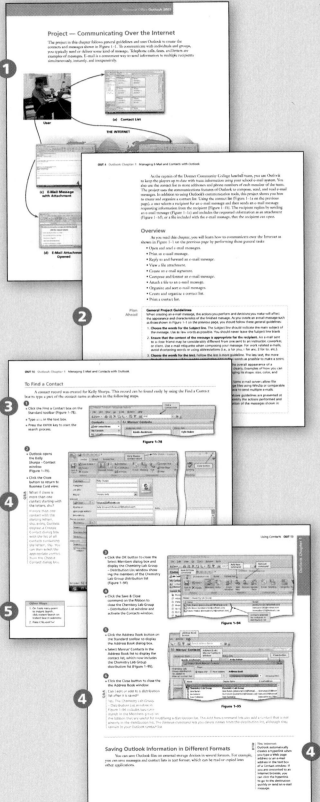

1 PROJECT ORIENTATION
Each chapter's project presents a practical problem and shows the solution in the first figure of the chapter. The project orientation lets you see firsthand how problems are solved from start to finish using application software and computers.

2 PROJECT PLANNING GUIDELINES AND PLAN AHEAD BOXES
Overall planning guidelines at the beginning of a chapter and Plan Ahead boxes throughout encourage you to think critically about how to accomplish the next goal before you actually begin working.

3 CONSISTENT STEP-BY-STEP, SCREEN-BY-SCREEN PRESENTATION
Chapter solutions are built using a step-by-step, screen-by-screen approach. This pedagogy allows you to build the solution on a computer as you read through the chapter. Generally, each step includes an explanation that indicates the result of the step.

4 MORE THAN JUST STEP-BY-STEP
BTW annotations in the margins of the book, Q&As in the steps, and substantive text in the paragraphs provide background information, tips, and answers to common questions that complement the topics covered, adding depth and perspective. When you finish with this book, you will be ready to use the Office programs to solve problems on your own. Experimental steps provide you with opportunities to step out on your own to try features of the programs, and pick up right where you left off in the chapter.

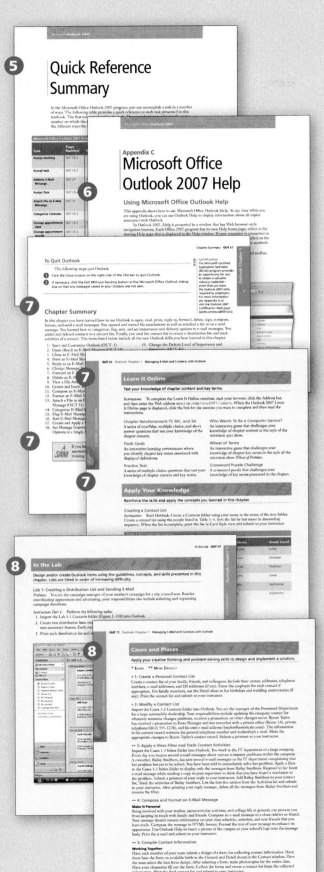

5 OTHER WAYS BOXES AND QUICK REFERENCE SUMMARY
Other Ways boxes that follow many of the step sequences and a Quick Reference Summary at the back of the book explain the other ways to complete the task presented, such as using the mouse, Ribbon, shortcut menu, and keyboard.

6 EMPHASIS ON GETTING HELP WHEN YOU NEED IT
The first project of each application and Appendix C show you how to use all the elements of Office Help. Being able to answer your own questions will increase your productivity and reduce your frustrations by minimizing the time it takes to learn how to complete a task.

7 REVIEW, REINFORCEMENT, AND EXTENSION
After you successfully step through a project in a chapter, a section titled Chapter Summary identifies the tasks with which you should be familiar. Terms you should know for test purposes are bold in the text. The SAM Training feature provides the opportunity for addional reinforcement on important skills covered in each chapter. The Learn It Online section at the end of each chapter offers reinforcement in the form of review questions, learning games, and practice tests. Also included are exercises that require you to extend your learning beyond the book.

8 LABORATORY EXERCISES
If you really want to learn how to use the programs, then you must design and implement solutions to problems on your own. Every chapter concludes with several carefully developed laboratory assignments that increase in complexity.

About Our New Cover Look

Learning styles of students have changed, but the Shelly Cashman Series' dedication to their success has remained steadfast for over 30 years. We are committed to continually updating our approach and content to reflect the way today's students learn and experience new technology.

This focus on the user is reflected in our bold new cover design, which features photographs of real students using the Shelly Cashman Series in their courses. Each book features a different user, reflecting the many ages, experiences, and backgrounds of all of the students learning with our books. When you use the Shelly Cashman Series, you can be assured that you are learning computer skills using the most effective courseware available.

We would like to thank the administration and faculty at the participating schools for their help in making our vision a reality. Most of all, we'd like to thank the wonderful students from all over the world who learn from our texts and now appear on our covers.

Microsoft Office Outlook 2007

1 Managing E-Mail and Contacts with Outlook

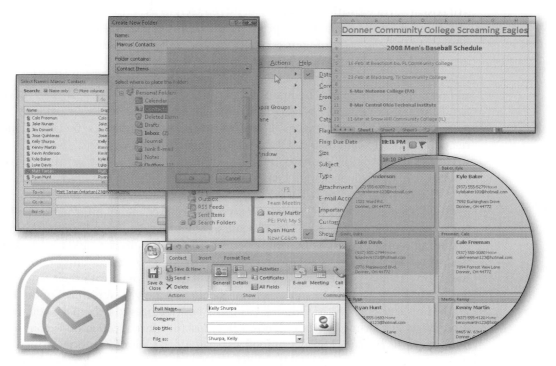

Objectives

You will have mastered the material in this chapter when you can:

- Start and quit Outlook
- Open, read, print, reply to, and delete electronic mail messages
- View a file attachment
- Create and insert an e-mail signature
- Compose, format, and send e-mail messages
- Insert a file attachment in an e-mail message
- Flag, categorize, sort, and filter e-mail messages

- Set e-mail importance, sensitivity, and delivery options
- Create a personal folder
- Create and print a contact list
- Use the Find a Contact feature
- Organize the contact list
- Track activities of a contact
- Use Outlook's Help

1 | Managing E-Mail and Contacts with Outlook

What Is Microsoft Office Outlook 2007?

Microsoft Office Outlook 2007, usually referred to as simply Outlook, is a powerful communications and scheduling program that helps you communicate with others (Figure 1–1), keep track of your contacts, and organize your calendar. Personal information management (PIM) programs such as Outlook provide a way for individuals and work-groups to organize, find, view, and share information easily. Outlook allows you to send and receive electronic mail (e-mail) and permits you to engage in real-time messaging with family, friends, or coworkers using instant messaging. Outlook also provides you with the means to organize your contacts. Users can track e-mail messages, meetings, and notes related to a particular contact. Outlook's Calendar, Contacts, Tasks, and Notes components aid in this organization. Contact information readily is available from the Outlook Calendar, Mail, Contacts, and Task components by accessing the Find a Contact feature.

    Electronic mail (e-mail) is the transmission of messages and files over a computer network. E-mail has become an important means of exchanging information and files between business associates, classmates and instructors, friends, and family. Businesses find that using e-mail to send documents electronically saves both time and money. Parents with students away at college or relatives who are scattered across the country find that communicating by e-mail is an inexpensive and easy way to stay in touch with their family members. In fact, exchanging e-mail messages is one of the more widely used features of the Internet.

    This latest version of Outlook has many new features to help make you more productive. For example, Outlook now offers Instant Search, which finds your information, no matter which folder it is in. Outlook also has added Color Categories, which let you apply the same color category to e-mail, calendar, and task items so you can visually locate all associated items. Outlook has added flags you can use to create and mark a follow-up item for tracking. The new To-Do Bar is a feature that integrates tasks, e-mail messages flagged for follow up, and calendar information in a toolbar located adjacent to the Reading pane.

    To illustrate the features of Outlook, this book presents a series of projects that use Outlook to create and send e-mail messages and create and manage a contact list.

Project Planning Guidelines

The process of composing an e-mail message that communicates specific information requires careful analysis and planning. As a starting point, establish why the message is needed. Once the purpose is determined, analyze the intended readers of the message and their unique needs. Then, gather information about the topic and decide what to include in the message. Finally, determine the document design and style that will be most successful at delivering the message. Creating a contact list is simply a matter of who you want to add to the list. The contact list can be used to store people you have frequent contact with via e-mail, telephone, or fax. The contact list can also be used as a mailing list. Each project in this book provides practical applications of these planning considerations.

Project — Communicating Over the Internet

The project in this chapter follows general guidelines and uses Outlook to create the contacts and messages shown in Figure 1–1. To communicate with individuals and groups, you typically send or deliver some kind of message. Telephone calls, faxes, and letters are examples of messages. E-mail is a convenient way to send information to multiple recipients simultaneously, instantly, and inexpensively.

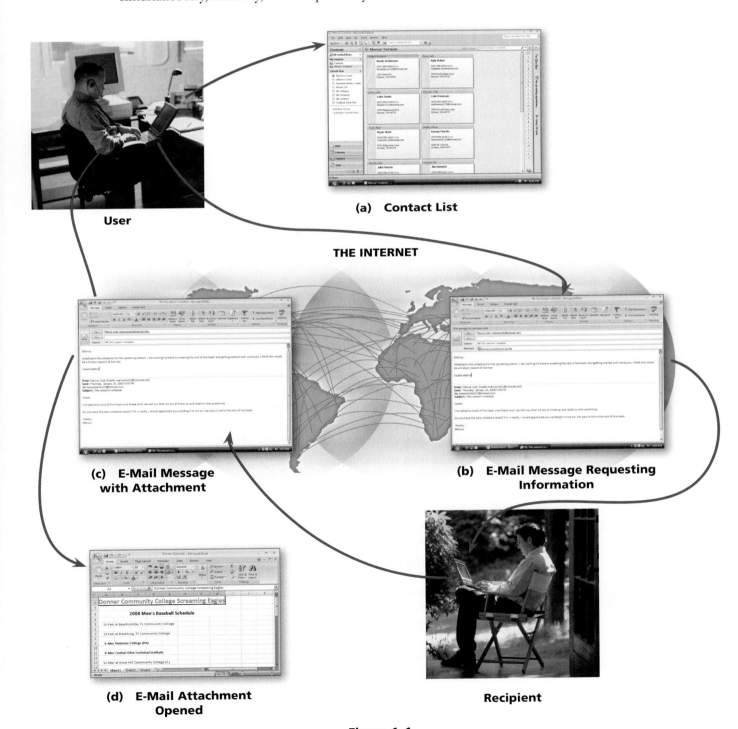

User

(a) Contact List

THE INTERNET

(c) E-Mail Message with Attachment

(b) E-Mail Message Requesting Information

(d) E-Mail Attachment Opened

Recipient

Figure 1–1

As the captain of the Donner Community College baseball team, you use Outlook to keep the players up to date with team information using your school e-mail system. You also use the contact list to store addresses and phone numbers of each member of the team. The project uses the communications features of Outlook to compose, send, and read e-mail messages. In addition to using Outlook's communication tools, this project shows you how to create and organize a contact list. Using the contact list (Figure 1–1a on the previous page), a user selects a recipient for an e-mail message and then sends an e-mail message requesting information from the recipient (Figure 1–1b). The recipient replies by sending an e-mail message (Figure 1–1c) and includes the requested information as an attachment (Figure 1–1d), or a file included with the e-mail message, that the recipient can open.

Overview

As you read this chapter, you will learn how to communicate over the Internet as shown in Figure 1–1 on the previous page by performing these general tasks:

- Open and read e-mail messages.
- Print an e-mail message.
- Reply to and forward an e-mail message.
- View a file attachment.
- Create an e-mail signature.
- Compose and format an e-mail message.
- Attach a file to an e-mail message.
- Organize and sort e-mail messages.
- Create and organize a contact list.
- Print a contact list.

Plan Ahead

General Project Guidelines

When creating an e-mail message, the actions you perform and decisions you make will affect the appearance and characteristics of the finished message. As you create an e-mail message such as those shown in Figure 1–1 on the previous page, you should follow these general guidelines:

1. **Choose the words for the Subject line.** The Subject line should indicate the main subject of the message. Use as few words as possible. You should never leave the Subject line blank.

2. **Ensure that the content of the message is appropriate for the recipient.** An e-mail sent to a close friend may be considerably different from one sent to an instructor, coworker, or client. Use e-mail etiquette when composing your message. For work related e-mails, avoid shortening words or using abbreviations (i.e., u for you, r for are, 2 for to, etc.).

3. **Choose the words for the text.** Follow the *less is more* guideline. The less text, the more likely the message will be read to completion. Use as few words as possible to make a point.

4. **Identify how to format various elements of the text.** The overall appearance of a message significantly affects its ability to communicate clearly. Examples of how you can modify the appearance, or format, of text include changing its shape, size, color, and position on the page.

5. **Alert the recipient when sending large file attachments.** Some e-mail servers allow file attachments up to a certain size. If possible, compress large files using WinZip or comparable software. If several attachments are required, you may have to send multiple e-mails.

When necessary, more specific details concerning the above guidelines are presented at appropriate points in the chapter. The chapter also will identify the actions performed and decisions made regarding these guidelines during the creation of the messages shown in Figure 1–1 on the previous page.

Starting and Customizing Outlook

If you are using a computer to step through the project in this chapter and you want your screen to match the figures in this book, you should change your screen's resolution to 1024×768. For information about how to change a computer's resolution, read Appendix E.

To Start and Customize Outlook

The following steps, which assume Windows Vista is running, start Outlook based on a typical installation. You may need to ask your instructor how to start Outlook for your computer.

Note: If you are using Windows XP, see Appendix F for alternate steps.

1

- Click the Start button on the Windows Vista taskbar to display the Start menu.

- Click All Programs at the bottom of the left pane on the Start menu to display the All Programs list.

- Click Microsoft Office in the All Programs list to display the Microsoft Office list (Figure 1–2).

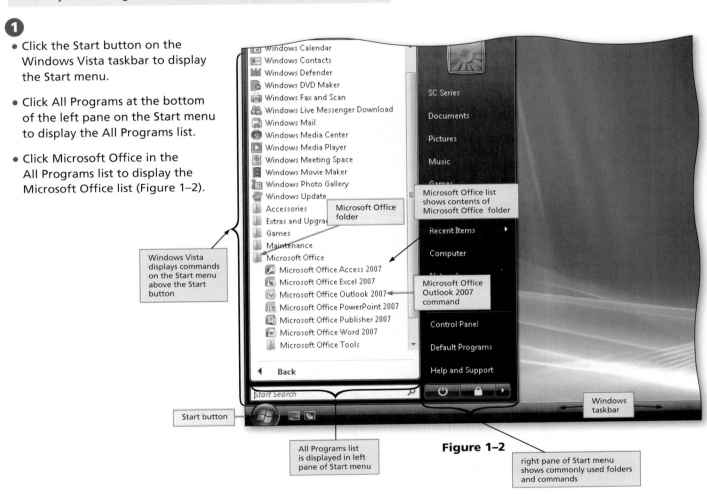

Figure 1–2

2

• Click Microsoft Office Outlook 2007 to start Outlook. If necessary, click the Mail button in the Navigation Pane and then click the Inbox folder in the Mail Folders pane to display the Inbox message pane (Figure 1–3).

• If the Inbox – Microsoft Office Outlook window is not maximized, click the Maximize button next to the Close button on its title bar to maximize the window.

Q&A

What is a maximized window?

A maximized window fills the entire screen. When you maximize a window, the Maximize button changes to a Restore Down button.

3

• Drag the right border of the Inbox message pane to the right so that the Inbox message pane and the Reading pane have the same width.

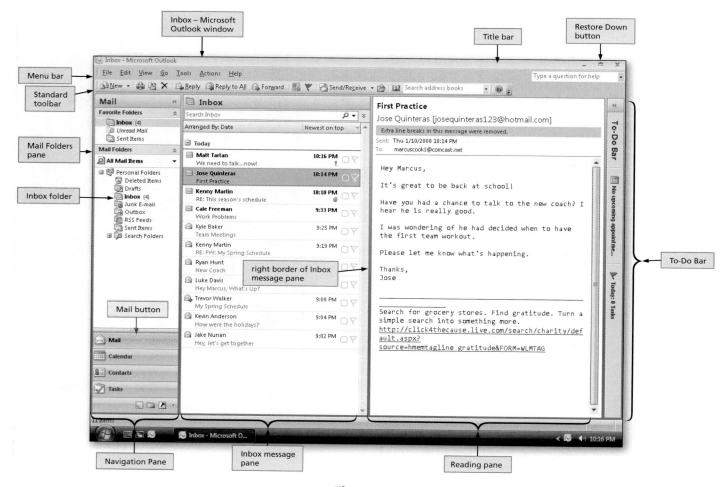

Figure 1–3

Other Ways

1. Double-click Outlook icon on desktop, if one is present

2. Click Microsoft Office Outlook 2007 on Start menu

The Inbox — Microsoft Outlook Window

The Inbox – Microsoft Outlook window shown in Figure 1–3 comprises a number of elements that you will use consistently as you work in the Outlook environment. Figure 1–4 illustrates the Standard toolbar, located below the title bar and the menu bar. The Standard toolbar contains buttons specific to Outlook. The button names indicate their functions. Each button can be clicked to perform a frequently used task, such as creating a new mail message, printing, or sending and receiving mail.

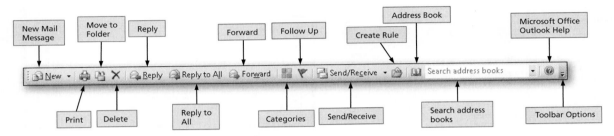

Figure 1–4

The Inbox – Microsoft Outlook window is divided into four panes: the Navigation Pane on the left side of the window, the Inbox message pane to the left of center, the Reading pane to the right of center, and the To-Do Bar on the far right side of the window (Figure 1–5 on the next page).

Navigation Pane   The **Navigation Pane** (Figure 1–5) is set up to help you navigate Microsoft Outlook while using any of the program's components (Mail, Calendar, Contacts, or Tasks). It comprises one or more panes and two sets of buttons. Although the two sets of buttons remain constant, the area of the Navigation Pane above the buttons changes depending on the active Outlook component. When you click the Mail button, Outlook displays Mail in the title bar of the Navigation Pane. When using Mail, the Navigation Pane includes two panes: Favorite Folders and Mail Folders. The **Favorite Folders** pane contains duplicate names of your favorite folders in the Mail Folders pane. To add a folder in the Mail Folders pane to the list of favorite folders, right-click the folder and then click the Add to Favorite Folders.

Below the Favorite Folders pane, the **Mail Folders** pane contains a set of folders associated with the communications tools of Outlook Mail (Deleted Items, Drafts, Inbox, Junk E-mail, Outbox, RSS Feeds, Sent Items, and Search Folders).

The **Deleted Items folder** holds messages that you have deleted. As a safety precaution, you can retrieve deleted messages from the Deleted Items folder if you later decide to keep them. Deleting messages from the Deleted Items folder permanently removes the messages from Outlook. The **Drafts folder** retains copies of messages that you are not yet ready to send. The **Inbox folder** is the destination for incoming mail. The **Junk E-mail folder** is the destination folder for unwanted messages or messages of an unknown origin. You can customize the settings for Outlook to direct only messages that meet certain criteria to the Inbox folder. Messages not meeting those criteria are sent to the Junk E-mail folder. The **Outbox folder** temporarily holds messages you send until Outlook delivers the messages. The **RSS Feeds folder** is new to Outlook. **Really Simple Syndication (RSS)** feeds allow you to receive current information from sources that are updated frequently, such as news headlines or blogs, without having to visit the various Web sites. The **Sent Items folder** retains copies of messages that you have sent. The **Search Folders folder** is actually a group of folders that allows you to group your messages easily in one of three ways – messages for follow up, large messages, or unread messages.

BTW

The Inbox Window
The screen in Figure 1–3 on the previous page shows how the Inbox window looks after you have received several e-mail messages. Your screen may look different depending on your screen resolution and Outlook settings.

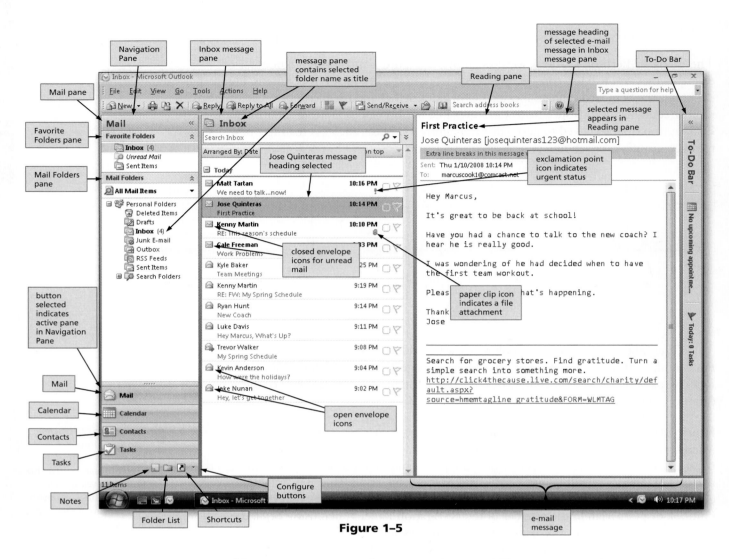

Figure 1–5

Folders can contain e-mail messages, faxes, and files created in other Windows applications. Folders in bold type followed by a number in parentheses, such as **Inbox** (4), indicate the number of messages in the folder that are unopened. Other folders may appear on your computer instead of or in addition to the folders shown in Figure 1–5.

The two sets of buttons at the bottom of the Navigation Pane contain shortcuts to the major components of Outlook (Mail, Calendar, Contacts, Tasks, Notes, Folder List, Shortcuts, and Configure buttons).

Message Pane The Inbox **message pane** (shown in Figure 1–5) lists the contents of the folder selected in the Mail Folders pane. In Figure 1–5, the Inbox folder is selected. Thus, the message pane lists the e-mails received.

Figure 1–6 shows the Arranged By shortcut menu that appears when you click or right-click the Arranged By column header in the Inbox message pane. The command you choose on the Arranged By shortcut menu causes Outlook to display a column header to the right indicating the sort order within the Arranged By grouping. In Figure 1–5, the Arranged By option is Date. This predefined pairing of a grouping and a sort (Arranged By: Date/Newest on top) is called an **arrangement**. Predefined arrangements allow you to sort your messages in various ways.

Several small icons may appear to the right of a message: an **exclamation point icon** indicates that the message is high priority and should be read immediately, a **paper clip icon** indicates that the message contains an attachment. A message heading that appears in bold

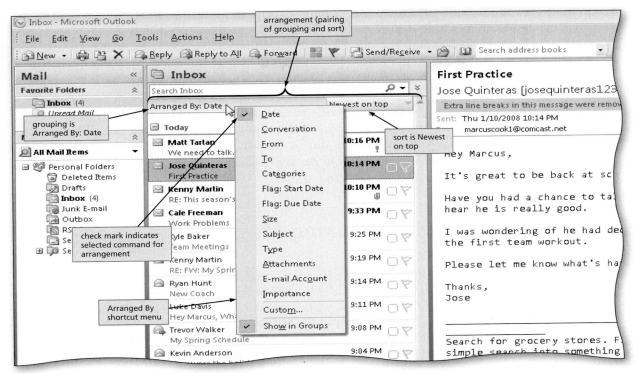

Figure 1–6

type with a **closed envelope icon** to the left identifies an unread e-mail message. An **open envelope icon** indicates a read message. In Figure 1–5, the second e-mail message is highlighted and therefore is displayed in the Reading pane on the right. The closed envelope icon and bold message heading indicate the e-mail message has not been read. The e-mail messages on your computer may be different.

The closed envelope icon is one of several icons called **message list icons**, which appear to the left of the message heading. Message list icons indicate the status of the message. The icon may indicate an action that was performed by the sender or one that was performed by the recipient. The actions may include reading, replying to, forwarding, digitally signing, or encrypting a message. Table 1–1 contains a partial list of message list icons and the action performed on the e-mail message.

Table 1–1 Message List Icons and Actions			
Message List Icon	**Action**	**Message List Icon**	**Action**
	The message has been opened.		The message is in progress in the Drafts folder.
	The message has not been opened.		The message is digitally signed and unopened.
	The message has been replied to.		The message is digitally signed and opened.
	The message has been forwarded.		

Reading Pane The Reading pane (Figure 1–5) contains the text of the selected e-mail message. The message header appears at the top of the Reading pane and contains the e-mail subject (First Practice), the sender's name and/or e-mail address (Jose Quinteras [josequinteras123@hotmail.com]), and the recipient's e-mail address (marcuscook1@ comcast.net). Outlook displays the text of the selected message below the message header. Using the View menu, you can display the Reading pane to the right of the message pane (vertically), as shown in Figure 1–5 on page OUT 8, or you can display it at the bottom of the message pane (horizontally) according to your personal preference.

To-Do Bar   The To-Do Bar is a new feature in Outlook 2007. The To-Do Bar keeps e-mail messages flagged for follow up, tasks, appointments, and other calendar information in one place. When displayed, the To-Do Bar contains a Date Navigator, an appointment list, and a task list. The To-Do Bar is displayed by clicking the double arrow button at the top of the To-Do Bar (Figure 1–5).

BTW

Reading E-Mail Messages
If Outlook is not the active window on your screen, it still provides a mail notification alert informing you when you receive a new message. Outlook displays a semitransparent ScreenTip momentarily by the Outlook icon in the notification area, showing the sender's name, subject of the message, and the first few words of the message body.

Working with Incoming Messages

Note: If you are stepping through this project on a computer and you want your screen to appear the same as in the figures in the Mail component section of this project, then you should ask your instructor to help you (or see page OUT 67) to import Marcus' Inbox from the Data Files for Students. Once you have imported Marcus' Inbox, click the plus sign (+) next to the Inbox folder in the Mail Folders list, and then select Marcus' Inbox folder. See the inside back cover of this book for instructions for downloading the Data Files for Students or see your instructor for information about accessing files for this book.

To Open (Read) an E-Mail Message

To view the complete message in its own window, it must be opened. The following step opens the e-mail message from Jose Quinteras.

1

- Double-click the Jose Quinteras message heading in the Inbox message pane to display the First Practice window (Figure 1–7).

- If necessary, maximize the window.

Q&A

What happens to the message heading in the message pane after the message is opened?

When you double-click the message heading in the message pane, Outlook changes the closed envelope icon to an opened envelope icon, and no longer displays the message heading in bold type.

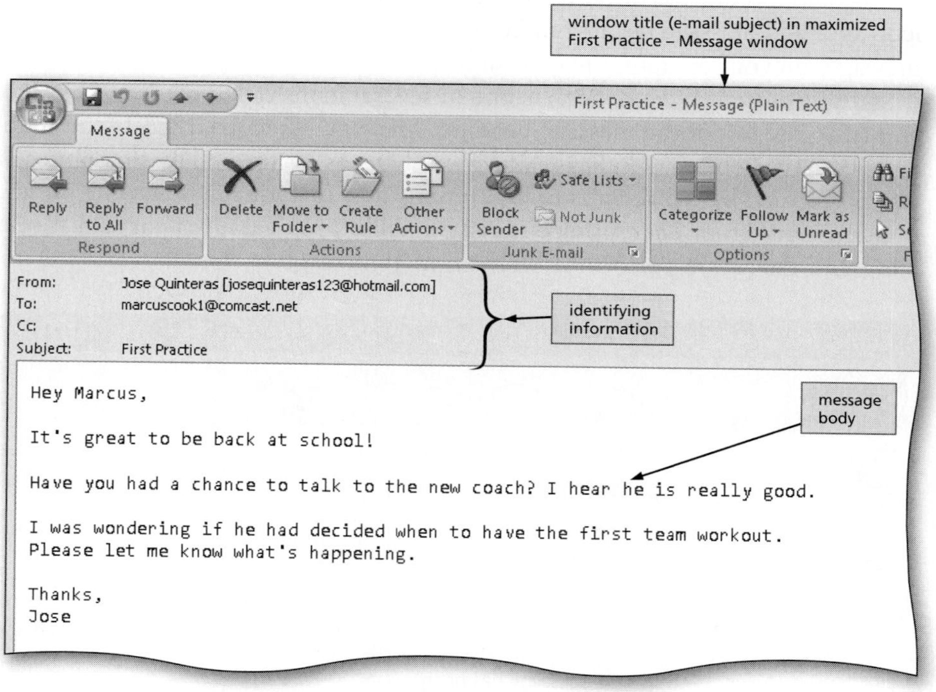

Other Ways

1. Right-click message heading, click Open on shortcut menu
2. Click message heading, on File menu point to Open, click Selected Items on Open submenu
3. Select message heading, press CTRL+O

Figure 1–7

Ribbon

The **Ribbon**, located near the top of the Outlook window, is the control center in Outlook (Figure 1–8a). The Ribbon provides easy, central access to the tasks you perform while creating or working with a message, contact, calendar item, or task. The Ribbon consists of tabs, groups, and commands. Each **tab** surrounds a collection of groups, and each group contains related commands. Figure 1–8a illustrates the Ribbon for the Message window.

When you open a message, the Message window Ribbon displays the Message tab. The Message tab contains the more frequently used commands.

To display more of the document in the document window, some users prefer to minimize the Ribbon, which hides the groups on the Ribbon and displays only the Message tab (Figure 1–8b). To use commands on a minimized Ribbon, click the top-level tab.

Each time you open a message, the Ribbon appears the same way it did the last time you used Outlook. The chapters in this book, however, begin with the Ribbon appearing as it did at the initial installation of the software. If you are stepping through this chapter on a computer and you want your Ribbon to match the figures in this book, read Appendix E.

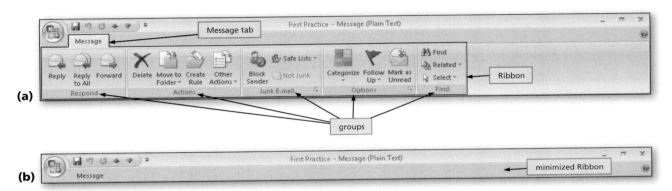

Figure 1–8

Some commands on the Ribbon display an image to help you remember their function. When you point to a command on the Ribbon, all or part of the command glows in shades of yellow and orange, and an **Enhanced ScreenTip** appears on the screen. An Enhanced ScreenTip is an on-screen note that provides the name of the command, available keyboard shortcut(s), a description of the command, and, sometimes, instructions for how to obtain help about the command (Figure 1–9). Enhanced ScreenTips are more detailed than a typical ScreenTip, which usually only displays the name of the command.

BTW

Minimizing the Ribbon
If you want to minimize the Ribbon, right-click the Ribbon and then click Minimize the Ribbon on the shortcut menu, double-click the active tab, or press CTRL+F1. To restore a minimized Ribbon, right-click the Ribbon and then click Minimize the Ribbon on the shortcut menu, double-click any top-level tab, or press CTRL+F1. To use commands on a minimized Ribbon, click the top-level tab.

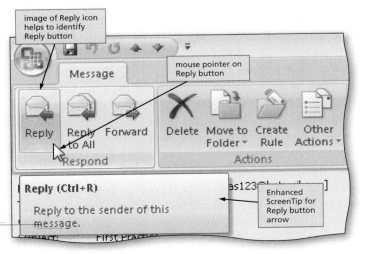

Figure 1–9

The lower-right corner of some groups on the Ribbon has a small arrow, called a **Dialog Box Launcher**, that when clicked displays a dialog box or a task pane with additional options for the group (Figure 1–10). When presented with a dialog box, you make selections and must close the dialog box before returning to the document. A **task pane**, by contrast, is a window that can remain open and visible while you work in the document.

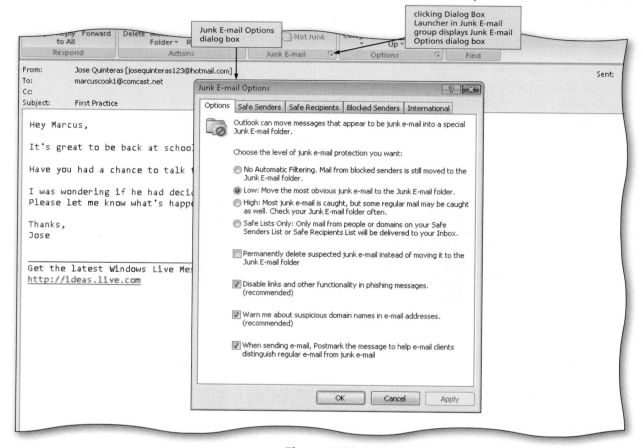

Figure 1–10

Quick Access Toolbar

The **Quick Access Toolbar**, located by default above the Ribbon, provides easy access to frequently used commands (Figure 1–11a). The commands on the Quick Access Toolbar always are available, regardless of the task you are performing. Initially, the Quick Access Toolbar contains the Save, Undo, and Redo commands. If you click the Customize Quick Access Toolbar button, Outlook provides a list of commands you quickly can add to and remove from the Quick Access Toolbar (Figure 1–11b).

You also can add other commands to or delete commands from the Quick Access Toolbar so that it contains the commands you use most often. As you add commands to the Quick Access Toolbar, its commands may interfere with the document title on the title bar. For this reason, Outlook provides an option of displaying the Quick Access Toolbar below the Ribbon (Figure 1–11c).

Each time you start Outlook, the Quick Access Toolbar appears the same way it did the last time you used Outlook. The chapters in this book, however, begin with the Quick Access Toolbar appearing as it did at the initial installation of the software. If you are stepping through this chapter on a computer and you want your Quick Access Toolbar to match the figures in this book, you should reset your Quick Access Toolbar. For more information about how to reset the Quick Access Toolbar, read Appendix E.

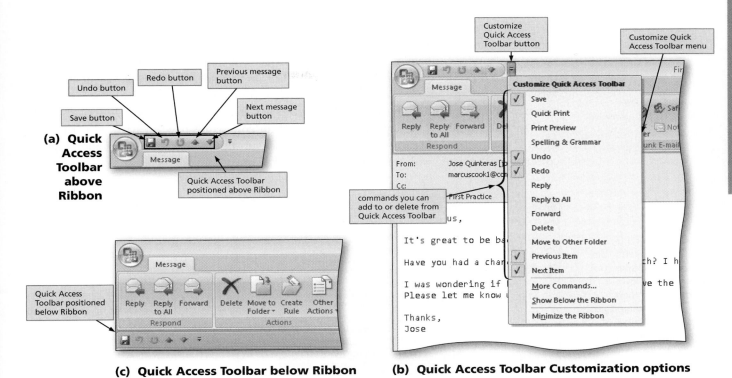

(a) **Quick Access Toolbar above Ribbon**

(c) **Quick Access Toolbar below Ribbon**   (b) **Quick Access Toolbar Customization options**

Figure 1–11

Office Button

While the Ribbon is a control center for creating documents, the **Office Button** is a central location for managing Outlook items. When you click the Office Button, located in the upper-left corner of the window, Outlook displays the Office Button menu (Figure 1–12). A **menu** contains a list of commands.

BTW

Quick Access Toolbar Commands
To add a Ribbon command to the Quick Access Toolbar, right-click the command on the Ribbon and then click Add to Quick Access Toolbar on the shortcut menu. To delete a command from the Quick Access Toolbar, right-click the command on the Quick Access Toolbar and then click Remove from Quick Access Toolbar on the shortcut menu. To display the Quick Access Toolbar below the Ribbon, right-click the Quick Access Toolbar and then click Show Quick Access Toolbar below the Ribbon on the shortcut menu.

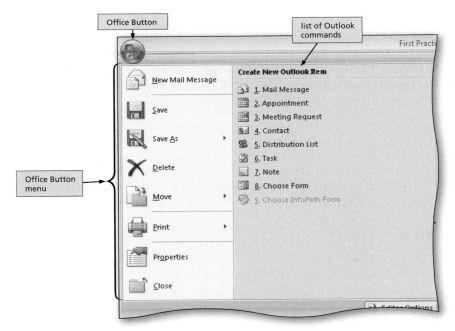

Figure 1–12

When you click the New Mail Message command, Outlook opens the message window to compose a new mail message. When you click the Save command, Outlook saves any changes you may have made to the message. When you click the Save As, Move, Print, and Properties commands on the Office Button menu, Outlook displays a dialog box with additional options. When you click the Delete command, Outlook sends the current message to the Deleted Items folder. When you click the Close command, Outlook closes the Message window. The Save As, Move, and Print commands have an arrow to their right. If you point to this arrow, Outlook displays a **submenu**, which is a list of additional commands associated with the selected command (Figure 1–13).

Spam Filters
If an individual or company is not receiving e-mail from you, it is likely that the recipient's ISP spam filter is not allowing it through to their mailbox. Try sending the message in Plain Text format, because spam filters are less likely to drop an e-mail in Plain Text format.

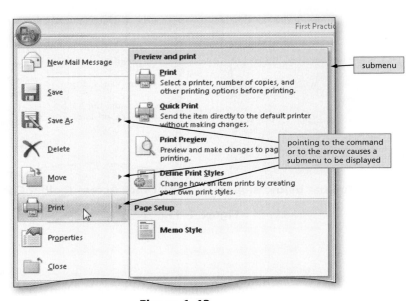

Figure 1–13

Key Tips

If you prefer using the keyboard instead of the mouse, you can press the ALT key on the keyboard to display a **Key Tip badge**, or keyboard code icon, for certain commands (Figure 1–14). To select a command using the keyboard, press its displayed code letter, or **Key Tip**. When you press a Key Tip, additional Key Tips related to the selected command may appear. For example, to select the New Mail Message command on the Office Button menu, press the ALT key, then press the F key, and then press the N key.

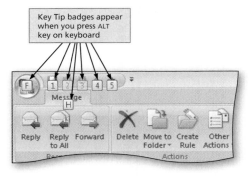

Figure 1–14

To remove the Key Tip badges from the screen, press the ALT key or the ESC key until all Key Tip badges disappear, or click the mouse anywhere in the Message window.

To Close an E-Mail Message

After reading the message from Jose, Marcus closes it. The following step closes the Message window.

1

- Click the Close button on the title bar (Figure 1–15) to close the Message window

Q&A

Why did the number next to the Inbox folder change from 4 to 3?

When you close the Message window, the Jose Quinteras message heading in the message pane no longer appears in bold type and the closed envelope icon changes to an open envelope icon to indicate the message has been opened. In addition, the Inbox folder in the Mail Folders pane indicates three messages remain unopened.

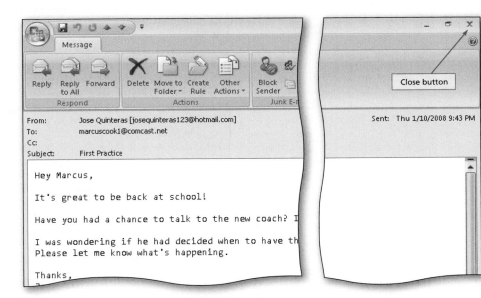

Figure 1–15

Other Ways

1. On Office Button Menu click Close
2. Press ALT+F4

To Print an E-Mail Message

Often, you will want to have a hard copy of your e-mail messages. You print the contents of an e-mail message from the Inbox window. The following steps print the e-mail message from Jose Quinteras.

1

- Point to the Print button on the Standard toolbar (Figure 1–16).

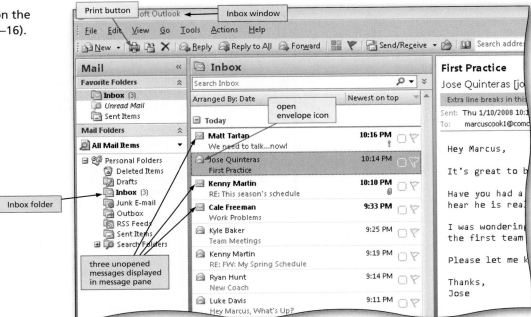

Figure 1–16

2

- Click the Print button to print the message shown in Figure 1–17.

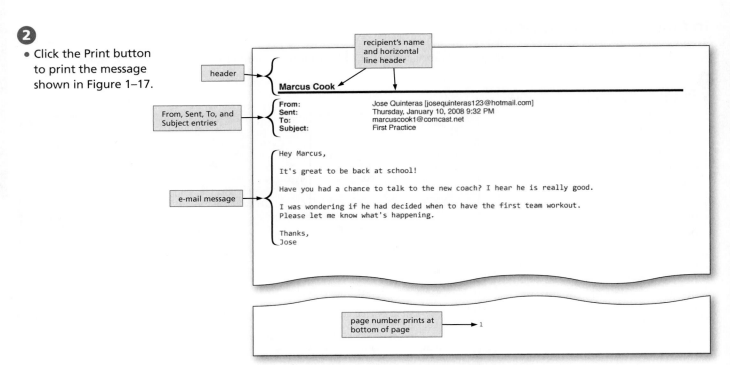

Figure 1–17

Other Ways

1. On File Menu click Print, click OK button	2. Press ALT+F, press P, press ENTER	3. Press CTRL+P, press ENTER

To Reply to an E-Mail Message

The Reply button allows you to reply quickly to an e-mail message using the sender's e-mail address. The following steps reply to the e-mail message from Jose Quinteras.

1

- If necessary, click the Jose Quinteras message heading in the message pane (Figure 1–18).

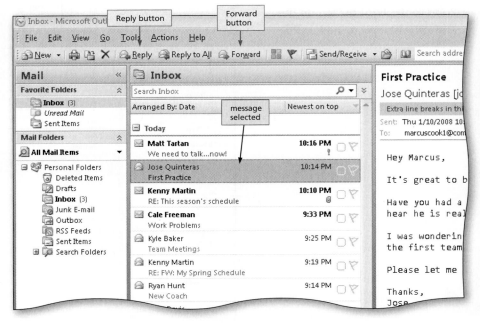

Figure 1–18

2

- Click the Reply button on the Standard toolbar to open the RE: First Practice - Message window.

- When Outlook displays the Message window for the reply, if necessary, double-click the title bar to maximize the window.

- Type the e-mail reply (Figure 1–19).

Q&A

Why is there RE: at the beginning of the Subject line and in the Title bar?

The RE: indicates it is the reply, the subject of the message identifies the title of the window, and Message indicates it is the Message window.

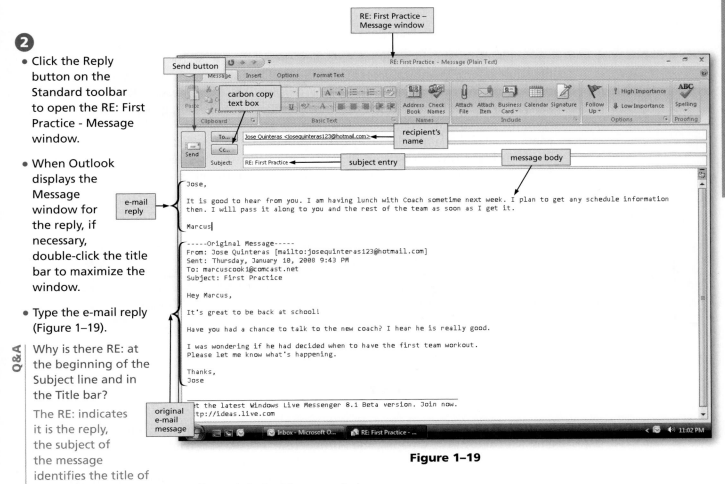

Figure 1–19

3

- Click the Send button to send the message and return to the Inbox window (Figure 1–20).

Q&A

What happened to the sent message?

Outlook closed the Message window and stores the reply e-mail in the Outbox folder while it sends the message. Outlook then moves the message to the Sent Items folder. The original message in the message pane now shows an open envelope icon with an arrow to indicate a reply has been sent.

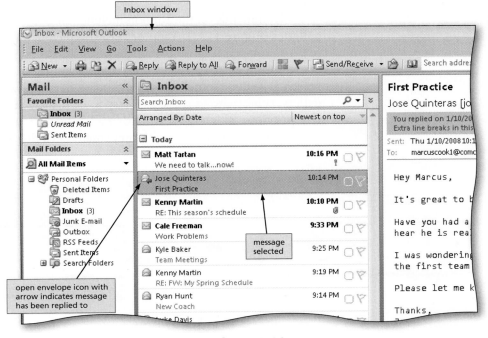

Figure 1–20

New Message Ribbon

The Ribbon for a reply message, new message, or forwarded message is similar to the Ribbon for a Word window (Figure 1–21). The Ribbon provides easy, central access to the tasks you perform while creating a message. The New Message Ribbon, in comparison to the Ribbon discussed earlier, consists of multiple tabs, groups, and commands. As in the previous Ribbon, each tab surrounds a collection of groups, and each group contains related commands. Many of the Ribbon commands will be inactive if the message format is Plain Text. To activate all of the commands, the message must be in HTML or Rich Text format. These formats are discussed later in this chapter.

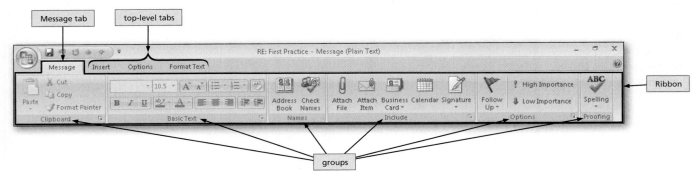

Figure 1–21

When you open a new mail Message window, the Ribbon displays four top-level tabs: Message, Insert, Options, and Format Text. The **Message tab**, called the primary tab, contains the more frequently used commands. To display a different tab on the Ribbon, click the top-level tab. That is, to display the Insert tab, click Insert on the Ribbon. To return to the Message tab, click Message on the Ribbon. The tab currently displayed is called the **active tab**.

Commands on the Ribbon include buttons, boxes (text boxes, check boxes, etc.), and galleries (Figure 1–22). A **gallery** is a set of choices, often graphical, arranged in a grid or list. You can scroll through choices on an in-Ribbon gallery by clicking the gallery's scroll arrows. Or, you can click a gallery's More button to view more gallery options on the screen at a time. Some buttons and boxes have arrows that, when clicked, also display a gallery; others always cause a gallery to be displayed when clicked. Most galleries support **live preview**, which is a feature that allows you to point to a gallery choice and see its effect in the document — without actually selecting the choice.

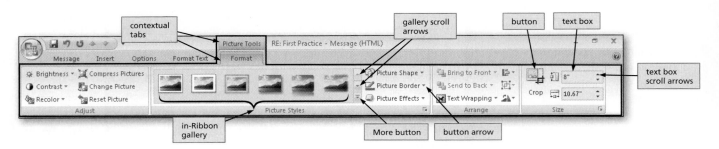

Figure 1–22

In addition to the top-level tabs, Outlook displays other tabs, called **contextual tabs**, when you perform certain tasks or work with objects such as pictures or tables. If you insert a picture in the message, for example, the Picture Tools tab and its related subordinate Format tab appear (Figure 1–22).

Message Formats

Outlook offers three message formats: Plain Text, HTML, and Rich Text, summarized in Table 1–2.

Table 1–2 Message Formats	
Message Format	**Description**
HTML	HTML format is the default format used when you create a message in Outlook. HTML supports the inclusion of pictures and basic formatting, such as text formatting, numbering, bullets, and alignment. HTML is the recommended format for Internet mail because the most popular e-mail programs use it.
Plain Text	Plain Text format is understood by all e-mail programs and is the most likely format to make it through a company's virus-filtering program. Plain text does not support basic formatting, such as bold, italic, colored fonts, or other text formatting. It also does not support pictures displayed directly in the message.
Rich Text	Rich Text Format (RTF) is a Microsoft format that only the latest versions of Microsoft Exchange and Outlook understand. RTF supports more formats than HTML or Plain Text, as well as linked objects and pictures.

To Change Message Formats

The following steps change the message format.

1
- With a Message window active, click the Options tab (Figure 1–23).

2
- Click the appropriate command (Plain Text, HTML, or Rich Text) in the Format group.

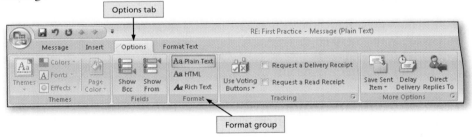

Figure 1–23

To Forward an E-Mail Message

You can forward an e-mail message to additional recipients. The following steps forward the Jose Quinteras e-mail message to the team's coach.

- With the Inbox window active, click the Jose Quinteras message header in the message pane.

- Click the Forward button on the Standard toolbar (Figure 1–24).

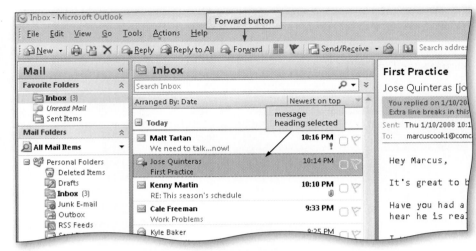

Figure 1–24

- When Outlook displays the Message window for the forwarded message, type kennymartin123@hotmail.com in the To text box as the recipient's e-mail address. (If you are stepping through this task, use an actual e-mail address in the To text box.)

- Enter the forwarding message in the message body (Figure 1–25).

- Click the Send button to forward the original message along with the new message to Kenny.

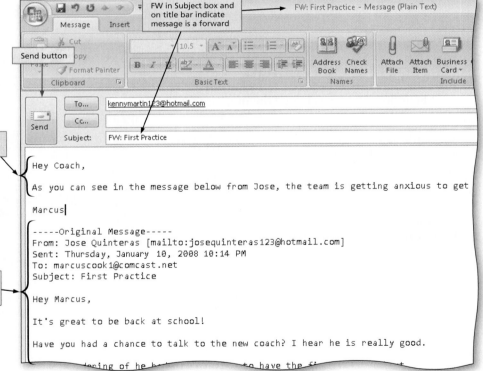

Figure 1–25

Other Ways

1. Right-click message heading, click Forward on shortcut menu

2. Press CTRL+F

To Delete an E-Mail Message

Deleting a message removes the e-mail message from the Inbox folder, saving disk space and making new messages easier to find. The following steps delete the e-mail message from Jose Quinteras.

1

- With the Inbox window active, click the Jose Quinteras message heading in the message pane to select the message (Figure 1–26).

Q&A

Why did the envelope icon for this message change to an open envelope with a forward pointing blue arrow instead of the backward pointing purple arrow?

The backward pointing purple arrow indicated that you replied to the message. The forward pointing blue arrow indicates that you have forwarded the message. The status of the envelope icon represents your last action with the message.

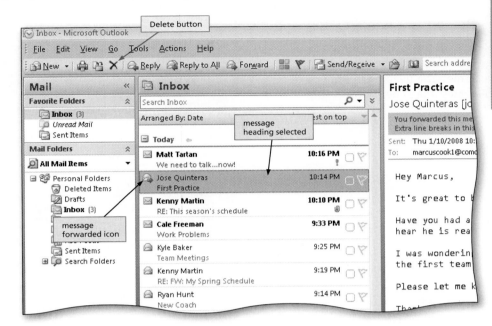

Figure 1–26

2

- Click the Delete button on the Standard toolbar to remove the message from your Inbox (Figure 1–27).

Q&A

Is the message permanently deleted?

Outlook moves the message to the Deleted Items folder. To permanently delete an e-mail message from the Deleted Items folder, click the Deleted Items folder icon in the Mail Folders pane, select the message in the Deleted Items message pane, click the Delete button, and then click the Yes button in the Microsoft Office Outlook dialog box.

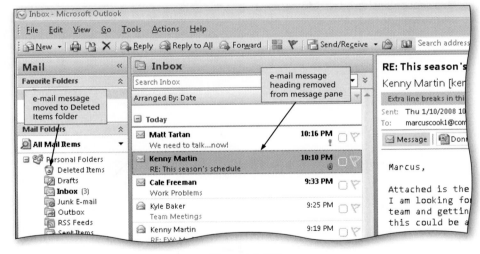

Figure 1–27

Other Ways

1. Drag e-mail message to Deleted Items folder in Mail Folders pane
2. On Edit menu click Delete
3. Press CTRL+D
4. Click e-mail message, press DELETE key

To View a File Attachment

A paper clip icon in a message heading indicates that the message contains a file attachment. The message from Kenny Martin (see Figure 1–28) contains an attachment — in this case, a schedule for the team. The following steps open the message and view the contents of the file attachment.

- With the Inbox window active, double-click the Kenny Martin message heading in the message pane (Figure 1–28).

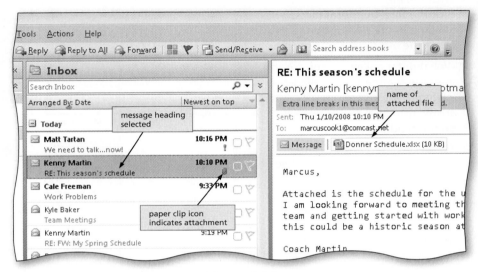

Figure 1–28

- If necessary, maximize the RE: This season's schedule – Message window (Figure 1–29).

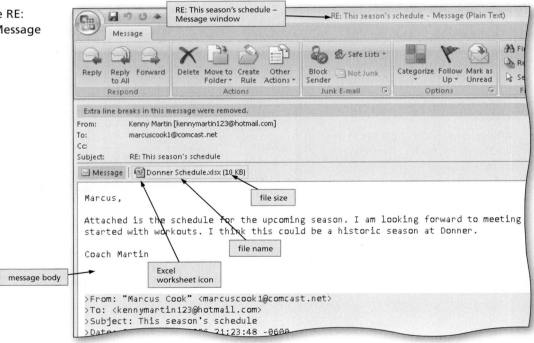

Figure 1–29

3

- Double-click the Donner Schedule icon in the Attachments area to open the Donner Schedule Microsoft Excel file (Figure 1–30).
- If Outlook displays the Opening Mail Attachment dialog box, click the Open button.

Q&A

What type of files can I open?

File attachments can be any type of file; however, files can be viewed only if your computer has the appropriate software. For example, if your computer does not have Excel installed, then you cannot view an Excel file attachment.

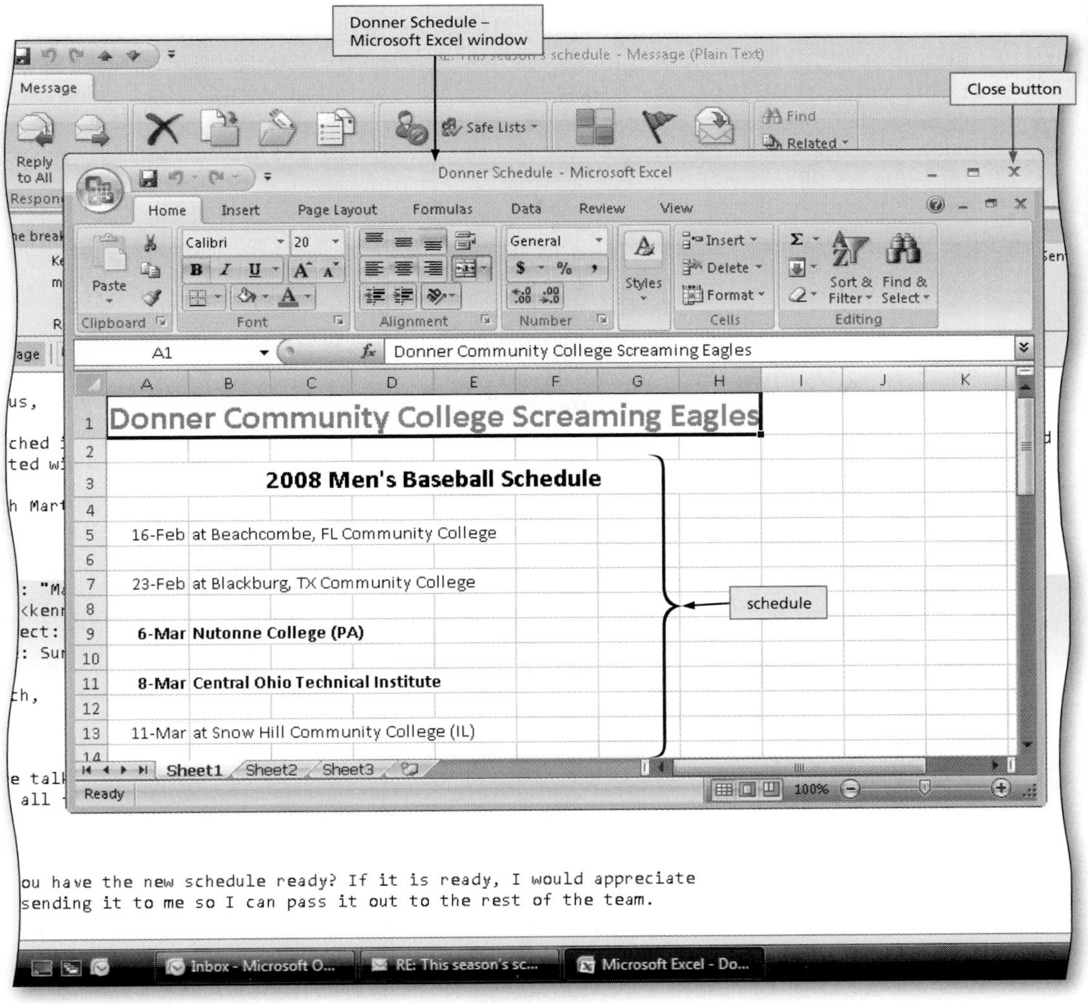

Figure 1–30

4

- After viewing the worksheet, click the Close button on the right side of the title bar in the Excel window to close the attachment and Excel.
- Click the Close button in the Message window.

Other Ways

1. Double-click file attachment name in Reading pane
2. Click Save button in Opening Mail Attachments dialog box to save attachment to hard drive or portable storage device
3. On File menu point to Save Attachments to save attachment to hard drive or portable storage device

Working with Outgoing Messages

Before composing a new mail message, you should create an e-mail signature to save time when sending messages.

An **e-mail signature** is a unique message automatically added to the end of an outgoing e-mail message. It can consist of text and/or pictures. The type of signature you add may depend on the recipient of the message. For messages to family and friends, a first name may be sufficient, while messages to business contacts may include your full name, address, telephone number, and other business information. Outlook allows you to create a different signature for each e-mail account created in Outlook.

To Create and Insert an E-Mail Signature

The following steps create and insert an e-mail signature in an e-mail message. The signature will be used by Marcus in his role as team captain.

- With the Inbox window active, click Tools on the menu bar to display the Tools menu (Figure 1–31).

Figure 1–31

- Click Options on the Tools menu to display the Options dialog box.

- Click the Mail Format tab to display the Mail Format sheet (Figure 1–32).

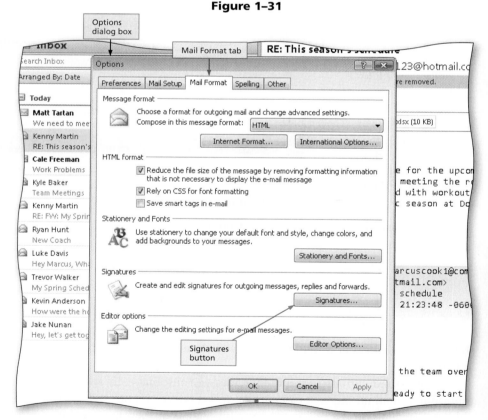

Figure 1–32

3

- Click the Signatures button to display the Signatures and Stationery dialog box (Figure 1–33).

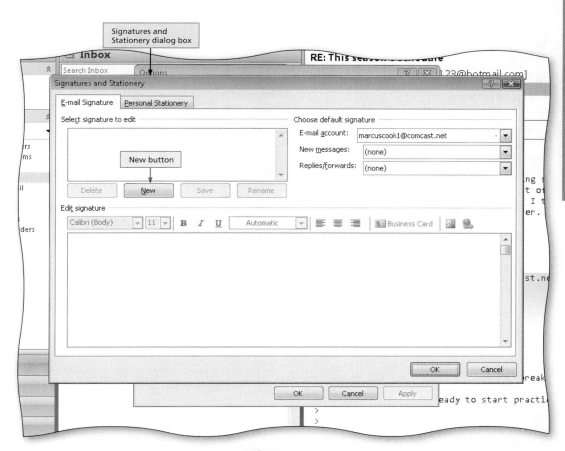

Figure 1–33

4

- Click the New button to display the New Signature dialog box.

- When Outlook displays the New Signature dialog box, type Team in the 'Type a name for this signature' text box (Figure 1–34).

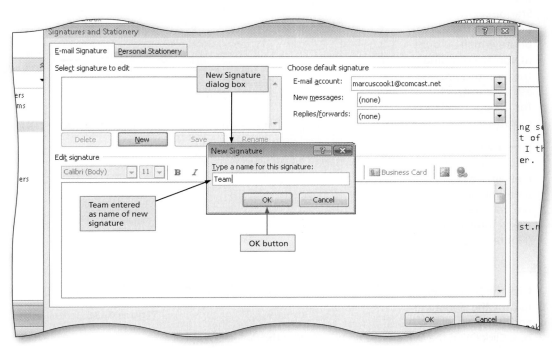

Figure 1–34

- Click the OK button.

- Click in the Edit signature area of the Signatures and Stationery dialog box and type `Marcus Cook – Team Captain` as the signature (Figure 1–35).

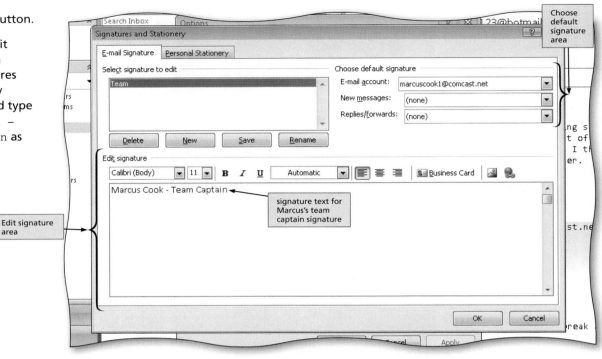

Figure 1–35

- In the Choose default signature area of the Signatures and Stationery dialog box, select the appropriate e-mail account (if you are stepping through this project, ask your instructor for the appropriate e-mail account).

- If necessary, select Team in the New messages box and the Replies/forwards box to select it as the default signature (Figure 1–36).

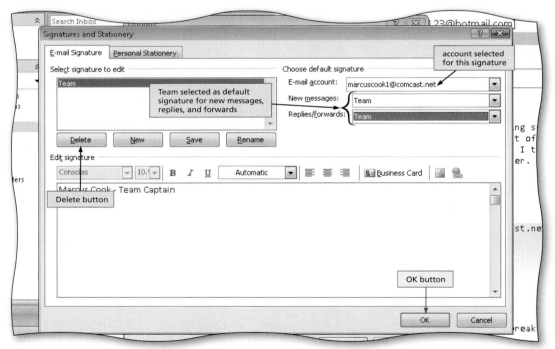

Figure 1–36

- Click the OK button to close the Signatures and Stationery dialog box. Click OK in the Options dialog box to close the dialog box.

Q&A

What do I do with my signature now that it is created?

Your signature will be inserted automatically in all new messages as well as reply and forward messages. You also can modify or remove your signatures at any time using the Signatures and Stationery dialog box.

Other Ways

1. Press ALT+T, press O

E-Mail Signatures for Multiple Accounts

You can create unique signatures for different accounts by adding new signatures and selecting a different account in the Choose default signature area of the Signatures and Stationary dialog box (Figure 1–36).

New Mail Messages

In addition to opening and reading, replying to, forwarding, and deleting e-mail messages, you will have many occasions to compose and send original e-mail messages. When you compose an e-mail message, you must know the e-mail address of the recipient of the message, enter a brief one-line subject that identifies the purpose or contents of the message, and then type the message in the message body.

You also can **format** an e-mail message to enhance the appearance of the message. Formatting refers to changing the style, size, and color of the text document.

BTW

E-Mail Signatures
Outlook allows you to add signatures to your e-mail messages that you create in Word 2007. Some of the advantages to creating them in Word is the ability to insert pictures and hyperlinks into the signature.

To Compose an E-Mail Message

The following steps compose a formatted e-mail message to Kenny Martin with an attachment.

1
- With the Inbox window active, point to the New Mail Message button on the Standard toolbar (Figure 1–37).

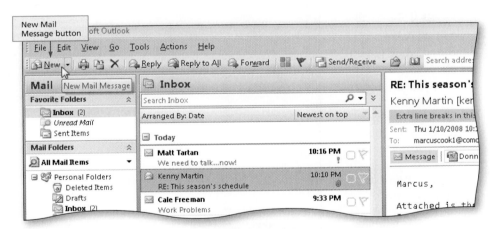

Figure 1–37

2
- Click the New Mail Message button to open the Untitled – Message window (Figure 1–38).

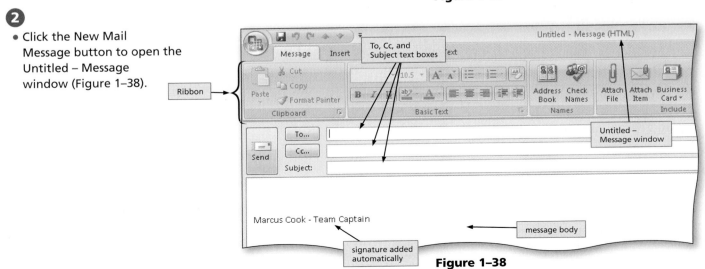

Figure 1–38

- Type kennymartin123@ hotmail.com in the To text box, click the Subject text box, and then type Draft Practice Schedule in the Subject text box (Figure 1–39).

- Press the TAB key to move the insertion point into the message body area.

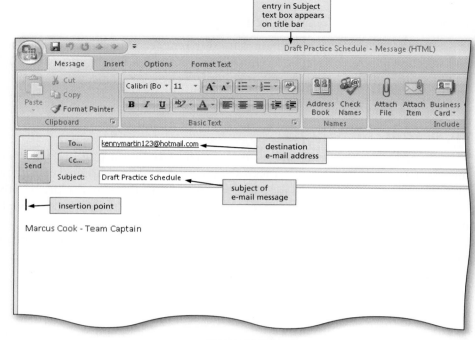

Figure 1–39

- Type the e-mail message (Figure 1–40).

Q&A

What if I make a mistake while typing a message?

When you enter a message, you can use the DELETE key and BACKSPACE key to correct errors. If you are using Microsoft Word as your e-mail editor and you have the appropriate Spelling options selected, then the spell checker will flag the misspelled words with a red wavy line. Furthermore, the message will be spell checked before it is sent.

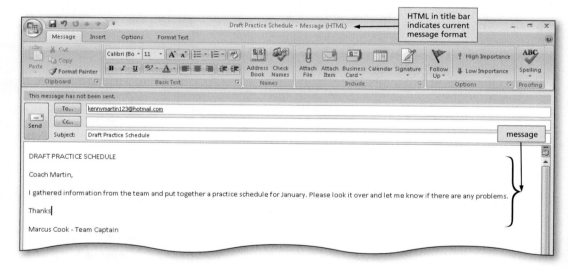

Figure 1–40

To Format an E-Mail Message

Outlook's default message format is HTML, which allows you to customize text with numbering, bullets, alignment, signatures, and linking to Web pages. The following steps center the text, DRAFT PRACTICE SCHEDULE, change the font size to 36-point, and change the color of the text to red. A **font size** is measured in points. A **point** is equal to 1/72 of one inch in height. Thus a font size of 36 points is approximately one-half inch in height.

1
- Highlight the text, DRAFT PRACTICE SCHEDULE, in the message body and then click the Format Text tab (Figure 1–41).

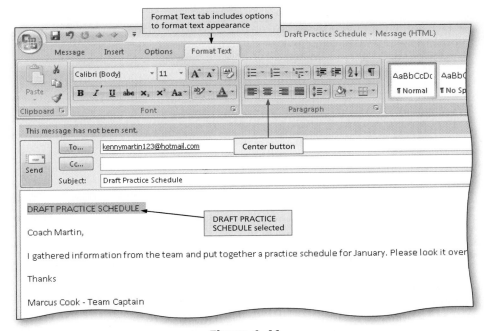

Figure 1–41

2
- Click the Center button in the Paragraph group on the Format Text tab to center the selected text (Figure 1–42).

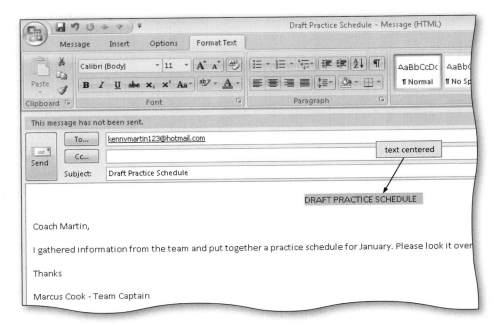

Figure 1–42

● Click the Font Color button in the Font group on the Format Text tab to change the color of the selected text to red (Figure 1–43).

Q&A

How do I pick a color other than red?

To select a font color, click the box arrow on the Font Color button to display a color palette. Simply click a color on the palette to change the color of the text.

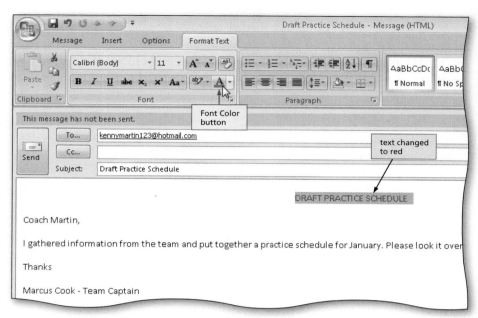

Figure 1–43

● Click the Font Size box arrow in the Font group on the Format Text tab to display the Font Size list (Figure 1–44).

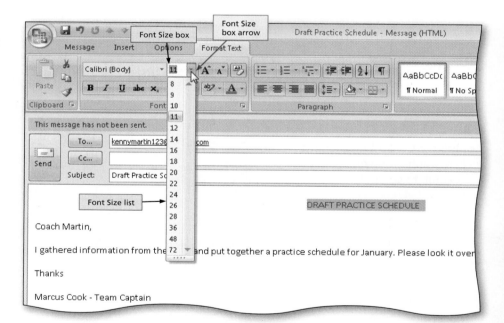

Figure 1–44

5

- Scroll down the Font Size list, click 36, and then click the selected text to remove the selection (Figure 1–45).

Why do I have to select the entire text to change the format?

Because centering is a paragraph format, you can simply click within the text, and then click the Center button. Font size, however, is a character format, so you must select the characters in the entire text before you select a new font size.

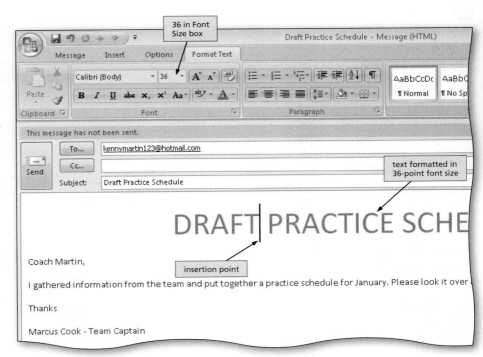

Figure 1–45

To Attach a File to an E-Mail Message and Send the Message

Outlook allows you to attach almost any kind of file to your message. You may need to send a Word document, an Excel worksheet, a picture, or other type of file. The following steps attach the Draft Practice Schedule.xlsx file to the e-mail message.

Note: If you are using Windows XP, see Appendix F for alternate steps.

1

- Click the Insert tab on the Ribbon and then click the Attach File button in the Include group to display the Insert File dialog box (Figure 1–46).

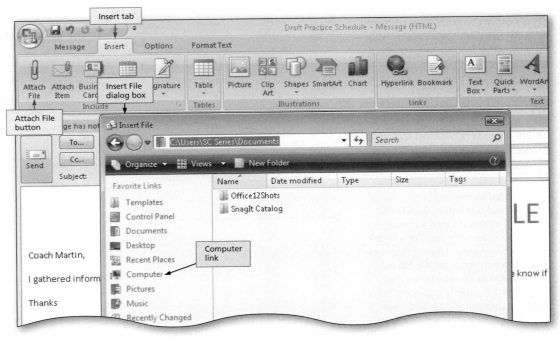

Figure 1–46

2

- With your USB flash drive connected to one of the computer's USB ports, if necessary, click Computer in the Favorite Links section and then scroll until UDISK 2.0 (E:) appears in the list of available drives.

- Double-click UDISK 2.0 (E:) to select the USB flash drive, drive E in this case, in the Look in list as the new open location.

- Click Draft Practice Schedule in the Insert File dialog box (Figure 1–47).

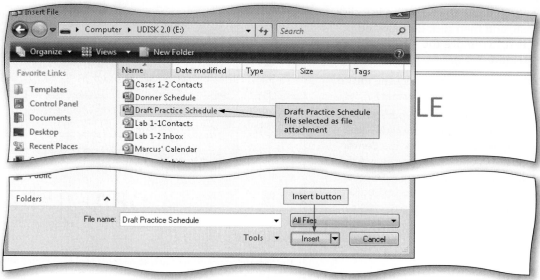

Figure 1–47

- Click the Insert button in the Insert File dialog box to insert the file into the message (Figure 1–48).

Q&A What if I have more than one file to send?

You can attach multiple documents to the same e-mail message. Simply perform the previous steps for each attachment. Keep in mind, however, that some Internet service providers limit the total size of e-mail messages you can attach. You should keep the sum of the file sizes attached to an e-mail message to less than 1 MB.

3

- Click the Send button to send the message and close the Message window (Figure 1–48).

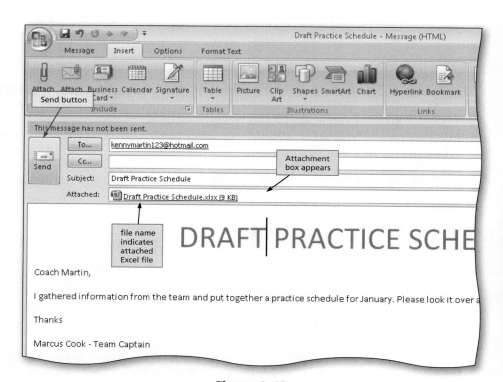

Figure 1–48

BTW

File Attachments
Outlook allows other ways for a file to be inserted into a message. You can drag a file from any folder on your computer to a message, or you can copy and paste a file into a message as an attachment by right-clicking the file, clicking Copy on the shortcut menu, and then in the Outlook message, clicking Paste on the Edit menu.

Organizing E-Mail Messages

Keeping track of your incoming messages can be a challenge, especially if you receive a lot of mail. Two features that can help you organize your messages are the Category box and Follow Up flag, located to the right of the message headings. The **Category box** option on an e-mail message can be assigned one of six different default colors, or you can create your own categories with different colors. Color selection and the meaning of each color are entirely at the discretion of the user. For example, you could assign red to indicate a message from your boss, yellow could mean a message from your best friend, and purple may be a message from your parents.

The **Follow Up flag** option on an e-mail message can be assigned one of five different flags, or you can customize your own Follow Up flag. These flags are used to remind you to follow up on an issue. When you select a flag, Outlook adds a reminder message in the Reading pane. Outlook also adds a task to the To-Do Bar.

To Categorize E-Mail Messages

Marcus would like to organize his messages. The following steps categorize, flag, and sort e-mail messages.

1

- With the Inbox window active, right-click the Kenny Martin message heading to display the message shortcut menu.

- Point to Categorize to display the Categories submenu (Figure 1–49).

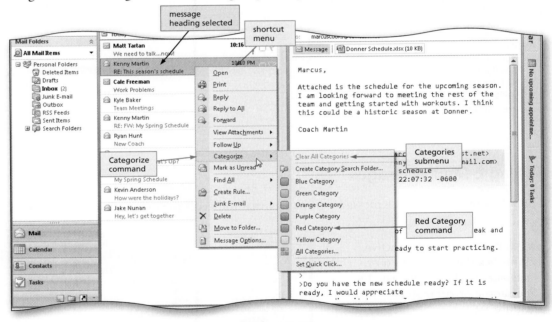

Figure 1–49

BTW

Junk E-Mail Filters

A useful feature in Outlook is the Junk E-mail Filter. The filter is on by default. It automatically evaluates whether an unread message should be sent to the Junk E-mail folder. While you can configure the Junk E-mail Filter to your own personal settings, the default settings evaluate several factors, such as content, time the message was sent, and who sent the message. To change junk e-mail settings, click Options on the Tools menu, and then click the Junk E-mail button in the Preferences sheet of the Options dialog box. Make the preferred changes in the Junk E-mail Options dialog box. Note that the Junk E-mail folder may not be available if you use an Exchange Server e-mail account.

2

- Click the Red Category command on the Categories submenu. If the Rename Category dialog box appears, click No.

- Repeat Steps 1 and 2 to categorize the remaining messages in the message pane (Figure 1–50).

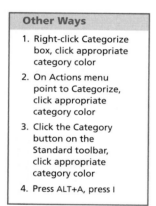

Other Ways

1. Right-click Categorize box, click appropriate category color
2. On Actions menu point to Categorize, click appropriate category color
3. Click the Category button on the Standard toolbar, click appropriate category color
4. Press ALT+A, press I

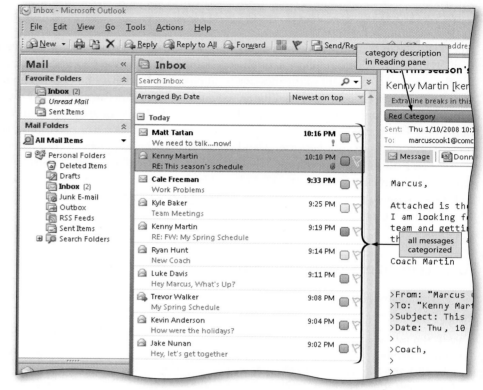

Figure 1–50

To Flag E-Mail Messages

The following steps mark a message with a flag that indicates the message needs to be dealt with today.

- With the Inbox window active, right-click the Kenny Martin message heading to display the message shortcut menu (Figure 1–51).

- Point to Follow Up to display the Follow Up submenu (Figure 1–51).

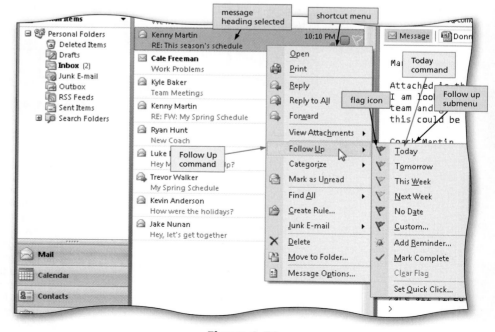

Figure 1–51

2

- Click the Today command on the Follow Up submenu to assign a Follow Up flag with today as the due date.

- Repeat Steps 1 and 2 to add Follow Up flags to the remaining messages in the message pane (Figure 1–52).

- Select different flags as necessary.

Q&A

What does the Follow Up message in the Reading pane mean?

You can select from five default Follow Up flags. The message in the Reading pane corresponds to that selection and assigns a Start date and Due date to the selection (today, tomorrow, this week, and next week).

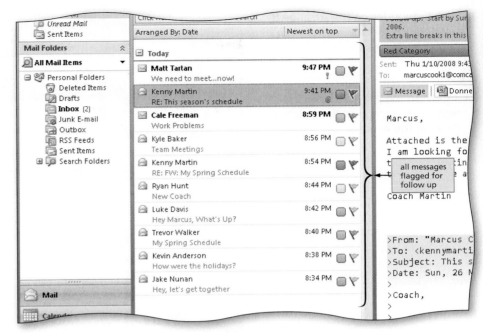

Figure 1–52

Other Ways		
1. Right-click Follow Up flag, click appropriate flag	2. On Actions menu point to Follow Up, click appropriate flag	3. Click the Follow Up button on the Standard toolbar, click appropriate flag
		4. Press ALT+A, press U

To Sort E-Mail Messages by Category Color

After categorizing and flagging the appropriate messages, you can sort the messages by category color. The following steps sort the messages by category color.

1

- With the Inbox window active, click View on the menu bar to open the View menu. Point to Arrange By to display the Arrange By submenu (Figure 1–53).

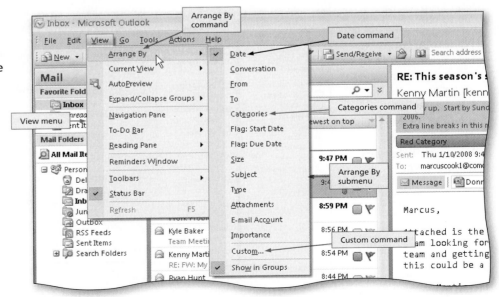

Figure 1–53

2

- Click Categories on the Arrange By submenu to sort the messages by Category (Figure 1–54).

3

- Return to the previous view by repeating Step 1 and then clicking Date on the Arrange By submenu.

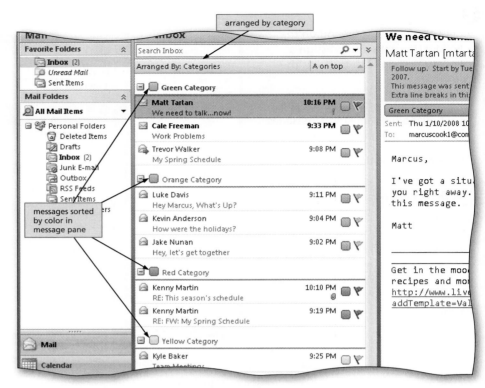

Figure 1–54

To Create and Apply a View Filter

The following steps create and apply a view filter to show only messages from Kenny Martin.

1

- With the Inbox window active, click View on the menu bar.

- Point to Arrange By on the View menu and then click Custom on the Arrange By sub-menu to display the Customize View: Messages dialog box (Figure 1–55).

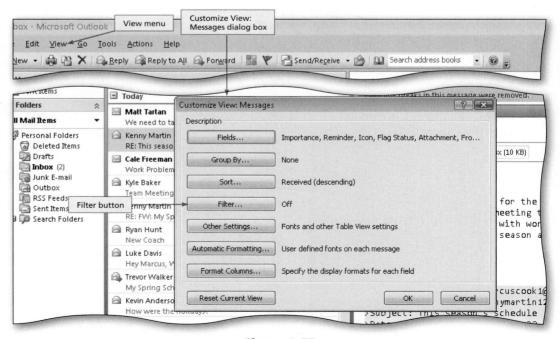

Figure 1–55

- Click the Filter button to display the Filter dialog box.

- Click the From text box (Figure 1–56).

- Type `Kenny Martin` in the From text box to specify that only e-mail messages from Kenny Martin are to appear.

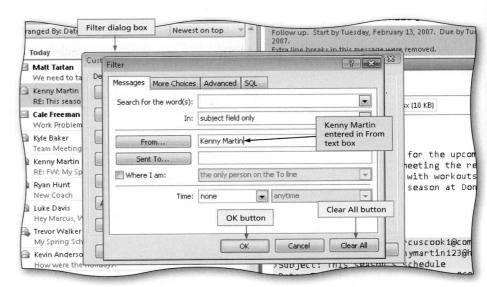

Figure 1–56

- Click the OK button in the Filter dialog box and the Customize View: Message dialog box to close both boxes and apply the view filter (Figure 1–57).

Q&A

How do I know that my other messages have not been deleted?

Outlook displays a message on the status bar and the Inbox pane title bar when a view filter is applied to a selected folder. It also shows the total number of messages remaining in the Inbox folder on the status bar.

4

- Repeat Steps 1 and 2 to display the Filter dialog box.

- Click the Clear All button in the Filter dialog box to remove the view filter.

- Close the Filter and Customize View: Message dialog boxes by clicking the OK button in each dialog box.

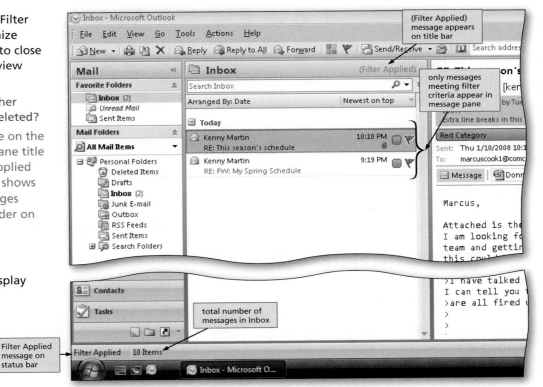

Figure 1–57

E-Mail Message Options

Outlook offers several ways in which you can customize your e-mail. You can either customize Outlook to treat all messages in the same manner, or you can customize a single message. Among the options available through Outlook are setting e-mail message importance and sensitivity. Setting **message importance** will indicate to the recipient the level of importance you have given to the message. For example, if you set the importance at high, a red exclamation point icon will appear with the message heading (Figure 1–58). Setting **message sensitivity** indicates whether the message is personal, private, or confidential. A message banner indicating the sensitivity of the message appears in the Reading pane below the sender's name in the message header, as shown in Figure 1–58.

Along with setting importance and sensitivity, Outlook also offers several delivery options. You can have replies to your message automatically forwarded, save sent messages in a location of your choice (default is Sent Items folder), or delay delivering a message until a specified date and time.

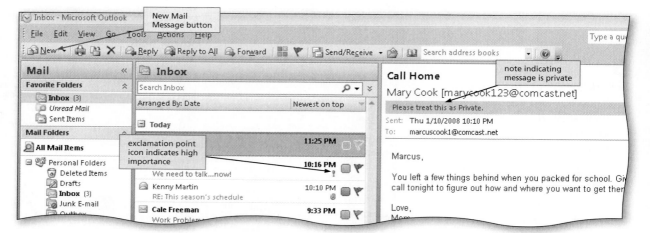

Figure 1–58

To Set Message Importance, Sensitivity, and Delivery Options in a Single Message

The following steps set message importance, sensitivity, and delivery options in a single message.

1

- With the Inbox window active, click the New Mail Message button on the Standard toolbar.

- Enter the message information (Figure 1–59).

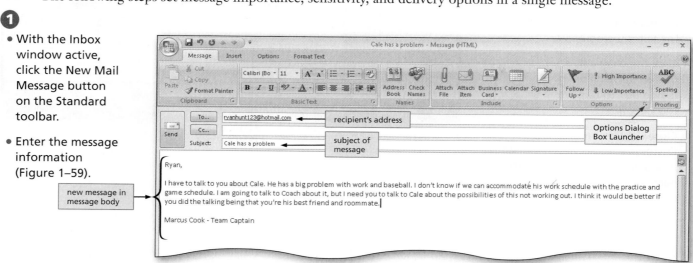

Figure 1–59

2

- Click the Options Dialog Box Launcher on the Ribbon to display the Message Options dialog box (Figure 1–60).

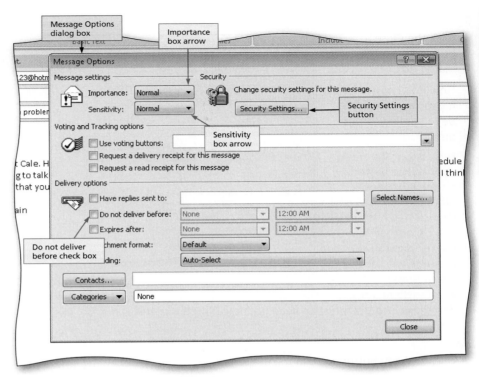

Figure 1–60

3

- Click the Importance box arrow and then select High in the Importance list.

- Click the Sensitivity box arrow and then select Private in the Sensitivity list.

- Click the 'Do not deliver before' check box in the Delivery options area to select it.

- Select January 14, 2008 in the calendar and 12:00 PM as the time in the respective delivery boxes (Figure 1–61).

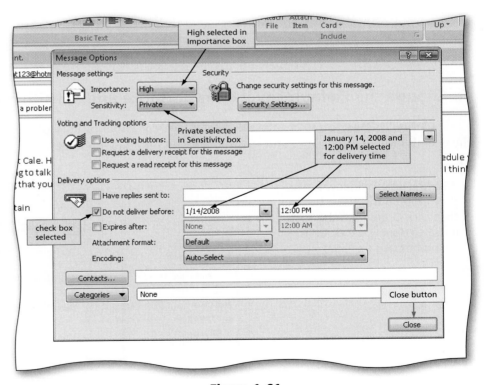

Figure 1–61

- Click the Close button to close the dialog box.

Q&A

How do I know that my settings have been applied to this message?

Notice that the High Importance button on the Ribbon is highlighted (Figure 1–62). While you cannot see it, the recipient of the message will receive the message with a red exclamation

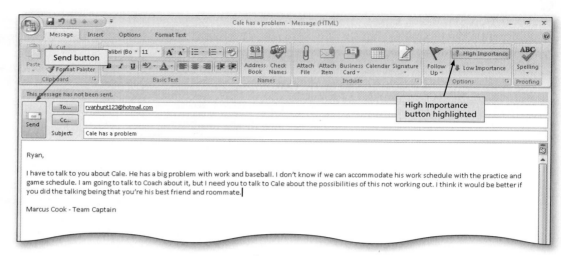

Figure 1–62

point icon and the message heading indicating the e-mail is private, like the one shown in Figure 1–58 on page OUT 38.

- Click the Send button to send the message.

Q&A

What does Outlook do with the message while it is waiting for the specified date and time to send the message?

Outlook stores the message in the Outbox folder until the specified date and time arrive. At that time, the message will be sent.

To Change the Default Level of Importance and Sensitivity

Outlook allows you to change the default level for either or both of these options. The following steps change the default level of importance and sensitivity for all outgoing messages.

- With the Inbox window active, click Tools on the menu bar and then click Options on the Tools menu to display the Options dialog box (Figure 1–63).

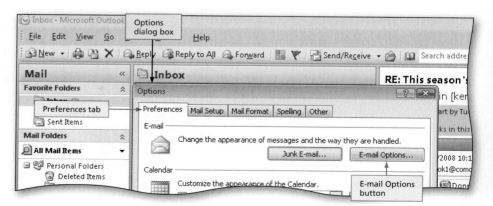

Figure 1–63

2

- In the Preferences sheet, click the E-mail Options button to display the E-mail Options dialog box (Figure 1–64).

- Click the Advanced E-mail Options button to open the Advanced E-mail Options dialog box.

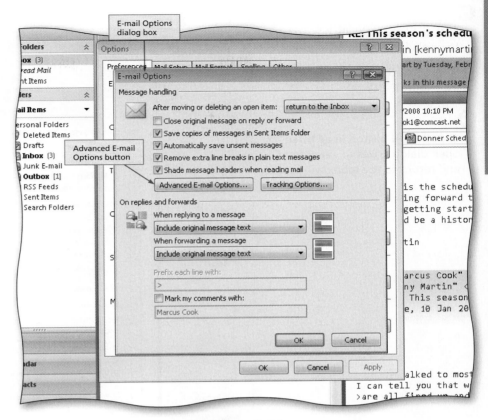

Figure 1–64

3

- Click the Set importance box arrow to display the importance options (Figure 1–65).

- Select High in the Set importance list.

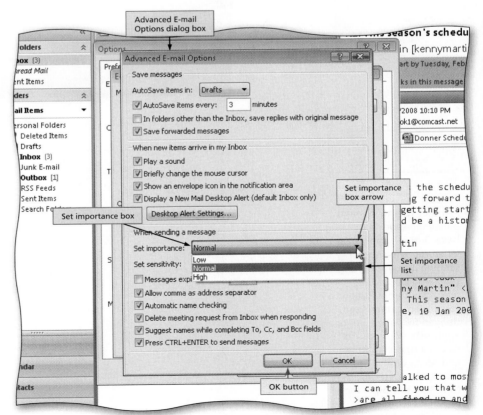

Figure 1–65

- Click the Set sensitivity box arrow to display the sensitivity options.

- Select Private in the Set sensitivity list (Figure 1–66).

- Click the OK button in all three open dialog boxes to close them and return to the Inbox window.

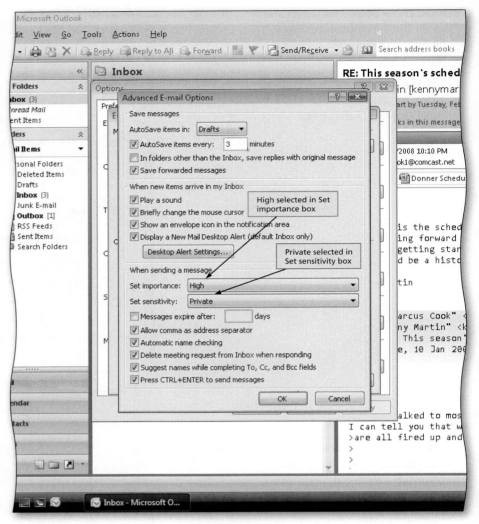

Figure 1–66

BTW

Rules
Another way to manage e-mail messages is to have Outlook apply rules when receiving and/or sending messages. Using rules, you can have messages automatically forwarded, categorized, flagged for follow up, or apply other options. To create a rule, click Rules and Alerts on the Tools menu, and then click the New Rule button in the E-mail Rules sheet of the Rules and Alerts dialog box.

Search Folders

Outlook offers a feature called the Search Folders folder in the Mail Folders pane (Figure 1–67). The **Search Folders folder** includes a group of folders that allows you to group and view your messages quickly in one of three ways: (1) Categorized Mail, (2) Large Mail, and (3) Unread Mail. **Categorized Mail** messages are messages to which you have assigned a category. These messages are sorted by color. **Large Mail** messages are messages containing very large file attachments. These messages are grouped by size: Large (100 to 500 KB), Very Large (500 KB to 1 MB), and Huge (1 to 5 MB). **Unread Mail** comprises messages that have not been opened or have not been marked as read even though you may have read them in the Reading pane. Figure 1–67 shows messages in the Categorized Mail folder.

BTW

Security Settings
Clicking the Security Settings button (Figure 1–60 on page OUT 39) opens a dialog box that allows you to apply certain security restrictions on a message, such as encrypting the message or adding a digital signature.

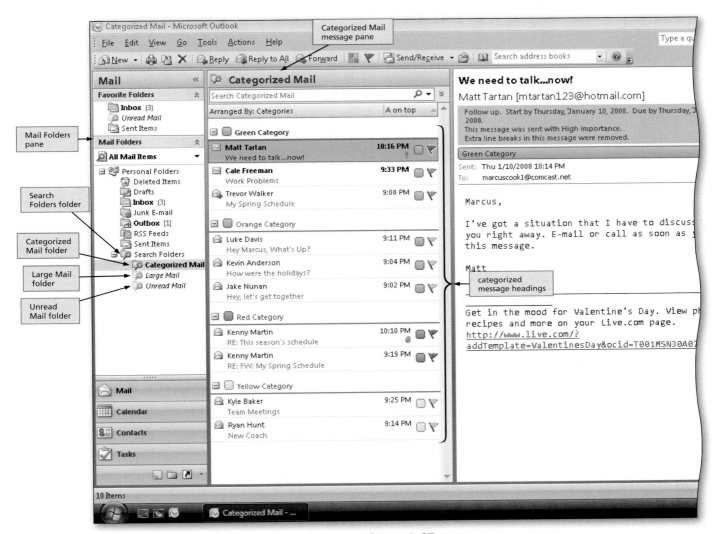

Figure 1–67

Using Contacts

The **Contacts component** of Outlook allows you to store information about individuals and companies. People with whom you communicate for school, business, or personal reasons are your **contacts**. To help organize information about personal contacts, some people keep names, addresses, and telephone numbers in business card files and address books. With the Outlook Contacts component, you can create and maintain important contact information in a **contact list**, which is stored in the Contacts folder. Your contact list is like an electronic address book that allows you to store names, addresses, e-mail addresses, and more. Once you have entered the information, you can retrieve, sort, edit, organize, or print your contact list. Outlook also includes a **Find option** that lets you search for a contact name in your address book while you are using the Calendar, Inbox, or other Outlook components.

When the Contacts folder is open, information about each contact appears on a business card in the default **Business Cards view**. Each card includes fields for name, address, and multiple telephone numbers (home, work, cellular, and so on), e-mail, and Web page addresses. You can choose which fields are displayed on the cards using the View menu.

Previously, an e-mail message was composed, signed, formatted, and sent to Kenny Martin. Kenny's e-mail address was typed into the To text box. The following sections show how to (1) create a personal folder; (2) create a contact list; (3) edit contact information; (4) print contact information; and (5) send an e-mail to a contact.

To Create a Personal Folder

The following steps create a personal folder for Marcus Cook.

- Click the Contacts button in the Navigation Pane to open the Contacts window.

- When Outlook displays the Contacts window, right-click Contacts in the My Contacts pane to display the Contacts shortcut menu (Figure 1–68).

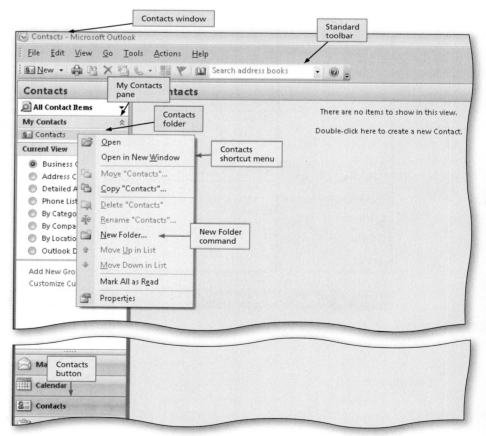

Figure 1–68

2

- Click New Folder on the Contacts shortcut menu to display the Create New Folder dialog box. Type `Marcus' Contacts` in the Name text box (Figure 1–69).

- If necessary, select Contact Items in the Folder contains list.

- Click Contacts in the Select where to place the folder list.

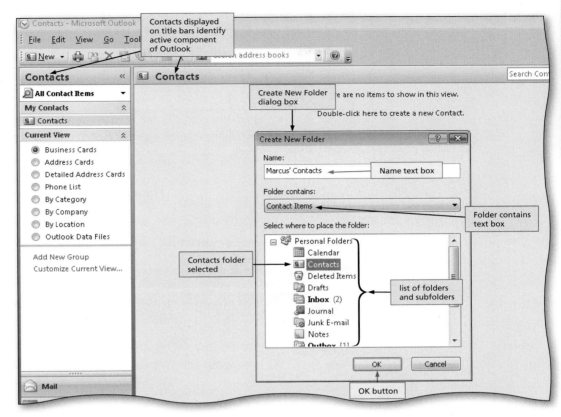

Figure 1–69

3

- Click the OK button to close the Create New Folder dialog box.

- In the Contacts window, click Marcus' Contacts in the My Contacts list (Figure 1–70).

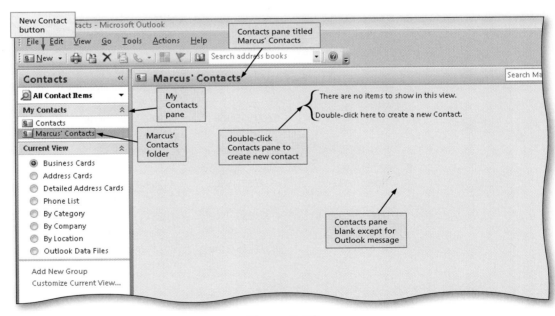

Figure 1–70

Other Ways		
1. On File menu point to New, click Folder on New submenu	2. On File menu point to Folder, click New Folder on Folder submenu 3. Press CTRL+SHIFT+E	

Figure 1–71 illustrates the Standard toolbar located below the menu bar in the Contacts window.

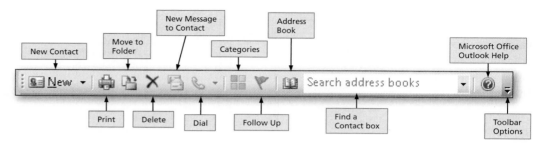

Figure 1–71

Next, you will create a contact list using the information included in Table 1–3.

Table 1–3 Contact Information			
Name	**Telephone**	**Address**	**E-Mail Address**
Kenny Martin	(937) 555-4120	8465 W. 63rd St. Donner, OH 44772	kennymartin123@hotmail.com
Jose Quinteras	(937) 555-7539	8868 Ashwood Lane Donner, OH 44772	josequinteras123@hotmail.com
Kelly Shurpa	(937) 555-9823	214 W. Lincoln Ave. Donner, OH 44772	kshurpa123@hotmail.com
Matt Tartan	(937) 555-0258	5246 Brookfield Ct. Donner, OH 44772	mtartan123@hotmail.com
Jim Osmont	(937) 555-6211	9812 River Rd. Donner, OH 44772	josmont123@hotmail.com
Cale Freeman	(937) 555-3080	7894 Forrest View Lane Donner, OH 44772	calefreeman123@hotmail.com
Kyle Baker	(937) 555-5279	7892 Buckingham Drive Donner, OH 44772	kylebaker101@hotmail.com
Ryan Hunt	(937) 555-1683	8792 Edgewater Lane Donner, OH 44772	ryanhunt123@hotmail.com
Luke Davis	(937) 555-2794	6776 Maplewood Blvd. Donner, OH 44772	lukedavis101@hotmail.com
Trevor Walker	(937) 555-8805	4476 Maplewood Blvd. Donner, OH 44772	trevwalker123@hotmail.com
Kevin Anderson	(937) 555-6309	1021 Ward Rd. Donner, OH 44772	kevanderson123@hotmail.com
Jake Nunan	(937) 555-2148	8924 65th Street Donner, OH 4477	jakenunan123@hotmail.com

To Create a Contact List

The following steps create a contact list.

1

- With the Contacts window active and Marcus' Contacts folder selected, click the New Contact button on the Standard toolbar (Figure 1–70 on page OUT 45) to open the Untitled-Contact window. If necessary, maximize the window.

- Type Kenny Martin in the Full Name text box (Figure 1–72).

- Click the Home text box in the Phone numbers area.

2

- Type 9375554120 as the home telephone number.

- Click the Addresses box arrow and select Home. (If the Location Information dialog box appears, enter your local area code and click the OK button to close the dialog box.)

- Click the text box in the Addresses area, type 8465 W. 63rd St. and then press the ENTER key.

- Type Donner, OH 44772 to complete the address entry.

- Click the E-mail text box.

- Type kennymartin123 @hotmail.com as the e-mail address and then press the TAB key to complete the contact information for Kenny Martin (Figure 1–73).

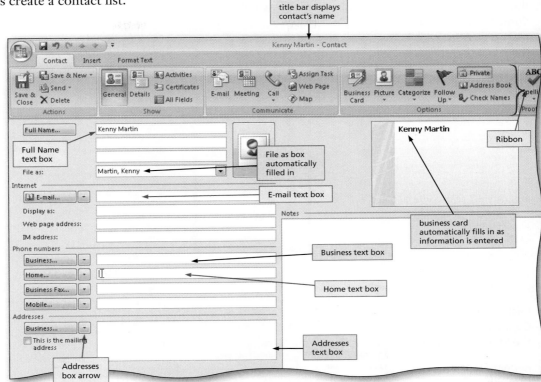

Figure 1–72

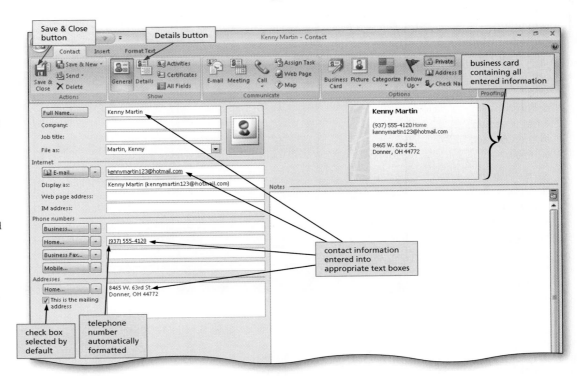

Figure 1–73

● Click the Save & Close button on the Ribbon to display the Marcus' Contacts window with the Kenny Martin business card in the Marcus' Contacts pane (Figure 1–74).

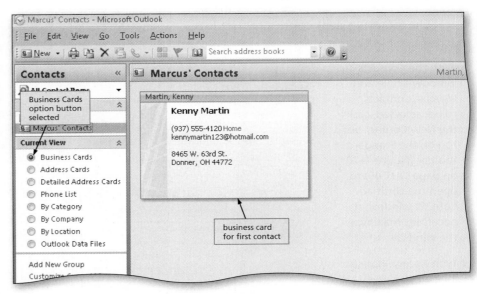

Figure 1–74

4

● Click the New Contact button on the Standard toolbar.

● Repeat Steps 2 through 4 to enter the 11 remaining contacts in Table 1–3 (Figure 1–75).

Q&A

Is it possible to store information different from what is shown in the Contact window?

By clicking the Details command in the Show group on the Ribbon (Figure 1–73 on page OUT 47), you can enter a contact's department, manager's name, nickname, and birthday information.

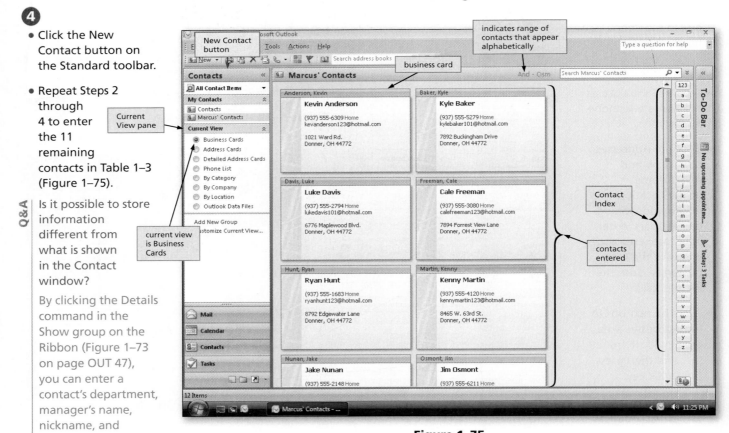

Figure 1–75

Other Ways	
1. On File menu point to New, click Contact on New submenu	2. On Actions menu click New Contact
	3. Press CTRL+SHIFT+C

To Change the View and Sort the Contact List

The following steps change the view from Business Cards to Phone List, sort the contact list in descending sequence, and then change back to Business Cards view.

1

- With the Marcus' Contacts – Microsoft Outlook window active, click Phone List in the Current View pane of the Navigation Pane.

- With the Phone List in ascending sequence by the File As field, click the File As column heading in the Contacts pane to display the contact list in descending sequence by last name (Figure 1–76).

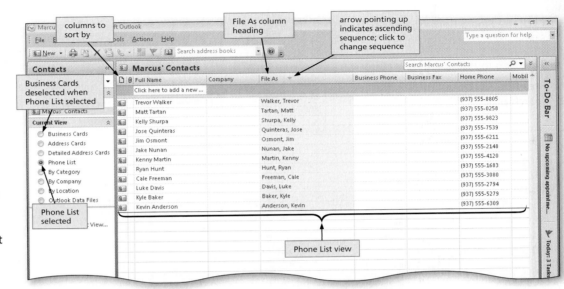

Figure 1–76

2

- After reviewing the contact list in Phone List view, click Business Cards in the Current View pane in the Navigation Pane to return to Business Cards view.

Are there other ways to sort Outlook information?

If you right-click a column heading in any Outlook component and point to the Arrange By command on the shortcut menu (Figure 1–77), you can see the Arrange By commands.

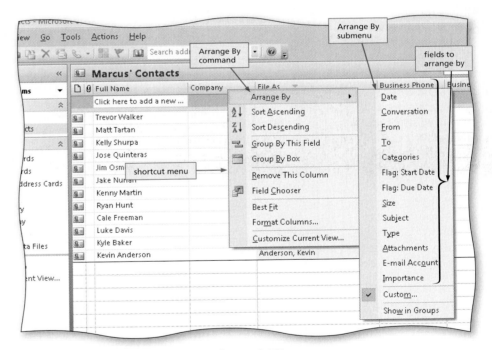

Figure 1–77

To Find a Contact

A contact record was created for Kelly Shurpa. This record can be found easily by using the Find a Contact box to type a part of the contact name as shown in the following steps.

1

- Click the Find a Contact box on the Standard toolbar (Figure 1–78).

- Type shu in the text box.

- Press the ENTER key to start the search process.

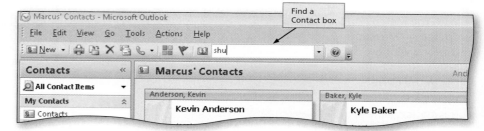

Figure 1–78

2

- Outlook opens the Kelly Shurpa – Contact window (Figure 1–79).

- Click the Close button to return to Business Card view.

Q&A

What if there is more than one contact starting with the letters, shu?

If more than one contact with the starting letters, shu, exists, Outlook displays a Choose Contact dialog box with the list of all contacts containing the letters, shu. You can then select the appropriate contact from the Choose Contact dialog box.

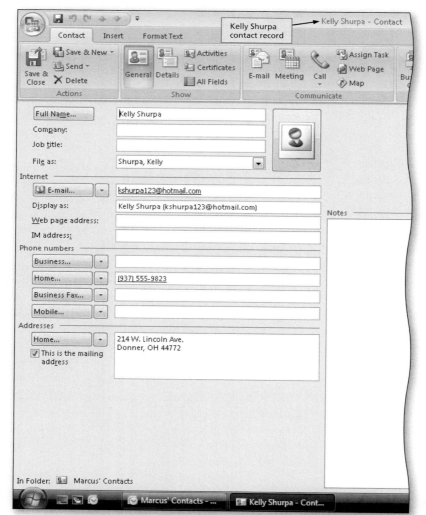
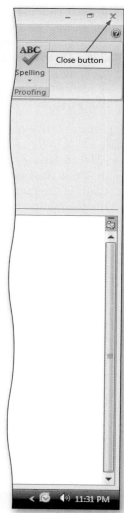

Figure 1–79

Other Ways

1. On Tools menu point to Instant Search, click Instant Search on Instant Search submenu

2. Press CTRL+SHIFT+F

To Organize Contacts

To help manage your contacts further, the contact list can be categorized and sorted using Outlook's default color categories, or using your own categories to group contacts by company, department, a particular project, a specific class, and so on. You also can sort by any part of the address; for example, you can sort by postal code for bulk mailings. The following steps assign the baseball players as a contact category with a color designation.

- Click Tools on the menu bar and then click Organize on the Tools menu.

- Click the name bar of the Kevin Anderson contact record.

- Hold down the CTRL key and then click the name bars of Cale Freeman and Ryan Hunt.

- Release the CTRL key.

- Click the 'Add contacts selected below to' box arrow to display a list of categories (Figure 1–80).

- Click Blue Category in the list.

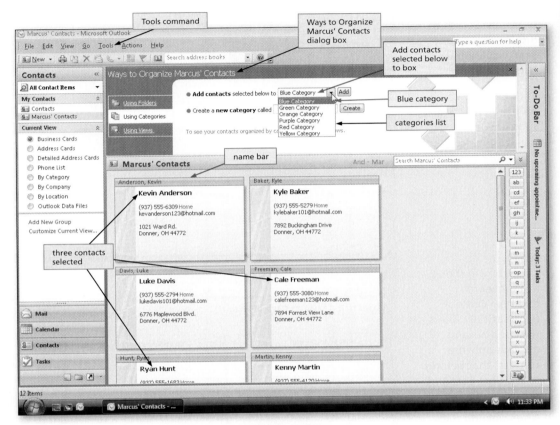

Figure 1–80

- Click the Add button to add the selected records to the Blue Category (Figure 1–81).

- Click the Close button in the Ways to Organize Marcus' Contacts dialog box to close it.

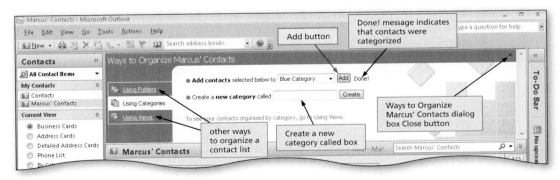

Figure 1–81

Other Ways
1. Press ALT+T, press Z

To Display the Contacts in a Category

The following steps use the Instant Search command to display contacts within a certain category.

- With the Contacts window active, click Tools on the menu bar and then point to Instant Search to display the Instant Search submenu (Figure 1–82).

- Click Instant Search on the Instant Search submenu.

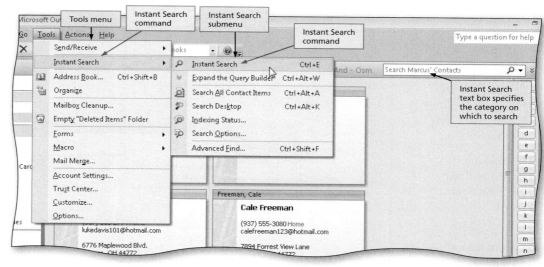

Figure 1–82

- Type Blue Category in the Instant Search text box. Outlook automatically filters the contacts and displays only the contacts that belong to the Blue Category (Figure 1–83).

- After viewing the contacts in the Blue Category, click the Clear Search button to return to the full Contacts window.

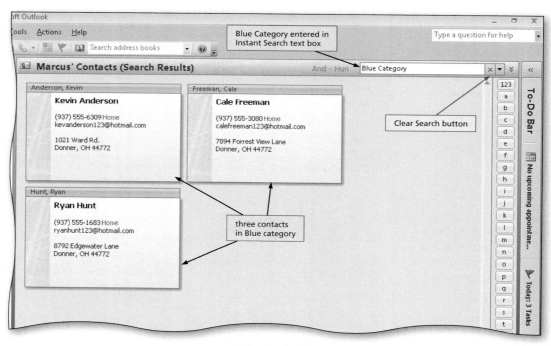

Figure 1–83

Other Ways

1. Press CTRL+E
2. Press ALT+T, press I

To Preview and Print the Contact List

The following steps preview and print the entire contact list.

1

- With the Contacts window active, click the Print button on the Standard toolbar to display the Print dialog box (Figure 1–84).

- Click the Preview button to display a preview of the printout (Figure 1–85 on the next page).

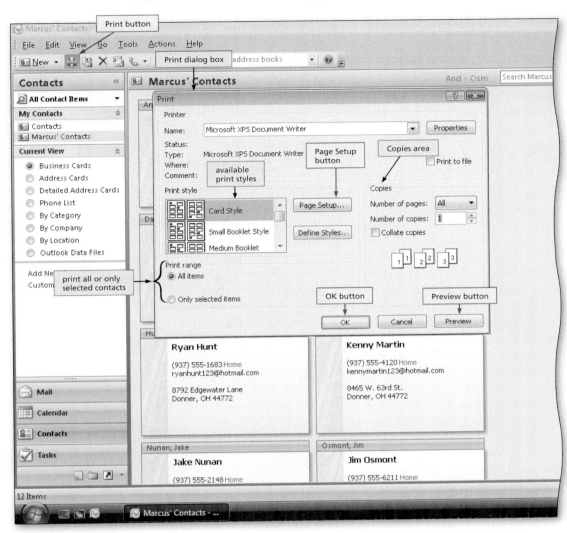

Figure 1–84

BTW

Contacts
You can organize contacts from one or more Contacts folders in a personal distribution list. Outlook also detects duplicates and provides the option to merge the new information with the existing contact entry. You also can filter your contact list and then use the filtered list to begin a mail merge from Outlook.

2

- After viewing the preview of the printed contacts list, click the Close button.

- If the preview is acceptable, ready the printer.

- Click the Print button on the Standard toolbar.

- When Outlook displays the Print dialog box, click the OK button.

Q&A

What if I want to print just a single category of contacts?

If you display a category of contacts and then click the Print button, Outlook will print only the contacts in that category.

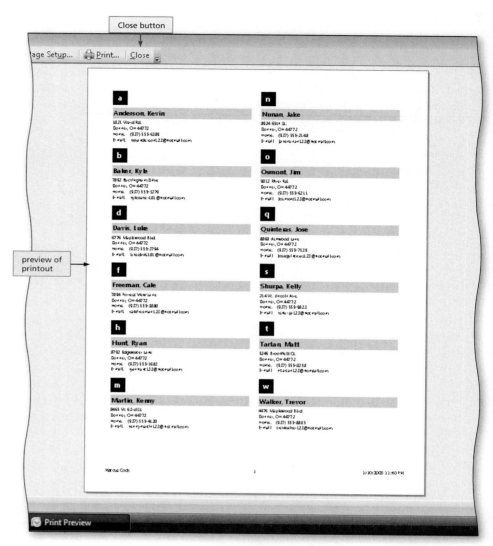

Figure 1–85

Other Ways

1. On File menu click Print
2. On File menu click Print Preview, click Print button in Print Preview window
3. Press CTRL+P

BTW

Business Contact Manager
Outlook 2007 with Business Contact Manager offers complete small business contact management capabilities to Outlook 2007. It allows you to organize customer and prospect information, manage sales and marketing activities, develop and track marketing activities, and centralize project information in one location. Among the capabilities of Business Contact Manager are tools for creating targeted mailing lists, personalizing and distributing print and e-mail marketing materials, and tracking results.

To Use the Contact List to Address an E-Mail Message

The following steps use the contact list to address an e-mail message to Matt Tartan.

1

- Click the Mail button in the Navigation Pane to display the Inbox window.

- Click the New Mail Message button on the Standard toolbar to display the Untitled – Message window (Figure 1–86).

- When Outlook displays the Untitled – Message window, if necessary, double-click its title bar to maximize it.

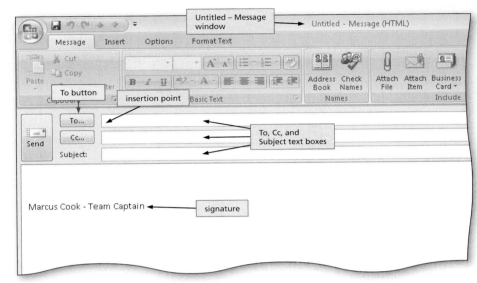

Figure 1–86

2

- Click the To button to display the Select Names dialog box (Figure 1–87).

- Click the Address Book box arrow.

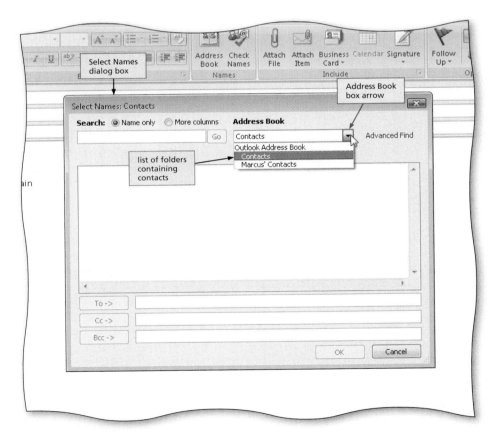

Figure 1–87

- Click Marcus' Contacts in the list.
- Click the Matt Tartan entry in the contact list (Figure 1–88).

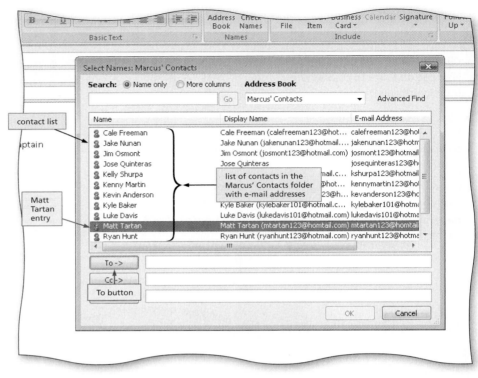

Figure 1–88

- Click the To button in the Message Recipients area to add Matt Tartan as the message recipient (Figure 1–89).

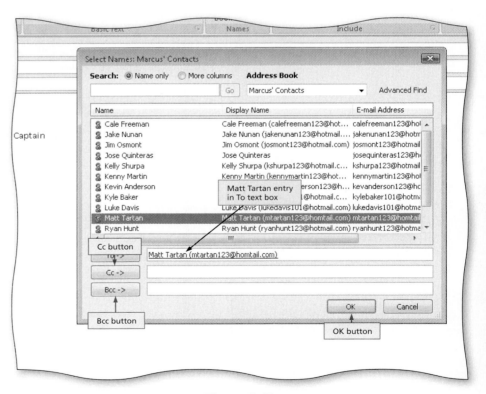

Figure 1–89

5

- Click the OK button to close the Select Names dialog box.

- Click the Subject text box and then type `Carwash Fund-raiser` as the entry (Figure 1–90).

- Press the TAB key to move the cursor to the message area.

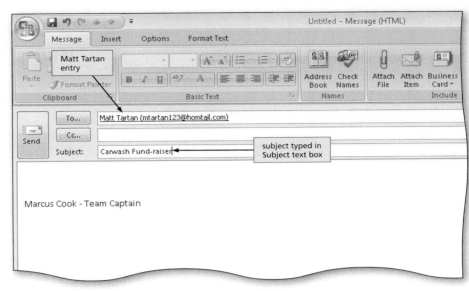

Figure 1–90

6

- Type the message (Figure 1–91).

- Click the Send button to send the message and close the Message window.

Q&A

Can I add more than one name to the To text box?

You can add as many names as you want to the To text box. You also can add names to the Cc text box. If you do not want those listed in the To text box or Cc text box to know you sent a copy to someone else, send a blind copy by adding the name to the Bcc text box.

Figure 1–91

Other Ways

1. Click Address Book command on Message window Ribbon

To Create a Distribution List

Outlook can send the same message to a group of recipients using a distribution list. The following steps create a distribution list titled Chemistry Lab Group that includes four members from Marcus' Contacts list.

- With the Contacts window active, click the New Contact button arrow on the Standard toolbar to display the New Contact menu (Figure 1–92).

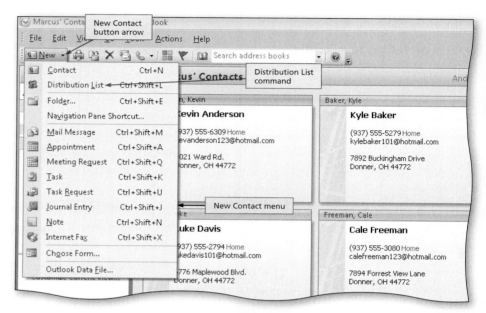

Figure 1–92

- Click Distribution List to display the Untitled – Distribution List window. Type Chemistry Lab Group in the Name text box, and then click the Select Members button on the Ribbon to display the Select Members dialog box.

- Click the Address Book box arrow and click Marcus' Contacts.

- Select Jake Nunan and then click the Members button to add Jake to the Chemistry Lab Group distribution list.

- Add Kyle Baker and Trevor Walker to the list in the same manner (Figure 1–93).

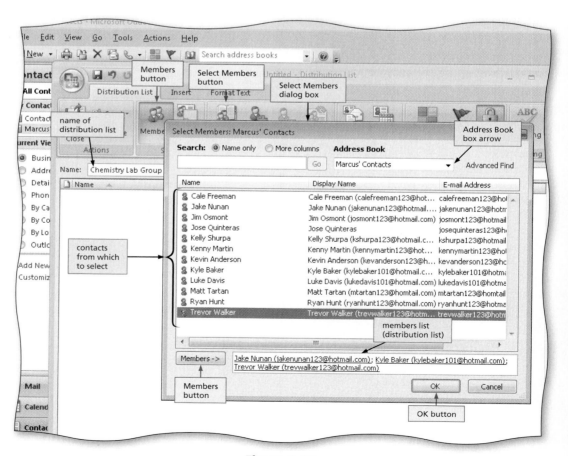

Figure 1–93

- Click the OK button to close the Select Members dialog box and display the Chemistry Lab Group – Distribution List window showing the members of the Chemistry Lab Group distribution list (Figure 1–94).

- Click the Save & Close command on the Ribbon to close the Chemistry Lab Group – Distribution List window and activate the Contacts window.

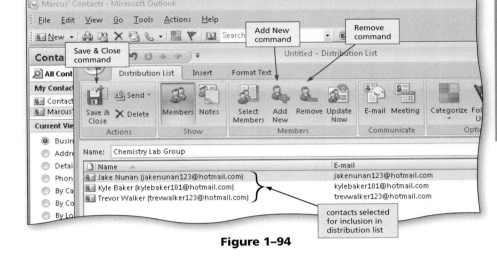

Figure 1–94

- Click the Address Book button on the Standard toolbar to display the Address Book dialog box.
- Select Marcus' Contacts in the Address Book list to display the contact list, which now includes the Chemistry Lab Group distribution list (Figure 1–95).

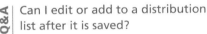

- Click the Close button to close the the Address Book window.

Q&A

Can I edit or add to a distribution list after it is saved?

Yes. The Chemistry Lab Group – Distribution List window in Figure 1–94 includes two commands in the Members group on the Ribbon that are useful for modifying a distribution list. The Add New command lets you add a contact that is not already in the distribution list. The Remove command lets you delete names from the distribution list, although they remain in your Outlook contact list.

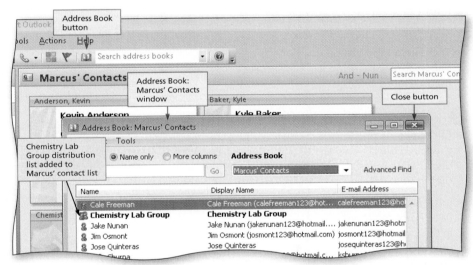

Figure 1–95

Saving Outlook Information in Different Formats

You can save Outlook files on external storage devices in several formats. For example, you can save messages and contact lists in text format, which can be read or copied into other applications.

BTW

The Internet
Outlook automatically creates a hyperlink when you type a Web page address or an e-mail address in the text box of a Contact window. If you are connected to an Internet browser, you can click the hyperlink to go to the destination quickly or send an e-mail message.

To Save a Contact List as a Text File and Display it in WordPad

The following steps save a contact list on a USB flash drive as a text file and display it in WordPad.

Note: If you are using Windows XP, see Appendix F for alternate steps.

 1

- Connect the USB flash drive containing the Data Files for Students to one of the computer's USB ports.

- With the Contacts window active, click the name bar of the first contact in the contact list.

- Press CTRL+A to select all the contacts.

- Click File on the menu bar to display the File menu (Figure 1–96).

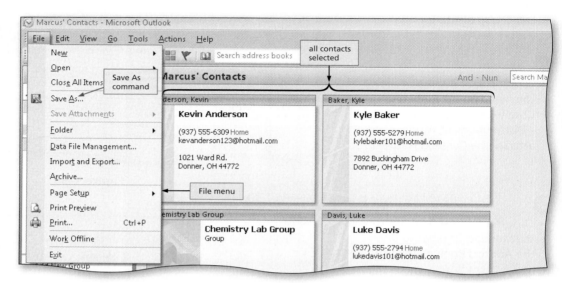

Figure 1–96

 2

- Click Save As on the File menu to display the Save As dialog box.

- If the Navigation Pane is not displayed in the Save As dialog box, click the Browse Folders button to expand the dialog box.

- If a Folders list is displayed below the Folders button, click the Folders button to remove the Folders list.

- Type `Marcus' Contacts` in the File name text box.

- If necessary, select Text Only in the Save as type box.

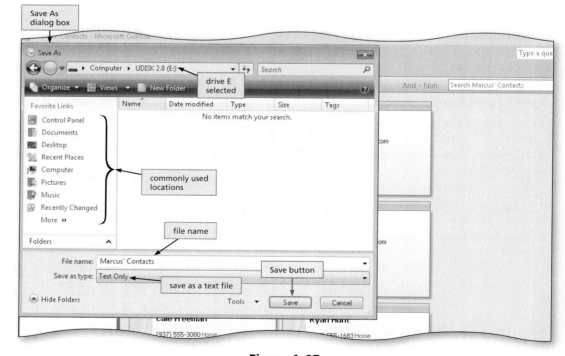

Figure 1–97

- If Computer is not displayed in the Favorite Links section, drag the top or bottom edge of the Save As dialog box until Computer is displayed.

- Click Computer in the Favorite Links section to display a list of available drives. If necessary, scroll until UDISK 2.0 (E:) appears in the list of available drives. Double-click UDISK 2.0 (E:) in the Computer list to select the USB flash drive, Drive E in this case, as the new save location. (Figure 1–97).

3

- Click the Save button in the Save As dialog box to save the file on the USB flash drive with the file name, Marcus' Contacts.
- Click the Start button on the Windows Vista taskbar to display the Start menu.
- Click All Programs at the bottom of the left pane on the Start menu to display the All Programs list. Click Accessories on the All Programs list, and then click WordPad on the Accessories list to open the WordPad text editor.
- When WordPad starts, click the Maximize button on the title bar, click File on the menu bar, and then click Open.
- When WordPad displays the Open dialog box, click the Files of type box arrow, select All Documents, click Computer in the Favorite Links section to display a list of available drives.
- If necessary, scroll until UDISK 2.0 (E:) appears in the list of available drives, and then double-click UDISK 2.0 (E:) in the Computer list to select the USB flash drive, Drive E in this case, as the new save location.
- Double-click Marcus' Contacts to display Marcus' Contacts as a text file (Figure 1–98).

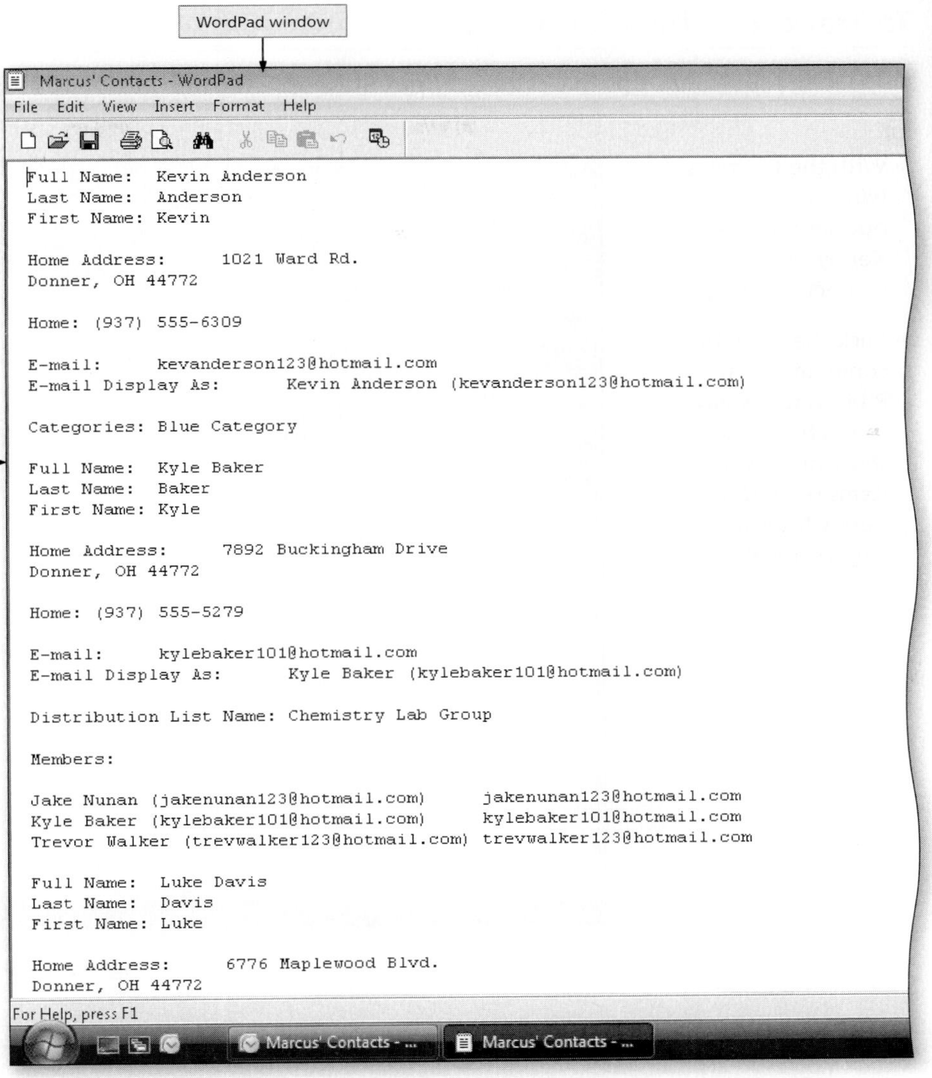
WordPad window
contact list viewed as a text file
Marcus' Contacts - WordPad
File Edit View Insert Format Help
Full Name: Kevin Anderson
Last Name: Anderson
First Name: Kevin
Home Address: 1021 Ward Rd.
Donner, OH 44772
Home: (937) 555-6309
E-mail: kevanderson123@hotmail.com
E-mail Display As: Kevin Anderson (kevanderson123@hotmail.com)
Categories: Blue Category
Full Name: Kyle Baker
Last Name: Baker
First Name: Kyle
Home Address: 7892 Buckingham Drive
Donner, OH 44772
Home: (937) 555-5279
E-mail: kylebaker101@hotmail.com
E-mail Display As: Kyle Baker (kylebaker101@hotmail.com)
Distribution List Name: Chemistry Lab Group
Members:
Jake Nunan (jakenunan123@hotmail.com) jakenunan123@hotmail.com
Kyle Baker (kylebaker101@hotmail.com) kylebaker101@hotmail.com
Trevor Walker (trevwalker123@hotmail.com) trevwalker123@hotmail.com
Full Name: Luke Davis
Last Name: Davis
First Name: Luke
Home Address: 6776 Maplewood Blvd.
Donner, OH 44772
For Help, press F1
Marcus' Contacts - ...
Marcus' Contacts - ...

Figure 1–98

4

- After viewing the text file, click the WordPad Close button.

Tracking Activities

When you are dealing with several contacts, it can be useful to have all associated e-mails, documents, or other items related to a contact available quickly. Outlook makes these items accessible through the Activities command in the Show group, located on the Contact window Ribbon. Clicking this command for a contact opens a list of all items related to that contact. Outlook searches for items linked only to the contact in the main Outlook folders (Contacts, Calendar, etc.); however, you can create and add new folders to be searched.

To Track Activities for a Contact

The following steps track the activities of Kenny Martin.

1

- With the Contacts window active, double-click the Kenny Martin contact heading.

- Click the Activities command on the Ribbon to display the Activities sheet showing a list of items related to Kenny Martin (Figure 1–99).

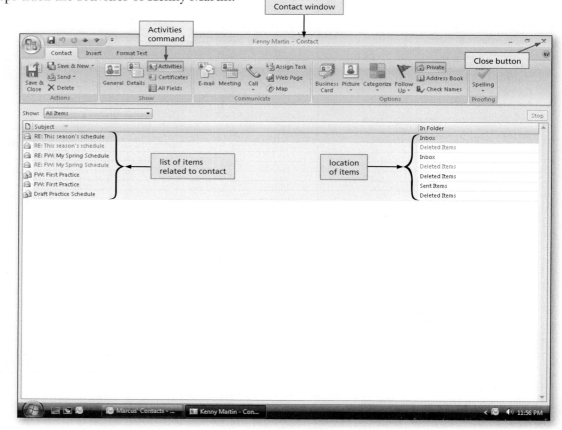

Figure 1–99

Outlook Help

The best way to become familiar with Outlook Help is to use it. Appendix C includes detailed information about Outlook Help and exercises that will help you gain confidence in using it.

Outlook Help

At any time while using Outlook, you can find answers to questions and display information about various topics through **Outlook Help**. The Help features can increase your productivity and reduce your frustrations by minimizing the time you spend learning how to use Outlook.

This section introduces you to Outlook Help. Additional information about using Outlook Help is available in Appendix C.

To Search for Outlook Help

Using Outlook Help, you can search for information based on phrases such as "send an e-mail message" or "format text," or key terms such as "copy," "save," or "format." Outlook Help responds with a list of search results displayed as links to a variety of resources. The following steps, which use Outlook Help to search for information about selecting text, assume you are connected to the Internet.

- Click the Microsoft Office Outlook Help button on the Standard toolbar to open the Outlook Help window.

- Type `format text` in the 'Type words to search for' text box at the top of the Outlook Help window (Figure 1–100).

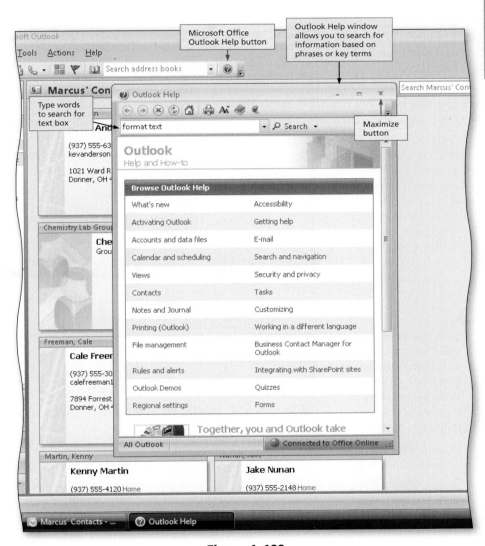

Figure 1–100

- Press the ENTER key to display the search results.

- Click the Maximize button on the Outlook Help window title bar to maximize the Help window (Figure 1–101).

Where is the Contacts window?

Outlook is open in the background, but the Outlook Help window is overlaid on top of the Microsoft Outlook window. When the Outlook Help window is closed, the Contacts window will reappear.

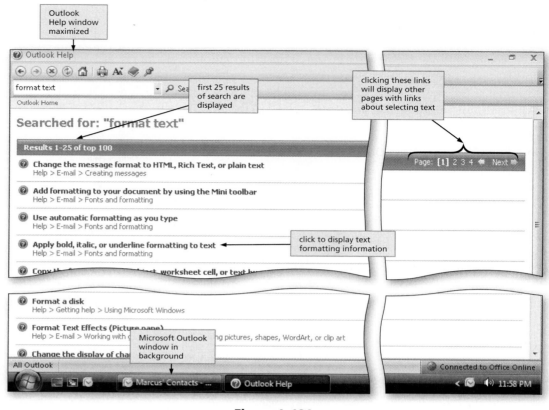

Figure 1–101

- Click the Apply bold, italic, or underline formatting to text link to display information regarding formatting text (Figure 1–102).

What is the purpose of the buttons at the top of the Outlook Help window?

Use the buttons in the upper-left corner of the Outlook Help window to navigate through the Help system, change the display, show the Outlook Help table of contents, and print the contents of the window.

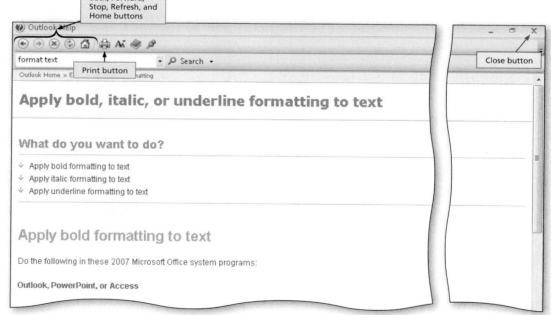

Figure 1–102

- Click the Close button on the Outlook Help window title bar to close the Outlook Help window and redisplay the Contacts window.

Other Ways
1. Press F1

To Quit Outlook

The following steps quit Outlook.

1 Click the Close button on the right side of the title bar to quit Outlook.

2 If necessary, click the Exit Without Sending button in the Microsoft Office Outlook dialog box so that any messages saved in your Outbox are not sent.

BTW

Certification
The Microsoft Certified Application Specialist (MCAS) program provides an opportunity for you to obtain a valuable industry credential – proof that you have the Outlook 2007 skills required by employers. For more information see Appendix G or visit the Outlook 2007 Certification Web page (scsite.com/out2007/cert).

Chapter Summary

In this chapter you have learned how to use Outlook to open, read, print, reply to, forward, delete, sign, compose, format, and send e-mail messages. You opened and viewed file attachments as well as attached a file to an e-mail message. You learned how to categorize, flag, sort, and set importance and delivery options to e-mail messages. You added and deleted contacts to a contact list. Finally, you used the contact list to create a distribution list and track activities of a contact. The items listed below include all the new Outlook skills you have learned in this chapter.

1. Start and Customize Outlook (OUT 5)
2. Open (Read) an E-Mail Message (OUT 10)
3. Close an E-Mail Message (OUT 15)
4. Print an E-Mail Message (OUT 15)
5. Reply to an E-Mail Message (OUT 16)
6. Change Message Formats (OUT 19)
7. Forward an E-Mail Message (OUT 20)
8. Delete an E-Mail Message (OUT 21)
9. View a File Attachment (OUT 22)
10. Create and Insert an E-Mail Signature (OUT 24)
11. Compose an E-Mail Message (OUT 27)
12. Format an E-Mail Message (OUT 29)
13. Attach a File to an E-Mail Message and Send the Message (OUT 31)
14. Categorize E-Mail Messages (OUT 33)
15. Flag E-Mail Messages (OUT 34)
16. Sort E-Mail Messages by Category Color (OUT 35)
17. Create and Apply a View Filter (OUT 36)
18. Set Message Importance, Sensitivity, and Delivery Options in a Single Message (OUT 38)
19. Change the Default Level of Importance and Sensitivity (OUT 40)
20. Create a Personal Folder (OUT 44)
21. Create a Contact List (OUT 47)
22. Change the View and Sort the Contact List (OUT 49)
23. Find a Contact (OUT 50)
24. Organize Contacts (OUT 51)
25. Display the Contacts in a Category (OUT 52)
26. Preview and Print the Contact List (OUT 53)
27. Use the Contact List to Address an E-Mail Message (OUT 55)
28. Create a Distribution List (OUT 58)
29. Save a Contact List as a Text File and Display it in WordPad (OUT 60)
30. Track Activities for a Contact (OUT 62)
31. Search for Outlook Help (OUT 63)
32. Quit Outlook (OUT 65)

If you have a SAM user profile, you may have access to hands-on instruction, practice, and assessment. Log in to your SAM account (http://sam2007.course.com) to launch any assigned training activities or exams that relate to the skills covered in this chapter.

BTW

Quick Reference
For a table that lists how to complete the tasks covered in this book using the mouse, Ribbon, shortcut menu, and keyboard, see the Quick Reference Summary at the back of this book, or visit the Outlook 2007 Quick Reference Web page (scsite.com/out2007/qr).

Learn It Online

Test your knowledge of chapter content and key terms.

Instructions: To complete the Learn It Online exercises, start your browser, click the Address bar, and then enter the Web address scsite.com/out2007/learn. When the Outlook 2007 Learn It Online page is displayed, click the link for the exercise you want to complete and then read the instructions.

Chapter Reinforcement TF, MC, and SA
A series of true/false, multiple choice, and short answer questions that test your knowledge of the chapter content.

Flash Cards
An interactive learning environment where you identify chapter key terms associated with displayed definitions.

Practice Test
A series of multiple choice questions that test your knowledge of chapter content and key terms.

Who Wants To Be a Computer Genius?
An interactive game that challenges your knowledge of chapter content in the style of the television quiz show.

Wheel of Terms
An interactive game that challenges your knowledge of chapter key terms in the style of the television show *Wheel of Fortune*.

Crossword Puzzle Challenge
A crossword puzzle that challenges your knowledge of key terms presented in the chapter.

Apply Your Knowledge

Reinforce the skills and apply the concepts you learned in this chapter.

Creating a Contact List
Instructions: Start Outlook. Create a Contacts folder using your name as the name of the new folder. Create a contact list using the people listed in Table 1–4. Sort the list by last name in descending sequence. When the list is complete, print the list in Card Style view and submit to your instructor.

Table 1–4 Contact Information				
Name	**Telephone**	**Address**	**E-mail Address**	**Grade Level**
Greg Sanders	(937) 555-4120	8465 W. 63rd St. Donner, OH 44772	gsanders@isp.com	Junior
Dan Gilbert	(937) 555-7539	8868 Ashwood Lane Donner, OH 44772	dgilbert@isp.com	Freshman
Heather Nichols	(937) 555-9823	214 W. Lincoln Ave. Donner, OH 44772	hnichols@isp.com	Freshman
Valerie Prince	(937) 555-0258	5246 Brookfield Ct. Donner, OH 44772	vprince@isp.com	Junior
Rafael Perez	(937) 555-6211	9812 River Rd. Donner, OH 44772	rperez@isp.com	Sophomore
Keith Lee	(937) 555-3080	7894 Forrest View Lane Donner, OH 44772	klee@isp.com	Sophomore

Extend Your Knowledge

Extend the skills you learned in this chapter and experiment with new skills. You may need to use Help to complete the assignment.

Categorizing Contacts and Creating a Distribution List

Instructions: Start Outlook. Using the contact list created in Apply Your Knowledge, create a category for each grade level (freshman, sophomore, junior, and senior) and categorize each student as follows: Greg Sanders – Junior, Dan Gilbert – Freshman, Heather Nichols – Freshman, Valerie Prince – Junior, Rafael Perez – Sophomore, Keith Lee – Sophomore.

Create a distribution list consisting of juniors and seniors. When the list is complete, print the list in Card Style view and submit to your instructor.

Make It Right

Analyze a document and correct all errors and/or improve the design.

Importing Subfolders for the In the Lab Exercises

Follow these steps to import subfolders for the following Make it Right and In the Lab exercises:

1. Connect the USB flash drive containing the Data Files for Students to your computer.

2. Click File on the Outlook menu bar and then click Import and Export.

3. In the Import and Export Wizard dialog box, click Import from another program or file and then click the Next button.

4. In the Import a File dialog box, click Personal Folder File (.pst) and then click the Next button.

5. In the Import Personal Folders dialog box, click the Browse button to access drive E (your USB flash drive letter may be different), select the appropriate subfolder, click Open, and then click the Next button.

6. In the Import Personal Folders dialog box, select the appropriate folder from which to import and then click the Finish button.

Continued >

Make It Right *continued*

Editing a Contact List

Instructions: Start Outlook. Import the MIR 1-1 Contacts folder (Figure 1–103) into Outlook. See the inside back cover of this book for instructions for downloading the Data Files for Students, or see your instructor for information on accessing the files required in this book.

The contact list contains 20 contacts. The five contacts in Table 1–5 need to have their information updated. Locate each contact using the Find a Contact box and change the applicable fields.

Print the revised contact list and submit it to your instructor.

Table 1–5 Revised Contact Information				
Name	**Telephone**	**Address**	**E-mail Address**	**Category**
Jennifer Craig	(916) 555-5686	354 Rutledge St. Condor, CA 95702	jcraig@isp.com	Blue
Andrew Brinckman	(916) 555-4565	8453 Whitcomb St. Condor, CA 95702	abrinckman@isp.com	Blue
Courtney Croel	(916) 555-2348	7456 Brummitt Rd. Condor, CA 95702	ccroel@isp.com	Blue
Ryan Bachman	(916) 555-7410	4654 Ashford Ct. Condor, CA 95702	rbachman@isp.com	Blue
Kris Davids	(916) 555-3647	678 E. 7th Ave. Condor, CA 95702	kdavids@isp.com	Blue

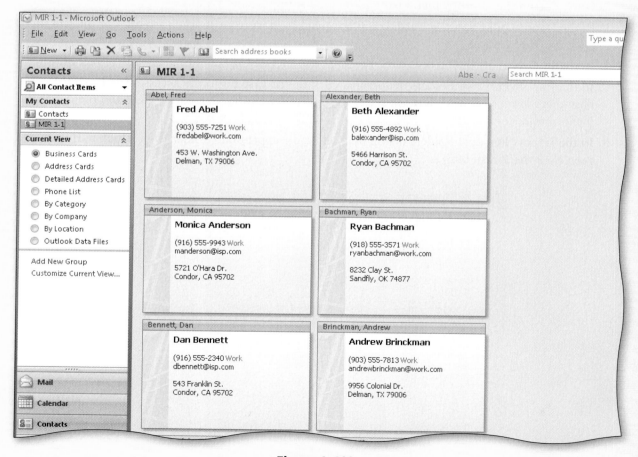

Figure 1–103

In the Lab

Design and/or create Outlook items using the guidelines, concepts, and skills presented in this chapter. Labs are listed in order of increasing difficulty.

Lab 1: Creating a Distribution List and Sending E-Mail

Problem: You are the campaign manager of your mother's campaign for a city council seat. Besides coordinating appearances and advertising, your responsibilities also include soliciting and organizing campaign donations.

Instructions Part 1:   Perform the following tasks:

1. Import the Lab 1-1 Contacts folder (Figure 1–104) into Outlook.

2. Create two distribution lists: one consisting of monetary donors, the other consisting of non-monetary donors. Each contact is categorized by type of donation.

3. Print each distribution list and submit to your instructor.

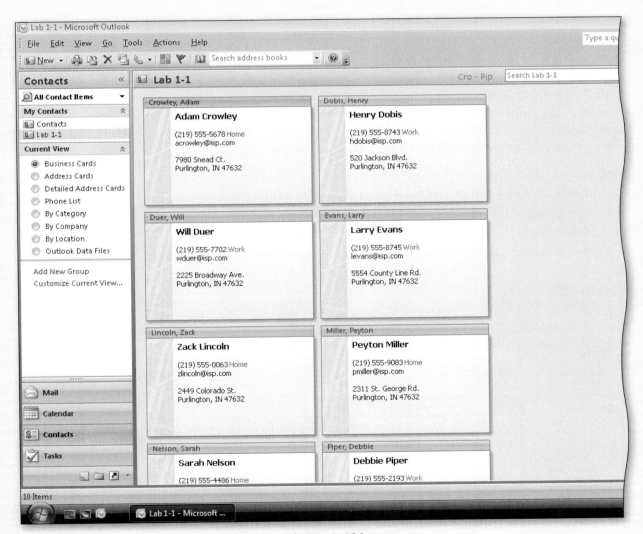

Figure 1–104

Continued >

In the Lab *continued*

Instructions Part 2:   Perform the following tasks:

1. Compose a message to each group created in Part 1. The message to monetary donors should thank them for their past support and request donations for this year's campaign. The message to non-monetary donors should thank them for their past support and include a request for the same contribution to this year's campaign.

2. Set the sensitivity for each message as confidential.

3. Using Microsoft Word, create a document called Campaign Platform, and include this file as an attachment with your e-mail messages.

4. Set the delivery for each message to March 1, 2008 at 10:00 a.m.

5. Format your messages to monetary donors as Plain Text and your messages to non-monetary donors as HTML.

6. Print each message and submit to your instructor.

Instructions Part 3:   Save the Lab 1-1 contact list as a text file. Open the file using WordPad. Print the contact list from WordPad and submit to your instructor.

In the Lab

Lab 2: Flagging and Sorting Messages

Problem: As student director of the Computer Help Center, you are responsible for responding to questions received by e-mail. Some questions require a more timely response than others, so you need a way to sort the questions first by urgency and then by time of receipt.

Instructions: Perform the following tasks:

1. Import the Lab 1-2 Inbox folder (Figure 1–105) into Outlook.

2. Read through each message and apply the appropriate Follow Up flag to each message (Today, Tomorrow, or This Week).

3. After you have flagged each message, sort the messages based on the Follow Up flag.

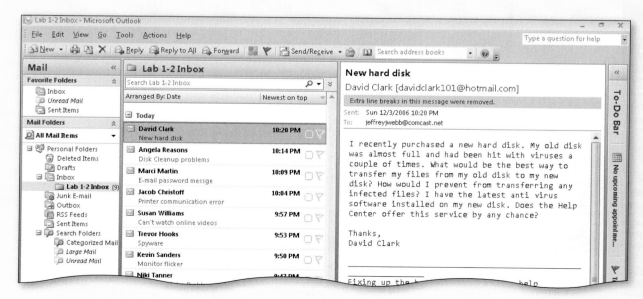

Figure 1–105

In the Lab

Lab 3: Creating an E-Mail Signature, Replying To, and Forwarding Messages

Problem: With all the Computer Help Center messages sorted and flagged, you now have to respond to the messages. You need to perform this task in an efficient manner, as it is the Computer Help Center's policy to respond to questions within three working days. Policy also requires that the name of the person responding, the Computer Help Center's telephone number, and its hours of operation appear on every reply.

Instructions Part 1: Perform the following tasks:

1. Create an e-mail signature consisting of your name, title (Student Director), a telephone number (555-1234), and hours of operation (8:00 a.m. – 8:00 p.m., Closed Sundays).

2. Click the New Message button on the Standard toolbar. Print the blank message containing the signature and submit to your instructor.

Instructions Part 2: Perform the following tasks:

1. Send a reply with the importance set at high to the messages flagged for follow up Today.

2. Forward the messages flagged for follow up Tomorrow. You may use fictitious e-mail addresses for this exercise, because the messages will not actually be sent.

3. Submit printouts of the replies to your instructor.

Instructions Part 3: Perform the following tasks:

1. Clear all the This Week Follow Up flags from the appropriate messages. Use Search Folders to display only the messages flagged for follow up. Make a list of the sender's name, subject, and Follow Up flag type and submit to your instructor.

2. Using information from Microsoft Outlook Help, create a unique signature for a separate e-mail account. See your instructor about setting up a separate e-mail account.

3. Print a blank message containing the signature and submit to your instructor.

Cases and Places

Apply your creative thinking and problem solving skills to design and implement a solution.

• Easier   •• More Difficult

• 1: Create a Personal Contact List

Create a contact list of your family, friends, and colleagues. Include their names, addresses, telephone numbers, e-mail addresses, and IM addresses (if any). Enter the employer for each contact if appropriate. For family members, use the Detail sheet to list birthdays and wedding anniversaries (if any). Print the contact list and submit to your instructor.

• 2: Modify a Contact List

Import the Cases 1-2 Contacts folder into Outlook. You are the manager of the Personnel Department for a large automobile dealership. Your responsibilities include updating the company contact list whenever someone changes positions, receives a promotion, or other changes occur. Byron Taylor has received a promotion to Parts Manager and was rewarded with a private office (Room 3A), private telephone ((812) 555-1278), and his own e-mail address (btaylor@autodealer.com). The information in his current record contains the general telephone number and dealership's e-mail. Make the appropriate changes to Byron Taylor's contact record. Submit a printout to your instructor.

•• 3: Apply a View Filter and Track Contact Activities

Import the Cases 1-3 Inbox folder into Outlook. You work in the IT department of a large company. Every day you receive several e-mail messages about various computer problems within the company. A coworker, Bailey Smithers, has sent several e-mail messages to the IT department complaining that her problem has yet to be solved. You have been told to immediately solve her problem. Apply a filter to the Cases 1-3 Inbox folder to display only the messages from Bailey Smithers. Respond to her latest e-mail message while sending a copy to your supervisor to show that you have found a resolution to the problem. Submit a printout of your reply to your instructor. Add Bailey Smithers to your contact list. Track the activities of Bailey Smithers. List the first five entries from the Activities list and submit to your instructor. After printing your reply message, delete all the messages from Bailey Smithers and remove the filter.

•• 4: Compose and Format an E-Mail Message

Make It Personal

Being involved with your studies, extracurricular activities, and college life in general, can prevent you from keeping in touch with family and friends. Compose an e-mail message to a close relative or friend. Your message should contain information on your class schedule, activities, and new friends that you have made. Compose the message in HTML format. Format the text of your message to enhance its appearance. Use Outlook Help to insert a picture of the campus or your school's logo into the message body. Print the e-mail and submit to your instructor.

•• 5: Compile Contact Information

Working Together

Have each member of your team submit a design of a form for collecting contact information. Have them base the form on available fields in the General and Detail sheets in the Contact window. Have the team select the best form design. After selecting a form, make photocopies for the entire class. Have your classmates fill out the form. Collect the forms and create a contact list from the collected information. Print the final contact list and submit to your instructor.

2 | Managing Calendars and Instant Messaging

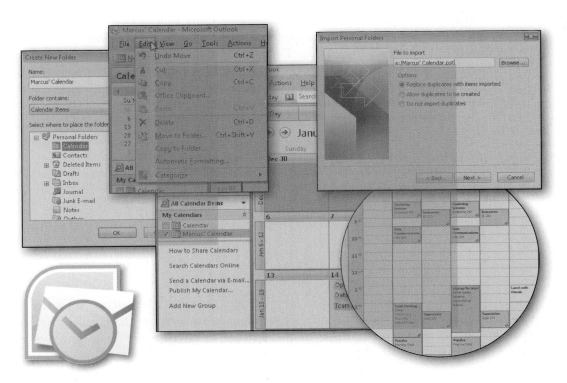

Objectives

You will have mastered the material in this project when you can:

- Start Outlook and open the Calendar folder

- Describe the components of the Calendar – Microsoft Outlook window and understand the elements of the Outlook Navigation Pane

- Enter, move, and edit one-time and recurring appointments

- Create an event

- Display the calendar in Day, Work Week, Week, and Month views

- Create and customize a task list and move it to a new folder

- Import, export, and delete personal subfolders

- Delegate tasks

- Schedule a meeting

- Customize the calendar

- Print the calendar in Daily Style, Weekly Style, and Monthly Style

- Enable and start instant messaging in Outlook

- Add an instant messaging address in the contact list

- Send an instant message and send a file with instant messaging

2 | Managing Calendars and Instant Messaging

Introduction

Whether you are CEO of a major company or president of an extracurricular activity group in school, you can take advantage of Outlook's features for scheduling and managing appointments, meetings, and tasks. You can view or print an Outlook calendar in Day, Week, or Month views (Figure 2–1). Using Outlook's Calendar component, you can schedule meetings and appointments, assign tasks for the other members of a group, and even keep track of meeting attendance and task progression. Outlook also allows you to store miscellaneous information using Notes.

Outlook is also helpful for scheduling personal time. Most individuals have multiple appointments to keep and tasks to accomplish in a day, week, or month. Outlook can organize activity-related information in a structured, readable manner.

Outlook has an instant messaging feature (bottom of Figure 2–1) that works in conjunction with Windows Messenger or MSN Messenger. This feature allows you to communicate instantaneously with people in your contact list who also use one of these instant messenger services.

Project — Calendar

Time management is a part of everyday life. Many people are constantly rearranging appointments, work schedules, or vacations in an attempt to efficiently utilize their time. The better you manage your professional or student life, the more time you will have for your personal life. Outlook is the perfect tool to maintain a personal schedule and help plan meetings. In this project, you use the basic features of Outlook to create a calendar of classes, work schedules, and extra-curricular activities for Marcus Cook, including scheduling meetings. In addition to creating the calendar, you learn how to print it in three views: Day, Week, and Month. The project also shows how to create a task list and delegate those tasks. Finally, you will learn how to use Windows Messenger with Outlook.

Overview

As you read through this chapter, you will learn how to create the calendar shown in Figure 2–1 by performing these general tasks:

- Enter appointments.
- Create recurring appointments.
- Move appointments to new dates.
- Schedule events.
- View and print the calendar.
- Create a task list.
- Assign tasks.

OUTLOOK CALENDAR

(a) Day View

(b) Week View

(c) Month View

(d) Daily Style Printout

(e) Weekly Style Printout

(f) Monthly Style Printout

INSTANT MESSAGING USING OUTLOOK

(g) Send Instant Message

(h) Receive Instant Message and Reply

Figure 2–1

- Accept a task assignment.
- Invite attendees to a meeting.
- Accept a meeting request.
- Propose and change the time of a meeting.
- Color code and label your calendar.
- Create and edit notes.
- Use AutoArchive.
- Use Windows Messaging with Outlook.

Plan Ahead

General Project Guidelines

When creating a schedule, the actions you perform and decisions you make will affect the appearance and characteristics of the finished schedule. As you create an appointment, task, or schedule a meeting as shown in Figure 2–1, you should follow these general guidelines:

1. **Determine what you need to schedule.** For students, a class list with room numbers and times would be a good start. For businesspeople, the schedule is a dynamic tool that will need frequent updating; however, you can schedule weekly staff meetings and other regular events or tasks.

2. **Determine if an activity is recurring.** Classes most likely recur through the semester. Work schedules can change week by week or month by month. If an activity happens regularly on the same day and time, it is recurring.

3. **Use good judgment when assigning a task.** If you are going to assign a task, you should be sure the person to whom you are assigning the task is capable of performing the task by the assigned due date.

4. **Be sure to have an agenda before scheduling a meeting.** A poorly organized meeting may be the least productive tool in the business world. Attendees become uninterested and sometimes angry knowing that their time could be better spent elsewhere. A carefully planned meeting with a defined agenda, however, can be a very productive tool if it is followed correctly.

When necessary, more specific details concerning the above guidelines are presented at appropriate points in the chapter. The chapter also will identify the actions you perform and decisions made regarding these guidelines during the creation of the schedule shown in Figure 2–1.

BTW

The Outlook 2007 Help System
Need Help? It is no further than the 'Type a question for help' box on the menu bar in the upper-right corner of the window. Click the box that contains the text, Type a question for help (Figure 2–2), type help, and then press the ENTER key. Outlook responds with a list of topics you can click to learn about obtaining help on an Outlook-related topic. To find out what is new in Outlook 2007, type what is new in Outlook in the 'Type a question for help' box.

Note: If you are stepping through this project on a computer, then you should set your system clock to January 10, 2008; otherwise, the steps and figures in the project will not match your computer.

Starting and Customizing Outlook

If you are using a computer to step through the project in this chapter and you want your screen to match the figures in this book, you should change your screen's resolution to 1024×768. For information about how to change a computer's resolution, read Appendix E.

To Start and Customize Outlook

The following steps, which assume Windows Vista is running, start Outlook based on a typical installation. You may need to ask your instructor how to start Outlook for your computer.

1
- Click the Start button on the Windows Vista taskbar to display the Start menu.

2
- Click All Programs at the bottom of the left pane on the Start menu to display the All Programs list, and then click Microsoft Office in the All Programs list to display the Microsoft Office list.

3
- Click Microsoft Office Outlook 2007 on the Microsoft Office list to start Outlook.

- If necessary, click the Calendar button in the Navigation Pane.

- If the Calendar – Microsoft Office Outlook window is not maximized, double-click its title bar to maximize the window (Figure 2–2).

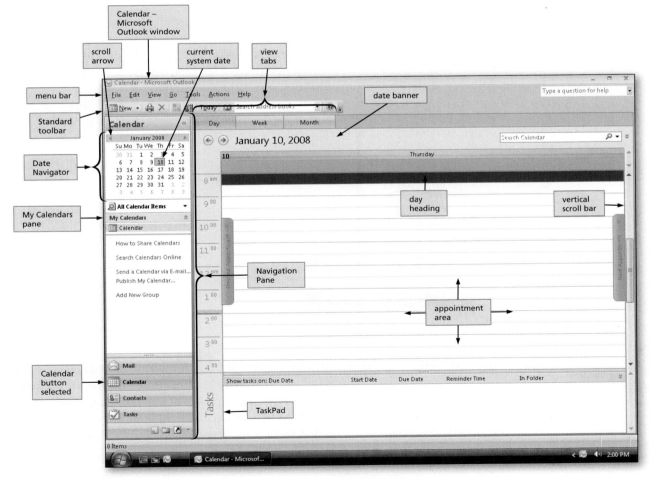

Figure 2–2

Calendars
Other users can give you access to their calendars. This allows you to make appointments, check free times, schedule meetings, check or copy contacts, or perform any other tasks that you can accomplish with your own calendar. This is useful when you need to schedule meetings or events that depend on other people's schedules.

The Calendar – Microsoft Outlook Window

The Calendar – Microsoft Outlook window shown in Figure 2–2 on the previous page includes a variety of features to help you work efficiently. It contains many elements similar to the windows in other Office applications, as well as some that are unique to Outlook. The main elements of the Calendar window are the Navigation Pane, the Standard toolbar, the appointment area, and the TaskPad. The following paragraphs explain some of the features of the Calendar window.

Navigation Pane   The **Navigation Pane** (Figure 2–2 on the previous page) includes two sets of buttons and two panes: the Date Navigator pane and My Calendars pane. The **Date Navigator** shows a calendar for the current month with scroll arrows. When you click the scroll arrows to move to a new date, Calendar displays the name of the month, week, or day in the current view in the appointment area. The current system date has a square around it in the Date Navigator. Dates displayed in bold in the Date Navigator indicate days on which an item is scheduled.

Below the Date Navigator, the My Calendars pane includes a list of available calendars on your computer. In this pane, you can select a single calendar to view, or view other calendars side-by-side with your calendar.

On the lower part of the Navigation Pane are two groups of buttons (Figure 2–3). The first group of buttons are shortcuts representing the standard items that are part of Microsoft Outlook: Mail, Calendar, Contacts, and Tasks. The second group of buttons are shortcuts to other functions of Outlook: Notes, Folder List, Shortcuts, and Configure buttons. When you click a shortcut, Outlook opens the corresponding folder.

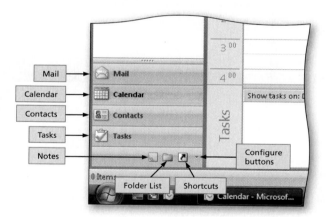

Figure 2–3

Appointment Area   The **appointment area** (Figure 2–2 on the previous page) contains view tabs, a date banner, a day heading and, under the day heading, time slots for the current view. The date currently selected in the Date Navigator appears in the date banner. By default, workday time slots are set from 8:00 a.m. to 5:00 p.m. in one-hour increments. Time slots outside this period are shaded. A vertical scroll bar allows backward and forward movement through the time slots.

Scheduled items, such as appointments, meetings, or events, are displayed in the appointment area. An **appointment** is an activity that does not involve other resources or people. A **meeting**, by contrast, is an appointment to which other resources or people are invited. Outlook's Calendar can be used to schedule several people to attend a meeting or only one person to attend an appointment (such as when you attend a class). An **event** is an activity that lasts 24 hours or longer, such as a seminar, birthday, or vacation. Scheduled events do not occupy time slots in the appointment area; instead, they are displayed in a banner below the day heading.

Standard Toolbar Figure 2–4 shows the Standard toolbar in the Calendar window. The button names indicate their functions. Each button can be clicked to perform a frequently used task, such as creating a new appointment or printing a calendar.

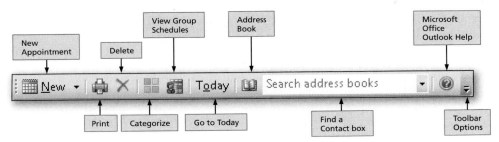

Figure 2–4

To Create a Personal Folder

As in other features of Outlook, such as Contacts, you can create multiple folders within the Calendar component. If you were the only person using Outlook on a computer, you could enter appointments and events directly into the main Calendar folder. In many school situations, however, several people share one computer and therefore, each user needs to create a separate folder in which to store their appointments and events. The following steps create a personal folder for Marcus Cook. Marcus will store his class, work, and baseball practice scheduling information in his personal folder.

1

• With the Calendar – Microsoft Office window active, right-click Calendar in the My Calendars pane to display the Calendar shortcut menu (Figure 2–5).

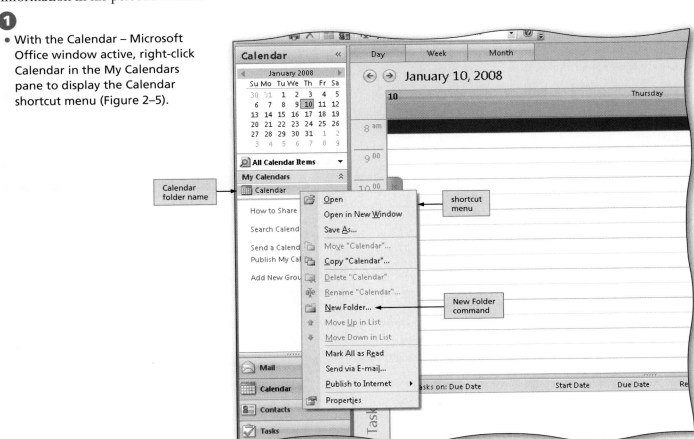

Figure 2–5

- Click New Folder on the Calendar shortcut menu to display the Create New Folder dialog box.

- Type `Marcus' Calendar` in the Name text box.

- If necessary, select Calendar Items in the Folder contains text box.

- Click Calendar in the 'Select where to place the folder' list box to specify where the folder will be stored (Figure 2–6).

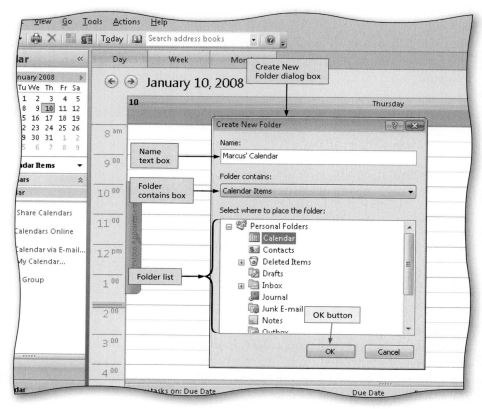

Figure 2–6

- Click the OK button to close the Create New Folder dialog box.

- Click the check box next to Marcus' Calendar in the My Calendars list to open Marcus' calendar.

- Click the check box next to Calendar to remove the existing check mark to remove the default calendar from view (Figure 2–7).

Q&A

Why does my view look different from what is shown?

Figure 2–7 shows the default view for Calendar. If this view does not appear on your computer, click View on the menu bar, point to Current View, and then make sure the Day/Week/Month option is selected.

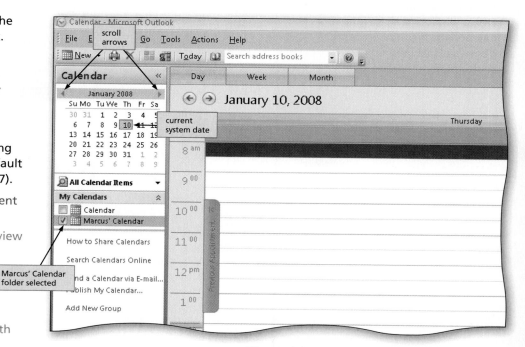

Figure 2–7

Other Ways
1. On the File menu point to Folder, click New Folder on Folder submenu
2. Press CTRL+SHIFT+E

Entering Appointments

Calendar allows you to schedule appointments, meetings, and events for yourself as well as for others who have given you permission to open their personal folders.

This section describes how to enter appointments, or in this case, classes, into Marcus Cook's personal folder, starting with classes for January 14, 2008. Work days and games are one-time appointments; classes and team meetings are recurring appointments.

When entering an appointment into a time slot that is not visible in the current view, use the scroll bar to bring the time slot into view. Once you enter an appointment, you can perform ordinary editing actions.

To Enter Appointments Using the Appointment Area

The following steps enter appointments using the appointment area.

1

- If necessary, click the scroll arrows in the Date Navigator to display January 2008.

- Click 14 in the January calendar in the Date Navigator to display it in the appointment area.

2

- Drag through the 8:00 a.m. – 9:00 a.m. time slot (Figure 2–8).

3

- Type Operating Systems as the first appointment.

4

- Drag through the 9:30 a.m. – 10:30 a.m. time slot.

- Type Data Communications as the second appointment.

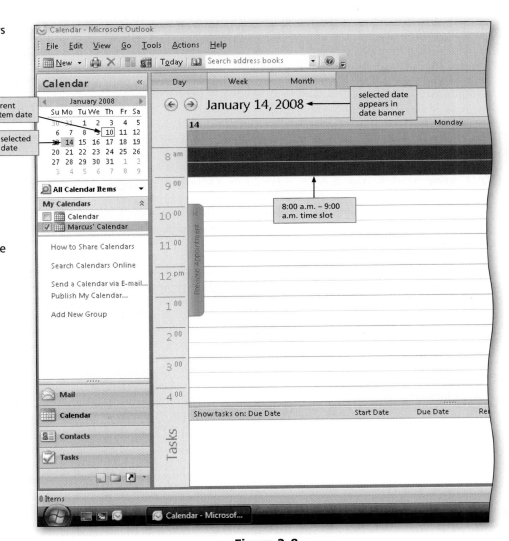

Figure 2–8

- Drag through the 11:30 a.m. –
12:30 p.m. time slot.

- Type Lunch with friends as
the third appointment and then
press the ENTER key (Figure 2–9).

Q&A

What if I make a mistake while
typing an appointment?

If you notice the error before
clicking outside the appointment
time slot or pressing the ENTER
key, use the BACKSPACE key to
erase the characters back to and
including the error. To cancel the
entire entry before clicking outside the appointment time slot or
pressing the ENTER key, press the
ESC key. If you discover the error
after clicking outside the appointment time slot or pressing the
ENTER key, click the appointment
and retype the entry.

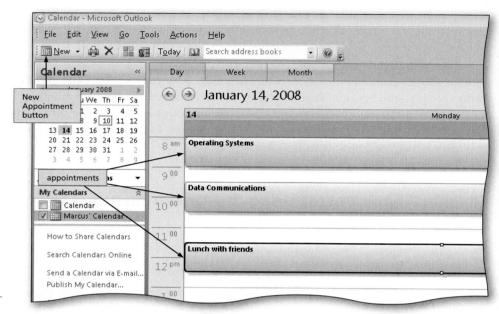

Figure 2–9

To Enter and Save Appointments Using the Appointment Window

Using the **Appointment window** is a slightly more involved process, but it allows the specification of
more detail about the appointment. The following steps enter an appointment at 2:00 p.m. to 4:00 p.m. using the
Appointment window.

1

- Drag through the 2:00 p.m. –
4:00 p.m. time slot and then click
the New Appointment button on
the Standard toolbar to open the
Untitled – Appointment
window. If necessary,
maximize the Untitled –
Appointment window
(Figure 2–10).

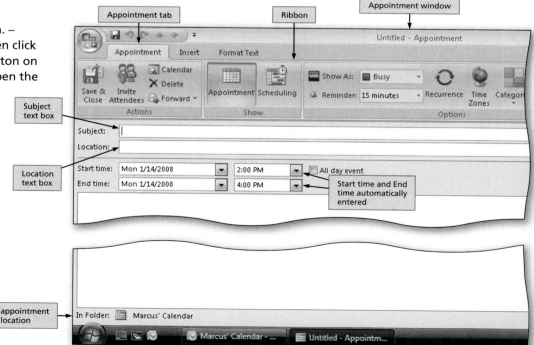

Figure 2–10

2

- Type Team Meeting in the Subject text box and then press the TAB key to move the insertion point to the Location text box.

- Type Union Conference Room #1 in the Location text box (Figure 2–11).

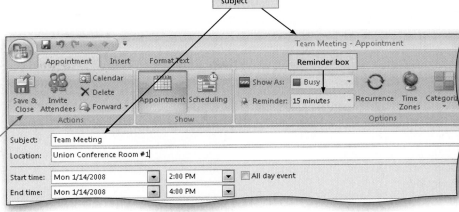

Figure 2–11

3

- Click the Save & Close button on the Ribbon to close the Team Meeting – Appointment window and return to the Calendar window (Figure 2–12).

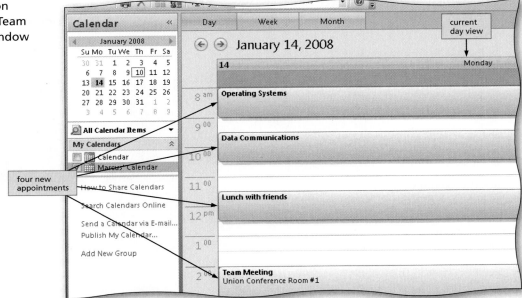

Figure 2–12

Other Ways

1. Double-click time slot, enter appointment
2. On Actions menu, click New Appointment
3. Right-click time slot, click New Appointment on shortcut menu
4. Press CTRL+N

Recurring Appointments

Many appointments are **recurring**, or occur at regular intervals. For example, a class held every Monday and Wednesday from 8:00 a.m. to 9:00 a.m. is a recurring appointment. In this project, Marcus' college classes and team meetings occur at regular weekly intervals. Typing these recurring appointments for each occurrence would be very time-consuming. Table 2–1 lists Marcus' recurring appointments.

Table 2–1 Recurring Appointments

Time	Appointment	Occurrence
8:00 a.m. – 9:00 a.m.	Operating Systems (Anderson 203)	Every Monday and Wednesday (30 times)
9:30 a.m. – 10:30 a.m.	Data Communications (Lilly 105)	Every Monday and Wednesday (30 times)
2:00 p.m. – 4:00 p.m.	Team Meeting (Union Conference Room #1)	Every other Monday (15 times)

BTW

Appointments
Appointments can be designated as busy, free, tentative, or out of office. The Private button in the Appointment window allows you to designate as private any appointments, tasks, meetings, or contacts. The private designation prevents viewing by other users with access to your calendar. Private calendar elements are identified with a lock symbol.

To Enter Recurring Appointments

By designating an appointment as recurring, the appointment needs to be added only once and then recurrence is specified for the days on which it occurs. The following steps enter recurring appointments.

- With Monday, January 14, 2008 displayed, double-click the words Operating Systems in the 8:00 a.m. – 9:00 a.m. time slot to open the Operating Systems – Appointment window.

- Click the Location text box and then type Anderson 203 to set the location of the class (Figure 2–13).

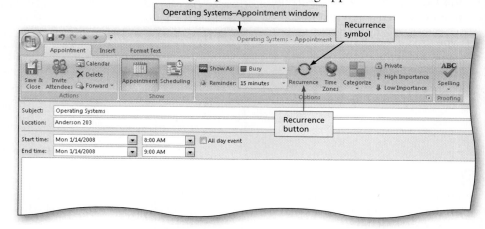

Figure 2–13

3

- Click the Recurrence button on the Ribbon to display the Appointment Recurrence dialog box.

- Click the Wednesday check box to select the days this appointment will recur.

- Click End after in the Range of recurrence area, double-click the End after text box, and then type 30 as the number of occurrences (Figure 2–14).

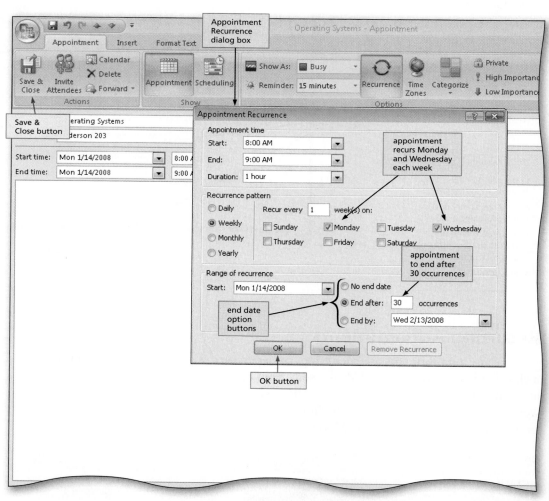

Figure 2–14

4

- Click the OK button to close the Appointment Recurrence dialog box.

- Click the Save & Close button on the Ribbon to close the Operating Systems – Recurring Appointment window and return to the Calendar window (Figure 2–15).

5

- Repeat Steps 1 through 4 to make the Data Communications and Team Meeting appointments recurring. Refer to Table 2–1 for the location, range, and ending dates.

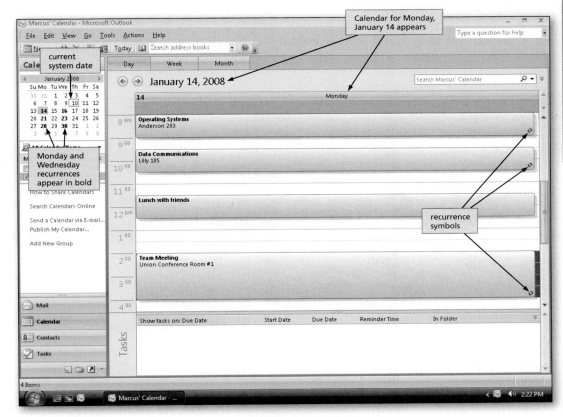

Figure 2–15

Completing Marcus' Calendar

With the Monday schedule entered, the next step is to move to the next day in the appointment area and complete the recurring appointments for every Tuesday and Thursday using the appointment information in Table 2–2.

Table 2–2 Additional Recurring Appointments

Time	Appointment	Occurrence
8:30 a.m. – 9:30 a.m.	Economics (EE 215)	Every Tuesday and Thursday (30 times)
2:30 p.m. – 3:30 p.m.	Supervision (Gyte 103)	Every Tuesday and Thursday (30 times)

To Move to the Next Day in the Appointment Area and Enter the Remaining Recurring Appointments

Because the recurring appointments start on Tuesday, Tuesday must be displayed in the appointment area. The following steps move to the next day using the Date Navigator and then enter the remaining recurring appointments.

- Click 15 in the January 2008 calendar in the Date Navigator to move to Tuesday, January 15, 2008.

- Drag through the 8:30 a.m. – 9:30 a.m. time slot (Figure 2–16).

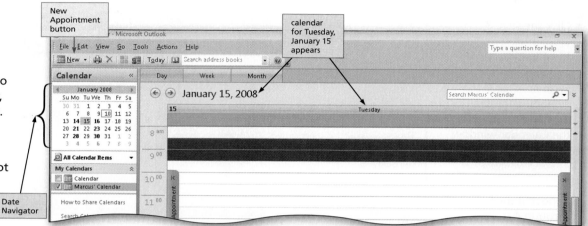

Figure 2–16

- Click the New Appointment button on the Standard toolbar to open the Untitled – Appointment window.

- Enter the recurring appointments listed in Table 2–2 on the previous page.

- Click the Save & Close button on the Ribbon to close the Appointment window and return to the Calendar window (Figure 2–17).

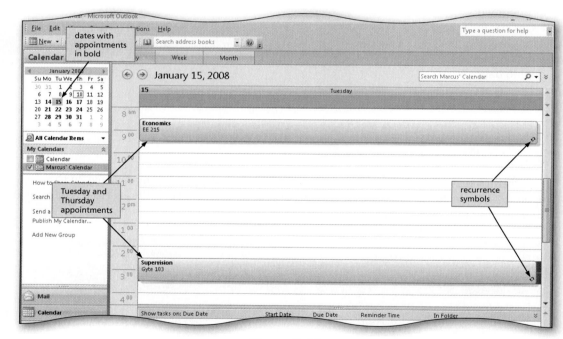

Figure 2–17

Q&A

What if I have appointments that recur other than weekly or semi-weekly?

Daily, weekly, monthly, or yearly recurrence patterns are possible in the Recurrence pattern options. An appointment can be set to occur a certain number of times or up to a certain day.

Other Ways

1. On Actions menu, click New Recurring Appointment

2. Press ALT+A, TYPE A

Natural Language Phrasing

In the steps just completed, dates and times were entered in the Appointment window using standard numeric entries. Outlook's **AutoDate function**, however, provides the capability of specifying appointment dates and times using **natural language phrases**. For example, you can type phrases, such as "next Tuesday," "two weeks from yesterday," or "midnight," and Outlook will calculate the correct date and/or time.

In addition to these natural language phrases, Outlook can convert abbreviations and ordinal numbers into complete words and dates. For example, you can type Feb instead of February or the first of September instead of 9/1. Outlook's Calendar application also can convert words such as "yesterday," and "tomorrow," and the names of holidays that occur on the same date each year, such as Valentine's Day. Table 2–3 lists various AutoDate options.

BTW

Moving a Recurring Appointment
If a recurring appointment is moved, only the selected instance of the appointment is moved. If all instances of an appointment need to be moved, open the appointment, click the Recurrence button on the Ribbon, and then change the recurrence pattern.

Table 2–3 AutoDate Options

Category	Examples
Dates Spelled Out	• July twenty-third, March 29th, first of December • this Fri, next Sat, two days from now • three weeks ago, next week • one month from today
Times Spelled Out	• noon, midnight • nine o'clock a.m., five twenty • 7 p.m.
Descriptions of Times and Dates	• now • yesterday, today, tomorrow • next, last • ago, before, after, ending, following • for, from, that, this, till, through, until
Holidays	• Cinco de Mayo • Christmas Day, Christmas Eve • Halloween • Independence Day • New Year's Day, New Year's Eve • St. Patrick's Day • Valentine's Day • Veteran's Day

To Enter Appointment Dates and Times Using Natural Language Phrases

Now that Marcus has entered his classes into his calendar, he will enter his work schedule. The following steps enter the date and time for the work schedule using natural language phrases.

- With Tuesday, January 15 displayed in the appointment area, click the New Appointment button on the Standard toolbar to open the Untitled – Appointment window.

- Type Sign up for work in the Subject text box and then press the TAB key to move to the location.

- Type Better Batter Baseball Instructional School in the Location text box and then press the TAB key once.

- Type next Wednesday in the Start time date box for the date (Figure 2–18).

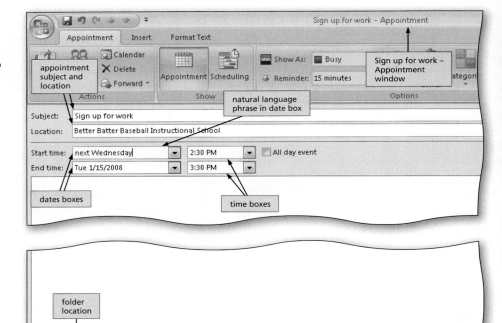

Figure 2–18

- Press the TAB key.

- Type one p.m. in the Start time time box.

- Press the TAB key twice to advance the cursor to the End time time box (Figure 2–19).

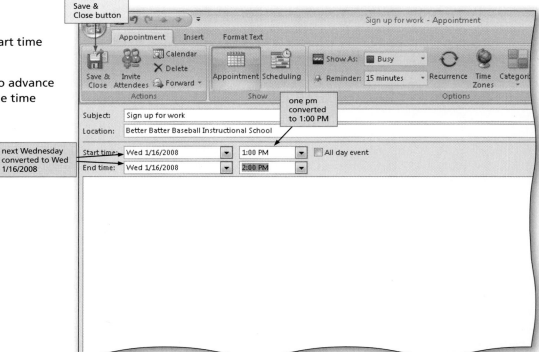

Figure 2–19

4

- Type `three forty five` in the End time time box and then press the ENTER key.

- Click the Save & Close button on the Ribbon to close the Sign up for work – Appointment window and return to the Marcus' Calendar window.

5

- Repeat Steps 1 through 4 to enter working at Better Batter Baseball Instructional School on January 26, 2008 from 9:00 a.m. to 1:00 p.m. Use work as the subject and Better Batter Baseball Instructional School as the location. Use natural language phrases to enter the dates and times. When you have completed entering the information, click the Save & Close button on the Ribbon to return to the Calendar window (Figure 2–20).

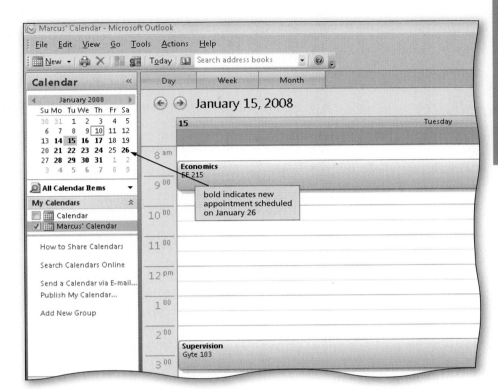

Figure 2–20

To Enter the Remaining One-Time Appointments

Table 2–4 contains the current week's practice schedule along with the schedule for the first seven games for the upcoming season. The following steps show how to enter the remaining one-time appointments.

Table 2–4 Additional One-Time Appointments			
Date	**Time**	**Appointment**	**Location**
1/14/2008	4:00 p.m. – 6:00 p.m.	Practice	Practice Field
1/15/2008	5:00 p.m. – 7:00 p.m.	Practice	Practice Field
1/16/2008	4:00 p.m. – 6:00 p.m.	Practice	Practice Field
1/17/2008	5:00 p.m. – 7:00 p.m.	Practice	Practice Field
1/19/2008	12:00 p.m. – 3:00 p.m.	Practice	Practice Field
2/16/2008	1:00 p.m. – 4:00 p.m.	Game	Beachcombe, FL
2/23/2008	11:00 a.m. – 2:00 p.m.	Game	Blackburg, TX
3/6/2008	7:00 p.m. – 10:00 p.m.	Game	Donner Field
3/8/2008	1:00 p.m. – 4:00 p.m.	Game	Donner Field
3/11/2008	7:00 p.m. – 10:00 p.m.	Game	Snow Hill, IL
3/15/2008	2:00 p.m. – 5:00 p.m.	Game	Donner Field
3/18/2008	7:00 p.m. – 10:00 p.m.	Game	Donner Field

① With the Calendar window active, click January 14, 2008 in the Date Navigator.

② Click the New Appointment button on the Standard toolbar.

③ Type `Practice` in the Subject text box, and then press the TAB key.

④ Type `Practice Field` in the Location text box, and then press the TAB key two times.

⑤ Type `4 p.m.` in the Start time time box, press the TAB key two times, and then type `six p.m.` in the End time time box.

⑥ Click the Save & Close button on the Ribbon.

⑦ Enter the remaining one-time appointments in Table 2–4.

Editing Appointments

Because schedules often need to be rearranged, Outlook provides several ways of editing appointments. Change the subject and location by clicking the appointment and editing the information directly in the appointment area, or double-click the appointment and make corrections using the Appointment window. You can specify whether all occurrences in a series of recurring appointments need to be changed, or a single occurrence can be altered.

To Delete an Appointment

Appointments sometimes are canceled and must be deleted from the schedule. For example, the schedule created thus far in this project contains appointments during the week of April 7, 2008. Because this week is Spring Break, no classes will meet and the scheduled appointments need to be deleted. The following steps delete an appointment from the calendar.

①

- Click the scroll arrow in the Date Navigator to display April 2008.

- Click 7 in the April 2008 calendar.

- Click the first appointment to be deleted, Operating Systems (Figure 2–21).

Editing Appointments
If you cannot remember the details about a specific appointment, you easily can check it. Click Tools on the menu bar, point to Instant Search, and then click Advanced Find to locate the appointment in question. In the Look for box, select Appointments and Meetings. You then may search for any word or subject.

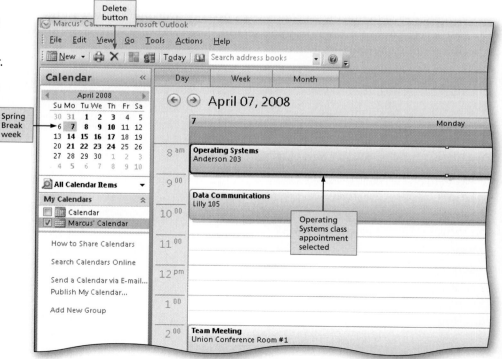

Figure 2–21

2

- Click the Delete button on the Standard toolbar to display the Confirm Delete dialog box (Figure 2–22).

- Click the OK button to delete the appointment and return to the Calendar window.

3

- Repeat Steps 1 and 2 to delete the remaining classes and meetings from the week of April 7, 2008.

Q&A

Can I use the DELETE key to delete an appointment?

Yes. Select the appointment and then press the DELETE key. If only individual characters are being deleted when you press the DELETE key, you are just editing the appointment. Try clicking outside the appointment and then select it again.

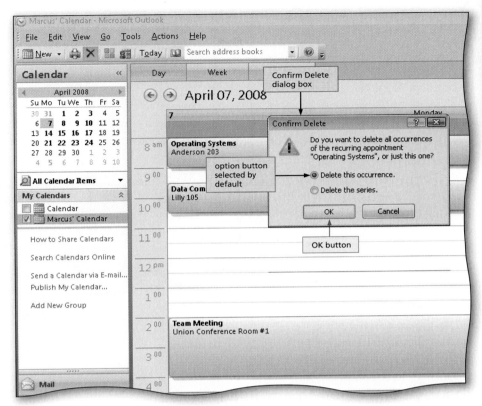

Figure 2–22

Other Ways
1. Right-click appointment to be deleted, click DELETE on the shortcut menu

To Move an Appointment to a New Time

Outlook provides several ways to move appointments. Suppose, for instance, that some of your friends cannot make it for lunch at 11:30 a.m. on Monday, January 14, 2008. The appointment needs to be rescheduled for 1:00 p.m. to 2:00 p.m. Instead of deleting and then retyping the appointment, simply drag it to the new time slot. The following steps move an appointment to a new time.

1

- Click the left scroll arrow in the Date Navigator to display January 2008.

- Click 14 in the January 2008 calendar in the Date Navigator.

- Position the mouse pointer over the Lunch with friends appointment (Figure 2–23).

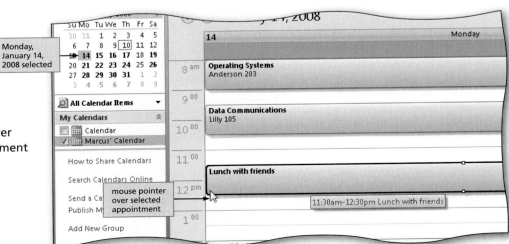

Figure 2–23

2

- Drag the appointment down to the 1:00 p.m. – 2:00 p.m. time slot.

- Release the mouse button to drop the appointment in the new time slot (Figure 2–24).

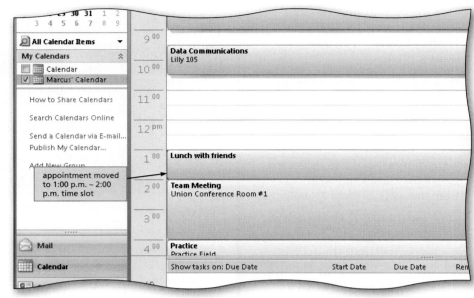

Figure 2–24

Other Ways

1. Double-click appointment, edit Start time date box in Appointment window

To Move an Appointment to a New Date

If an appointment is being moved to a new date but remaining in the same time slot, simply drag the appointment to the new date in the Date Navigator. The following steps move an appointment to a new date.

1

- Position the mouse pointer over the Lunch with friends appointment.

- Click and drag the appointment from the appointment area to the 18 in the January 2008 calendar (Figure 2–25).

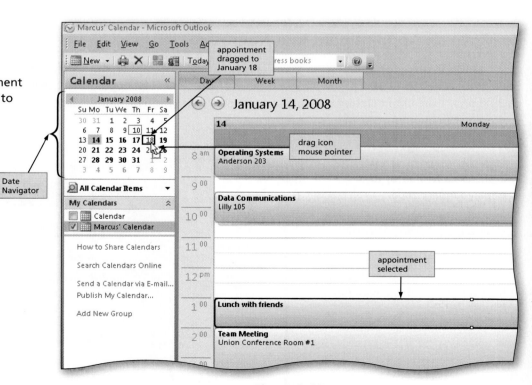

Figure 2–25

2

- Release the mouse button to complete moving the appointment (Figure 2–26).

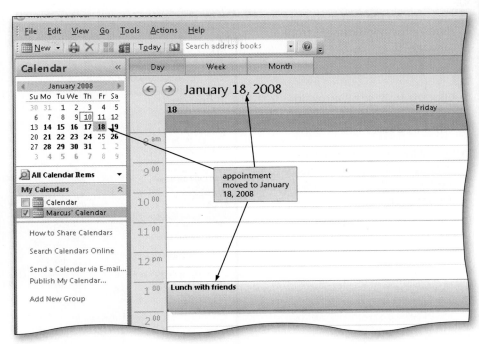

Figure 2–26

To Move an Appointment to a New Month

When moving an appointment to another month, you must cut and paste the appointment.

The baseball instructional school has decided to reschedule the Saturday time slot to a date in February. The new work date is moved from Saturday, January 26, 2008 to Saturday, February 2, 2008. The following steps show how to move an appointment to a new month using the cut and paste method.

- Click 26 in the January 2008 calendar in the Date Navigator.

- Click the Work appointment to select it.

- Click Edit on the menu bar to display the Edit menu (Figure 2–27).

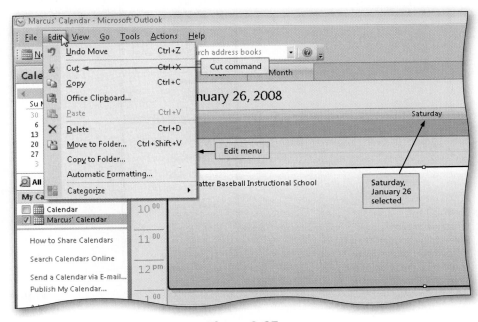

Figure 2–27

- Click Cut on the Edit menu to remove the appointment from January 26.

- Click the right scroll arrow in the Date Navigator to display February 2008.

- Click 2 in the February 2008 calendar in the Date Navigator to display it in the Appointment area (Figure 2–28).

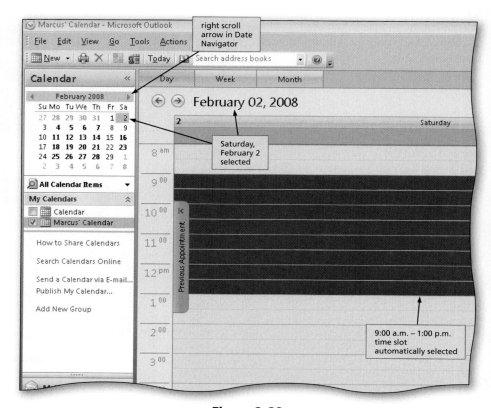

Figure 2–28

4

- Click Edit on the menu bar and then click Paste to complete moving the appointment to the new time slot (Figure 2–29).

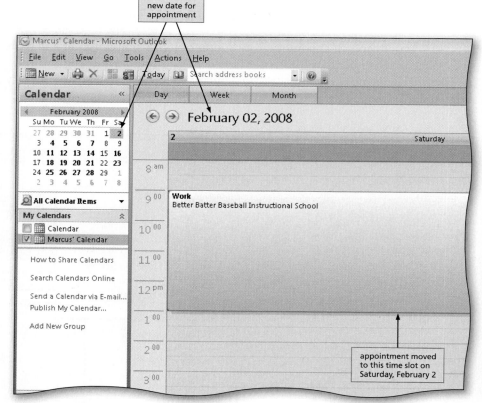

Figure 2–29

BTW

E-Mailing Appointments
To send an appointment to a coworker or classmate, right-click the appointment and click Forward on the shortcut menu.

Creating an Event

Outlook's Calendar folder allows you to keep track of important events. **Events** are activities that last 24 hours or longer. Examples of events include birthdays, conferences, weddings, vacations, holidays, and so on, and can be one-time or recurring. In Outlook, events differ from appointments in one primary way – they do not appear in individual time slots in the appointment area. When an event is scheduled, its description appears in a small **banner** below the day heading. The details of the event can be indicated as time that is free, busy, or out of the office during the event.

To Create an Event

The following steps enter a birthday as an event.

1
- If necessary, click the left scroll arrow to display January 2008 in the Date Navigator. Click 25 in the January 2008 calendar in the Date Navigator.

2
- Double-click the day heading at the top of the appointment area. When the Untitled - Event window opens, type Drew's Birthday in the Subject text box and then press the TAB key (Figure 2–30).

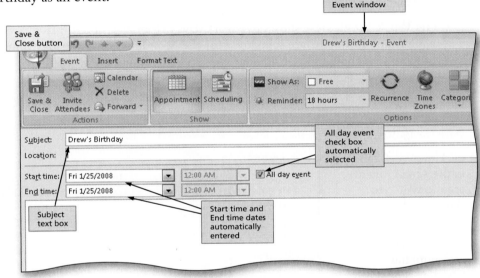

Figure 2–30

3
- Click the Save & Close button on the Ribbon to close the Event window and return to the Calendar window (Figure 2–31).

Q&A
Do I have to enter every holiday into the calendar?

No. Outlook contains a folder of typical holidays for various countries that can be added to your calendar automatically. To do this, click Options on the Tools menu. Click Calendar Options, and then click Add Holidays in the Calendar Option sheet.

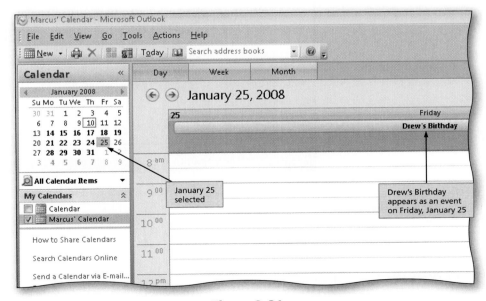

Figure 2–31

BTW

Locations
As appointments or events are entered with specific locations, the locations automatically are accumulated in a list. To access this list, open the appointment and click the Location box arrow. Frequently used locations can be selected from this list, thereby saving typing time.

Various Calendar Views

The default view type of the Calendar folder is the Day/Week/Month view. While in **Day/Week/Month view**, Outlook can display calendars in four different views: Day, Work Week, Week, and Month. So far in this project, you have used only the Day view, which is indicated by the Day tab selected in the Appointment area (Figure 2–31).

Some people may prefer a different view of their calendar, or you may need to use different views at various times. Now that the schedule is complete, it also can be displayed in Week or Month view. Although the screen looks quite different in Week and Month views, you can accomplish the same tasks as in Day view: you can add, edit, or delete appointments and events, and reminders can be set or removed.

To Change to Work Week View

The **Work Week view** shows five work days (Monday through Friday) in columnar style. This view lets you see how many appointments are scheduled for the Monday through Friday timeframe, eliminating the weekends. The following step changes the Calendar view to Work Week view.

- Click Tuesday, January 15 in the Date Navigator.

- Click the Week tab in the Appointment area to switch to Work Week view.

- If necessary, scroll up in the appointment area until the 8:00 a.m. time slot appears (Figure 2–32).

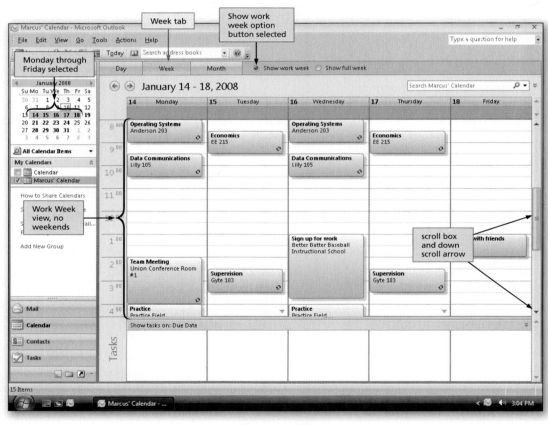

Figure 2–32

Other Ways

1. On the View menu click Work Week
2. Press ALT+V, type R
3. Press CTRL+ALT+2

To Change to Week View

The advantage of displaying a calendar in **Week view** is to see how many appointments are scheduled for any given week. In Week view, the seven days of the selected week appear in the appointment area. The following step displays the calendar in Week view.

1

• With the Week tab active, click the Show full week option button to switch to Week view (Figure 2–33).

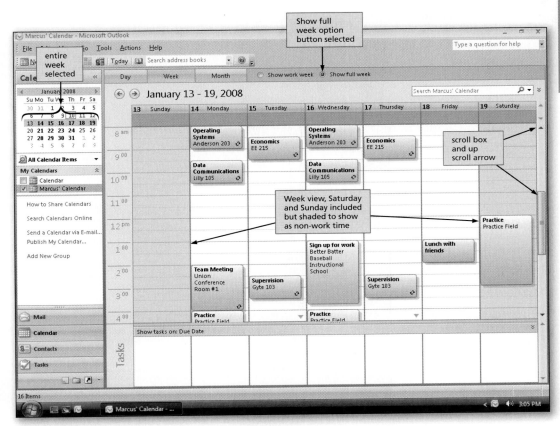

Figure 2–33

<table>
<tr><td colspan="2">**Other Ways**</td></tr>
<tr><td>1.</td><td>On the View menu click Week</td></tr>
<tr><td>2.</td><td>Press ALT+V, type W</td></tr>
<tr><td>3.</td><td>Press CTRL+ALT+3</td></tr>
</table>

To Change to Month View

The **Month view** resembles a standard monthly calendar page and displays a schedule for an entire month. Appointments are listed in each date frame in the calendar. The following step displays the calendar in Month view.

1

- Click the Month tab in the Appointment area to switch to Month view (Figure 2–34).

- Click the Day tab to return to Day view.

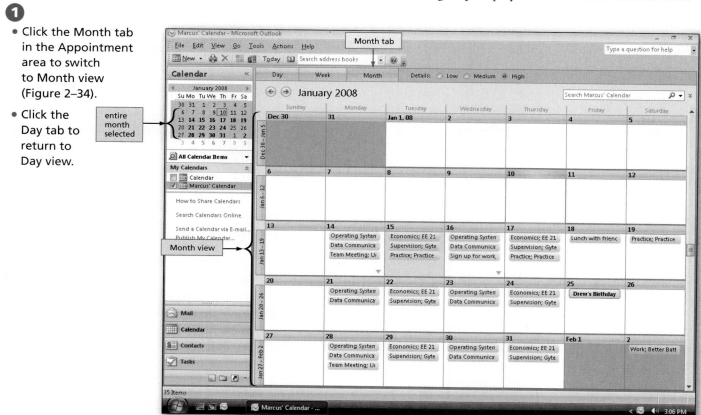

Figure 2–34

Organizing Tasks

BTW

Editing Tasks
You can drag a task from the Task list to the Calendar button in the Navigation Pane, thereby making a task an appointment.

With the daily appointments organized, you can use Tasks to organize the many duties and projects you need to complete each day. Tasks allow for the creation of a **task list** of items that need to be tracked through completion. **Tasks** can be simple to do items, daily reminders, assignments with due dates, or business responsibilities. Outlook can indicate whether a task is pending, in progress, complete, or has some other status.

When a task is complete, click the check box in the Sort by: Complete column to the left of the task's subject. A check mark called a **Completed icon** then appears in the Complete column and a line through the task indicates it is complete.

In this project, Table 2–5 contains tasks that occur once and will be later made into group tasks, assigned, or forwarded.

Table 2–5 Task List

Task	Due Date
Pick up hats and practice jerseys from coach	1/14/2008
Get Econ class book	1/15/2008
Set up meeting with advisor	1/11/2008
Make appointment with dentist	1/10/2008
Check on availability of parking lots for fund-raiser carwash	1/25/2008

To Create a Task List

The following steps create a task list.

1

• Click the Tasks button in the Navigation Pane to open the To-Do-List – Microsoft Outlook window.

2

• Click the Tasks folder in the My Tasks folder list to switch to the Tasks – Microsoft Outlook window.

• Click the Subject text box and then type `Pick up hats and practice jerseys from coach` as the first task.

• Press the TAB key and then type `1/14/2008` in the Due Date text box (Figure 2–35).

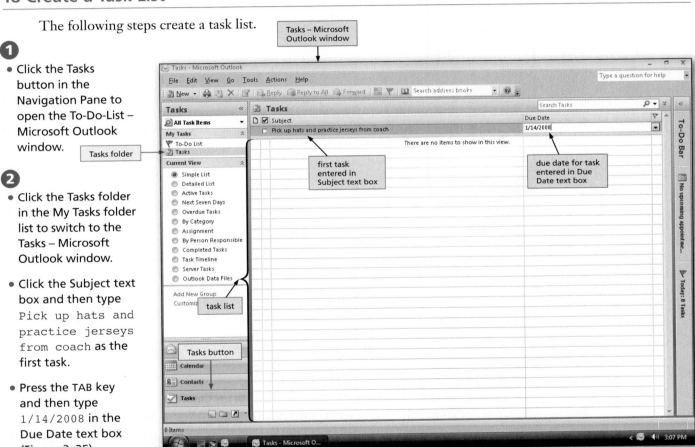

Figure 2–35

3

- Press the ENTER key.

- Repeat Steps 1 and 2 to enter the remaining tasks in Table 2–5.

- Click outside the task list to display the completed task list (Figure 2–36).

Q&A

Is there a way to add more detail to a task?

Yes. To add details to tasks, such as start dates, status, and priority, double-click a task in the task list to open a Task window.

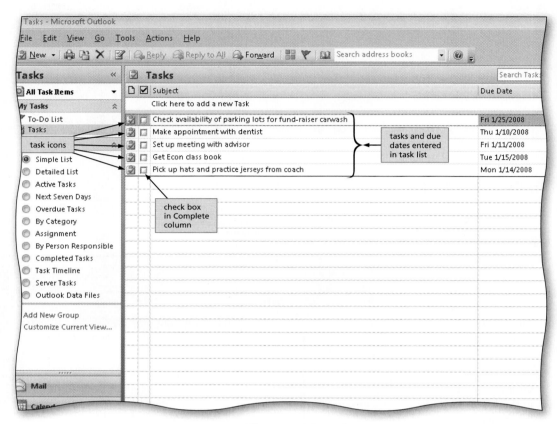

Figure 2–36

Other Ways

1. Click New Task button on Standard toolbar
2. On File menu point to New, click Task on New submenu
3. Press CTRL+N

Exporting, Deleting, and Importing Subfolders

The calendar is now ready to be saved to a USB flash drive. Saving your work to an external storage device allows you to take your schedule to another computer.

With many application software packages, a single file, such as a letter or spreadsheet, can be saved directly to an external storage device. With Outlook, however, each appointment, task, or contact is a file in itself. Thus, rather than saving numerous individual files, Outlook uses an **Import and Export Wizard** to guide you through the process of saving an entire subfolder. Transferring a subfolder to a USB flash drive is called **exporting**. Moving a subfolder back to a computer is called **importing**. Subfolders can be imported and exported from any Outlook application. Outlook then saves the subfolder to a USB flash drive, adding the extension **.pst**.

To Export a Subfolder to a USB Flash Drive

The following steps show how to export Marcus' Calendar subfolder to a USB flash drive.

- Connect the USB flash drive containing the Data Files for Students to one of the computer's USB ports.

- Click File on the menu bar and then click Import and Export to display the Import and Export Wizard dialog box.

2

- Click Export to a file in the Choose an action to perform list (Figure 2–37).

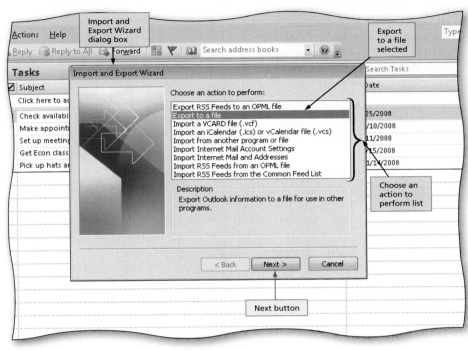

Figure 2–37

3

- Click the Next button.

- In the Export to a File dialog box, click Personal Folder File (.pst) and then click the Next button to display the Export Personal Folders dialog box.

- If necessary, scroll up until the Calendar folder is visible and then click the plus sign (+) to the left of the Calendar icon in the Select the folder to export from list to see Marcus' calendar in the list.

- Click Marcus' Calendar to select it as the folder to be exported (Figure 2–38).

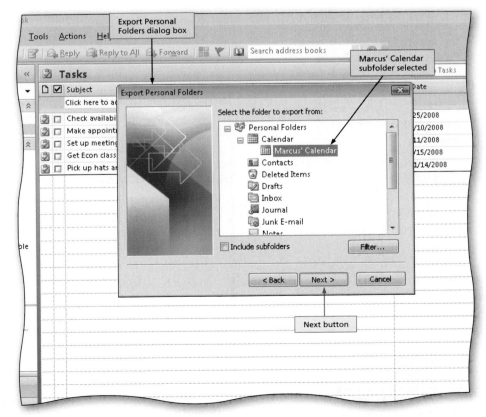

Figure 2–38

● Click the Next button.

● Type `e:\Marcus' Calendar.pst` in the Save exported file as text box and then click the 'Replace duplicates with items exported' option button (Figure 2–39). (If your USB flash drive is not labeled E, type the drive letter accordingly.)

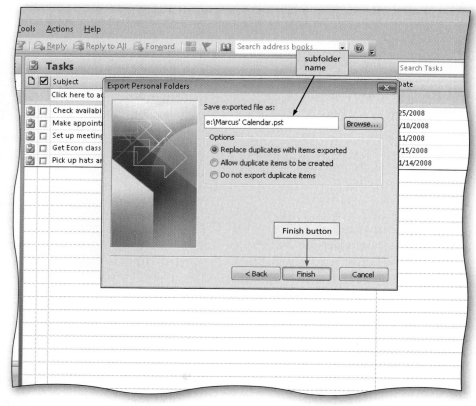

Figure 2–39

● Click the Finish button to display the Create Microsoft Personal Folders dialog box (Figure 2–40).

● Click the OK button to close the dialog box and return to the Tasks window.

Q&A

What programs can I use to view the exported subfolder?

Exported subfolders can be viewed only in Outlook. However, they can be saved as another file type, such as a text file, and then imported into other programs.

BTW

Saving

All appointments, events, meetings, and tasks are saved as separate files on your hard disk. As such, they can be edited, moved, copied, or deleted. These items can be saved as a group using the Import and Export Wizard on the File menu.

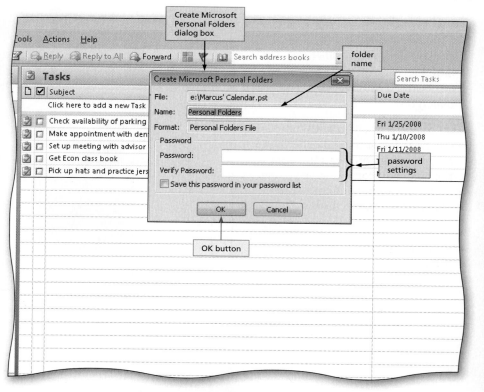

Figure 2–40

To Delete a Personal Subfolder

The Marcus' Calendar subfolder now has been exported to a USB flash drive. A copy of it is still present on the hard disk of your computer, however, and appears in Outlook's Folder List. To delete a subfolder from the computer entirely, use the Delete command. The following steps delete a personal subfolder. If you did not complete the previous set of steps, do not delete the Marcus' Calendar subfolder.

1

- Click the Calendar button in the Navigation Pane to display the Marcus' Calendar window.

- Right-click the date banner to display the shortcut menu (Figure 2–41).

2

- Click Delete "Marcus' Calendar" on the shortcut menu to delete the folder from Outlook's folder list.

- Click the Yes button in the dialog box that asks if you are sure you want to delete the folder.

Q&A

Is there a way to retrieve a deleted folder?

Yes. Outlook sends the deleted sub-folder to the **Deleted Items** folder in the Folder List. If you accidentally delete a subfolder without first exporting it to an external storage device, you can still open the subfolder by double-clicking it in the Deleted Items folder in the Folders List.

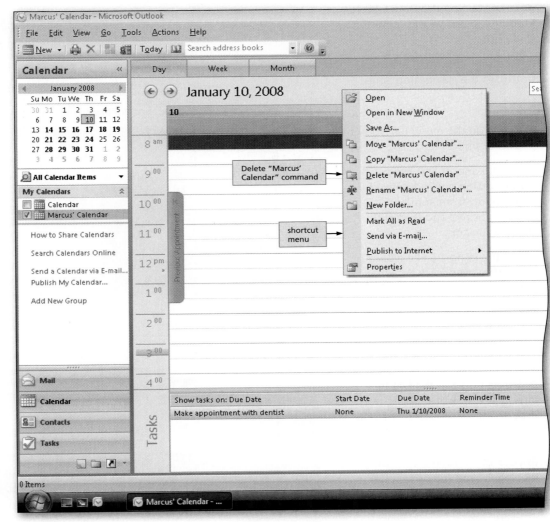

Figure 2–41

Other Ways

1. On File menu point to Folders, click Delete "Calendar" on Folders submenu

2. Press ALT+F, press F, press D

To Import a Subfolder

Earlier, the Calendar subfolder containing Marcus' appointment and event files was exported to a USB flash drive. The following steps import the same Calendar subfolder from the USB flash drive as well as other Data files to be used later in the chapter.

- If necessary, connect the USB flash drive containing the Data Files for Students to one of the computer's USB ports.

- If necessary, click the Calendar button in the Navigation Pane.

- Click File on the menu bar and then click Import and Export.

- When the Import and Export Wizard dialog box is displayed, click 'Import from another program or file' and then click the Next button.

- When the Import a File dialog box is displayed, click Personal Folder File (.pst) and then click the Next button.

- In the Import Personal Folders dialog box, type e:\Marcus' Calendar.pst in the File to Import text box or click the Browse button to access the USB flash drive and select the Marcus' Calendar subfolder (Figure 2–42). (If your USB flash drive is not labeled E, type the drive letter accordingly.)

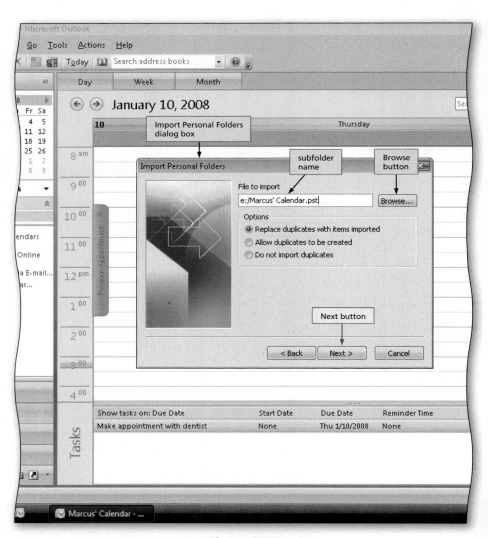

Figure 2–42

4

- Click the Next button to display the Import Personal Folders dialog box.

- Click Calendar in the 'Select the folder to import from' list (Figure 2–43).

5

- Click the Finish button to close the dialog box and return to the Calendar window.

6

- Repeat Steps 1 through 5 twice, once to import Marcus' Contacts subfolder (selecting the Contact folder in Step 4) and once to import Marcus' Inbox subfolder (selecting the Inbox folder in Step 4) from the Chapter 2 folder in the Data Files for Students.

Importing
Other contact information can be imported through the Import and Export Wizard on the File menu. This wizard allows you to copy to Outlook information that was created and saved in other applications.

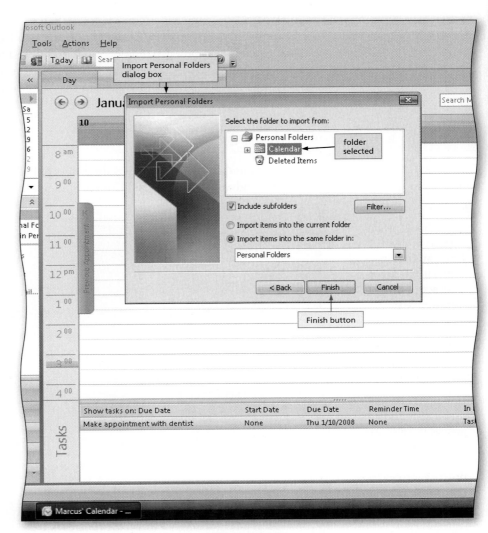

Figure 2–43

Meeting and Task Management

If you are in charge of an organization or group, you likely will have to schedule meetings and delegate tasks to other members of the group. Using your contact list, Outlook allows you to easily perform these functions. The following sections illustrate how to assign tasks and schedule meetings with individuals in the Marcus' Contact list.

To Assign a Task to Another Person

Using the task list previously created in this project and the imported Marcus' Contacts contact list, the following steps assign a task to an individual in the Marcus' Contacts contact list.

1

- Click the Contacts button in the Navigation Pane and then click Marcus' Contacts in the My Contacts list.

- Click the Tasks button in the Navigation Pane to display the Task window.

- Double-click the Pick up hats and practice jerseys from coach task to display the Pick up hats and practice jerseys from coach – Task window.

- Double-click the title bar to maximize the window (Figure 2–44).

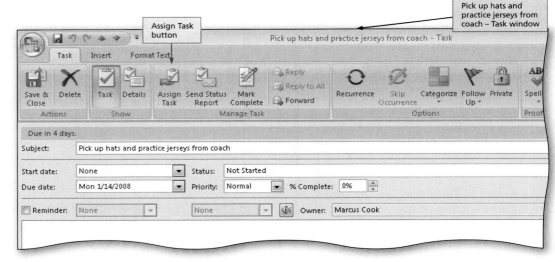

Figure 2–44

2

- Click the Assign Task button on the Ribbon.

- Type Jake Nunan in the To text box (Figure 2–45).

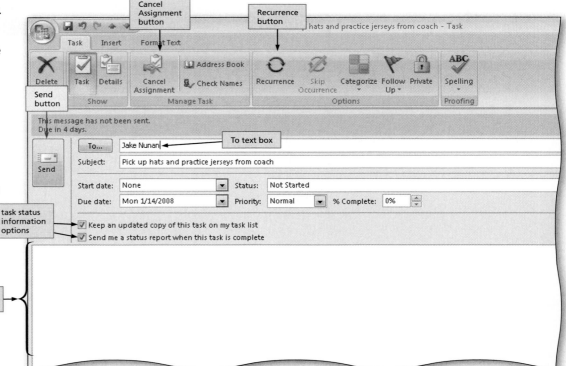

Figure 2–45

3

- Click the Send button to send the task to Jake Nunan and close the task window (Figure 2–46).

Q&A

Can I assign a task to more than one person at a time?

Yes. Outlook does allow you to assign a task to more than one person at a time; however, in order to have Outlook keep you up to date on the progress of a task, you must divide the work into separate tasks and then assign each task individually.

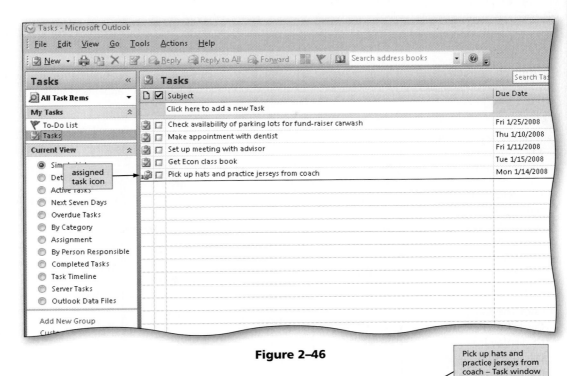

Figure 2–46

4

- Double-click the Pick up hats and practice jerseys from coach task to open the task window (Figure 2–47).

5

- Click the Close button on the Pick up hats and practice jerseys from coach task to close the task window.

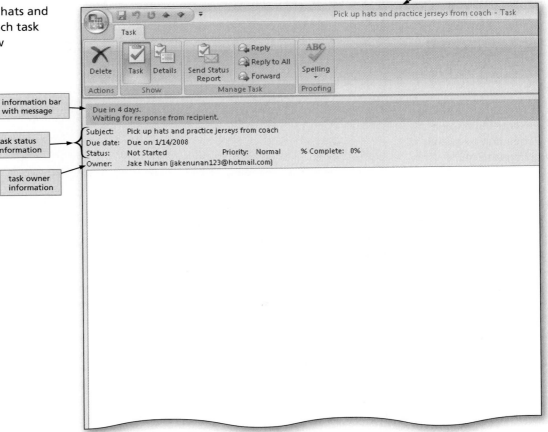

Figure 2–47

To Accept a Task Assignment

When a recipient receives a task assignment, it appears in his or her Inbox. Then, the recipient has the option to accept or decline the task. The following steps show how to accept a task assignment.

Note: The steps on pages OUT 108 through OUT 110 are for demonstration purposes only, thus, if you are stepping through this project on a computer, then you must have someone send you a task request so it appears in the Inbox as shown in Figure 2–48.

- If necessary, click the Mail button in the Navigation Pane.

- If necessary, click the plus sign (+) next to the Inbox folder in the All Mail Items list, and then select the Marcus' Inbox folder.

- Click the Mary Cook Task Request to display it in the Reading pane (Figure 2–48).

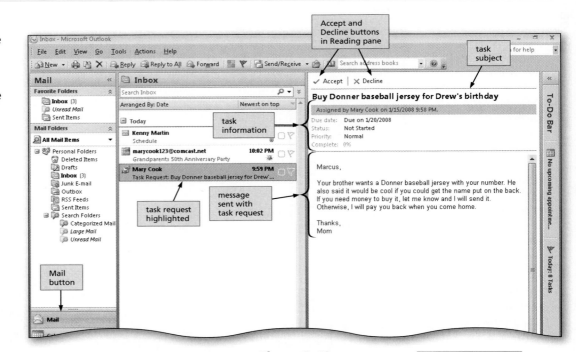

Figure 2–48

- Double-click the Task Request message heading to open it (Figure 2–49).

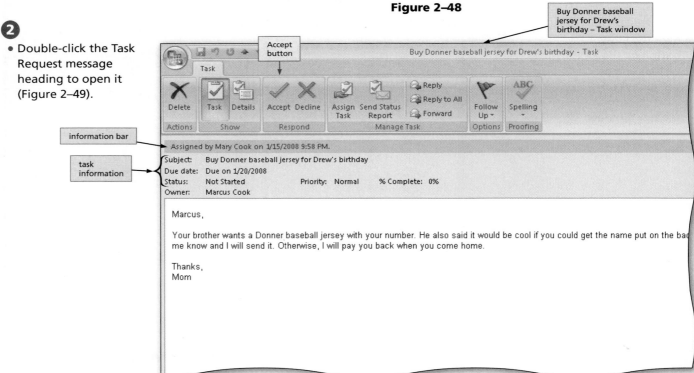

Figure 2–49

- Click the Accept button on the Ribbon to display the Accepting Task dialog box (Figure 2–50).

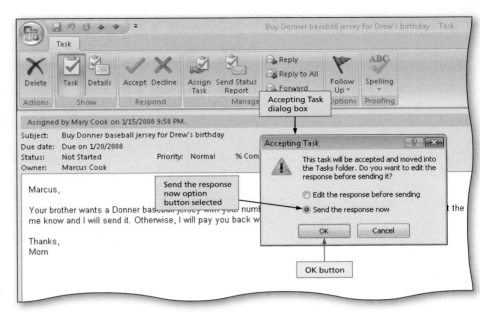

Figure 2–50

- Click the 'Send the response now' option button, and then click the OK button to send the response and close the Accepting Task dialog box.

- Click the Task button in the Navigation Pane to display the Task List. If necessary, click Tasks in the My Tasks list in the Navigation Pane (Figure 2–51).

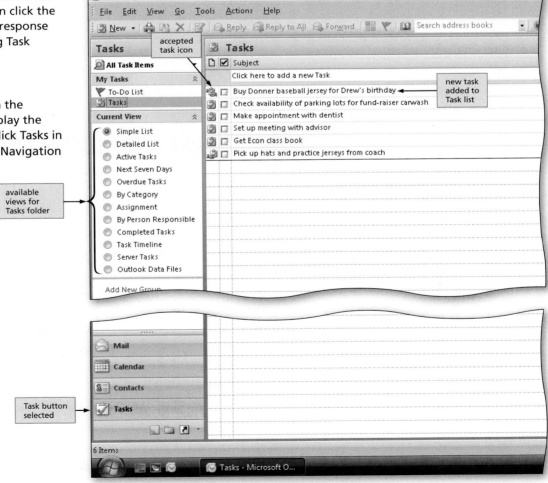

Figure 2–51

6

• When a recipient accepts a task request, the requestor receives a message indicating that the task has been accepted (Figure 2–52).

information bar indicating task has been accepted

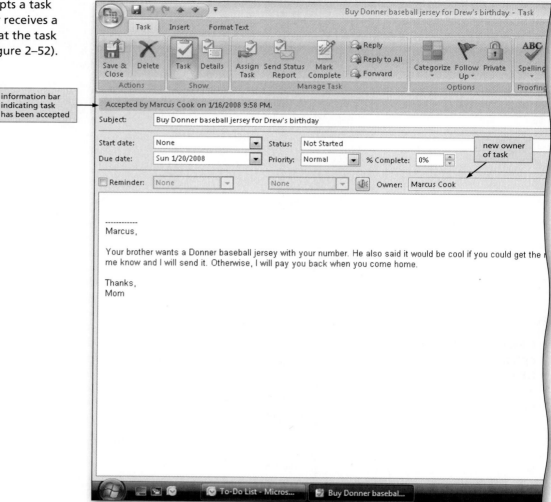

Figure 2–52

TO CUSTOMIZE THE TASKS WINDOW

The default view for the task list is shown in Figure 2–51 on the previous page. This view contains the Task icon, the completed task check box, the task description, and the due date. Outlook allows you to add or delete columns, or **fields**, so you can display only the information you want to view. To modify the current view of the task list, you would follow these steps.

1. On the View menu, point to Current View, and then click Customize Current View in the Current View submenu.

2. When the Customize View: Simple List dialog box is displayed, click the Fields button.

3. To add a new field, select a field in the Available fields list, and then click the Add button.

4. To delete a field, select a field in the Show these fields in this order list, and then click the Remove button.

5. When you are finished customizing the view, click the OK buttons in both open dialog boxes.

For the same reason you created a separate folder for calendar items, you may want to create a separate folder for tasks and move the current task list to that folder. The following steps describe how to create a personal tasks folder and move the current task list to that folder.

To Move Tasks to a New Personal Folder

1. With the Tasks window active, right-click the Tasks title bar above the task list.
2. Click New Folder on the shortcut menu.
3. When the Create New Folder dialog box is displayed, type Marcus' Tasks in the Name text box and select Tasks in the select where to place the folder list. Click the OK button.
4. Click the first task in the task list, then, while holding the SHIFT key, click the last task in the task list to select all the tasks in the task list.
5. Right-click the task list. Click Move to Folder on the shortcut menu.
6. When the Move Items dialog box is displayed, select Marcus' Tasks in the Move the selected items to the folder list. Click the OK button.

BTW

Updating Tasks
To send a status report for a task on which you are working, open the task. Click Send Status Report on the Ribbon. If the task was assigned to you, the person who sent the task request will automatically be added to the update list.

To Schedule Meetings

Earlier in this chapter, you added an appointment for a team meeting. Outlook allows you to invite multiple attendees to a meeting by sending a single invitation. The following sections show how to invite attendees for that meeting.

1

- With the Calendar window active, click January 14 in the Date Navigator.

- Double-click the Team Meeting appointment to open the Team Meeting – Recurring Appointment window.

- When the Open Recurring Item dialog box is displayed, if necessary, click Open this occurrence, and then click the OK button.

- Double-click the title bar to maximize the window.

- Click the Scheduling button on the Ribbon to display the Scheduling sheet (Figure 2–53).

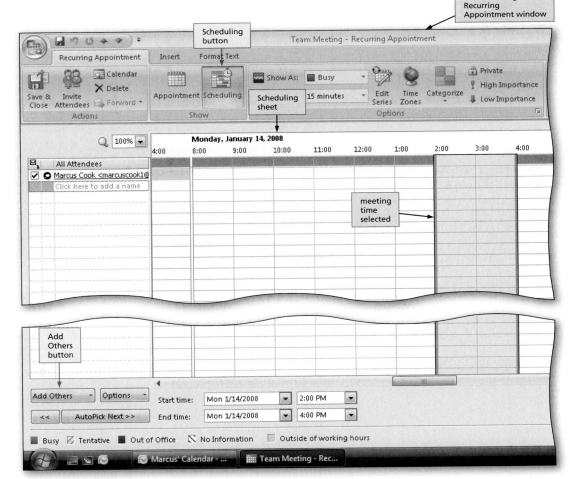

Figure 2–53

- Click the Add Others button, and then click Add From Address Book to display the Select Attendees and Resources dialog box (Figure 2–54).

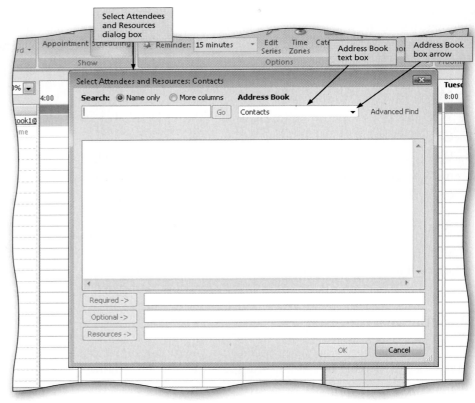

Figure 2–54

- Click the Address Book box arrow, and then click Marcus' Contacts.

- While holding the SHIFT key, click Trevor Walker to select the entire list.

- Click the Required button to add the selected names to the Required text box (Figure 2–55).

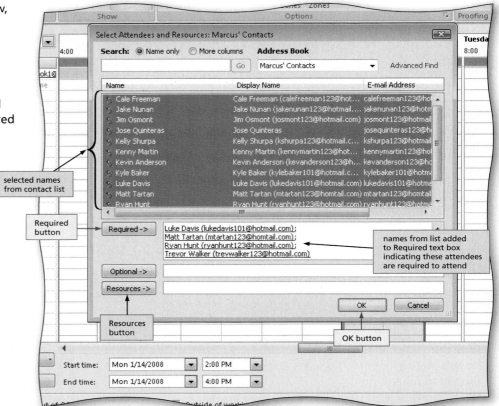

Figure 2–55

- Click the OK button to close the Select Attendees and Resources dialog box and display the Team Meeting – Recurring Appointment window (Figure 2–56).

- If the Microsoft Office Internet Free/Busy dialog box appears, click the Cancel button.

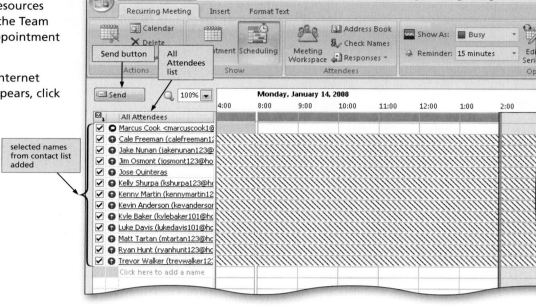

Figure 2–56

- Click the Send button to close the Meeting window and display the Calendar window (Figure 2–57).

Figure 2–57

- Double-click the Team Meeting appointment and click OK in the Open Recurring Item dialog box to open the appointment to see the invitation recipients and whether any replies to the invitation have been received (Figure 2–58).

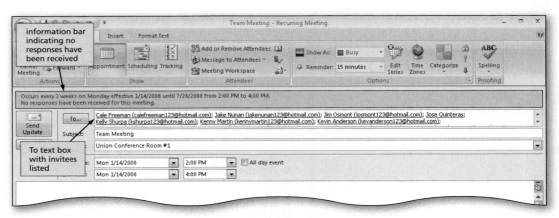

Figure 2–58

To Reply to Meeting Requests

Once you receive a meeting request, you will either accept it or decline it. A meeting request will appear in your Inbox similar to the one shown in Figure 2–59. Outlook allows you to choose from four responses: Accept, Tentative, Decline, or Propose New Time. The following steps accept a meeting request.

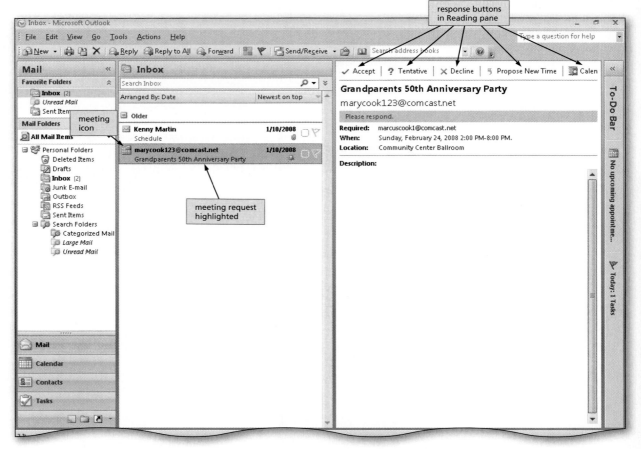

Figure 2–59

1

- If necessary, click the Mail button in the Navigation Pane to display the Inbox folder and then click the Grandparents 50th Anniversary Party message to select it (Figure 2–60).

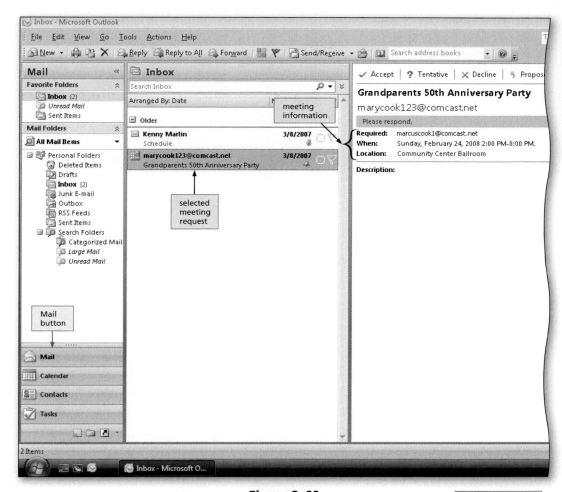

Figure 2–60

2

- Double-click the Grandparents 50th Anniversary Party message heading to open it (Figure 2–61).

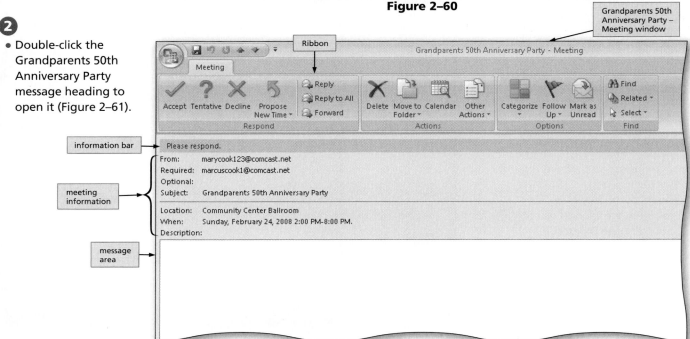

Figure 2–61

• Click the Accept button on the Ribbon to display the Microsoft Office Outlook dialog box (Figure 2–62).

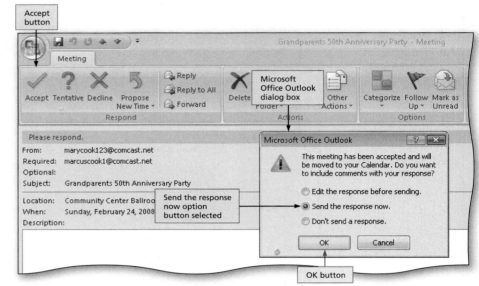

Figure 2–62

• Select the 'Send the response now' option button, and then click the OK button to close the dialog box and display the Inbox window.

• Click the Calendar button in the Navigation Pane.

• Click the right scroll arrow in the Date Navigator so the February 2008 calendar appears.

• Click 24 in the Date Navigator to display February 24 in the appointment area (Figure 2–63).

Q&A

How does the person organizing the meeting know whether I have accepted or declined a meeting request?

When a meeting is accepted, the meeting organizer receives a message indicating that the request has been accepted. If the meeting request is declined, the request is moved to the Deleted Items folder, and the meeting organizer receives a message indicating that the request was declined.

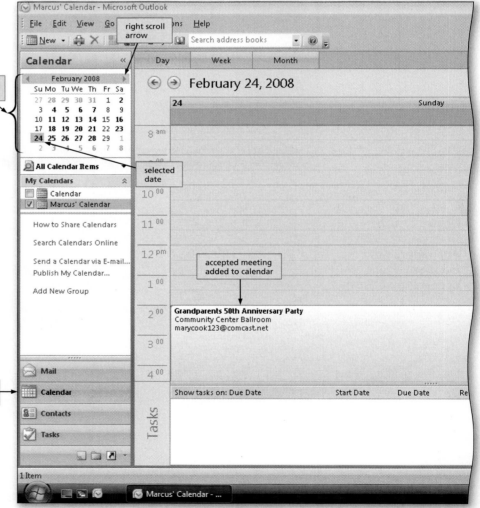

Figure 2–63

TO PROPOSE A NEW MEETING TIME

One of the available responses to a meeting request is to propose a new time. When you click the Propose New Time button, Outlook allows you to send a response to the meeting organizer indicating that you tentatively accept the request, but propose the meeting be held at a different time. To propose a new time for a meeting, you would perform the following steps.

1. Double-click the appropriate meeting request to open the request.

2. Click the Propose New Time button on the Ribbon.

3. When the Propose New Time dialog box is displayed, drag through the time slot that you want to propose, or enter the appropriate information in the Meeting start time and Meeting end time time boxes.

4. Click the Propose Time button.

5. When the New Time Proposed – Meeting Response window opens, click the Send button.

TO CHANGE THE TIME OF A MEETING AND SEND AN UPDATE

Once someone has proposed a new meeting time, it may be necessary to update the meeting request to the other potential attendees. Other reasons to update a meeting request may be that you have added or removed attendees, changed the meeting to a recurring series, or moved the meeting to a different date. To change the time of a meeting and send an update, you would perform the following steps.

1. With the Calendar window active, drag the meeting to its new time.

2. When the Microsoft Office Outlook dialog box is displayed, select the 'Save changes and send an update' option.

3. Click OK. If the appointment opens, click the Send button.

Q&A

What if a meeting needs to be canceled?

If you need to cancel a meeting, open the meeting window, click Cancel Meeting on the Ribbon, and then click OK in the Confirm Delete dialog box. Click the Send Cancellation button to send the cancellation and remove the meeting from the calendar.

Creating and Editing Notes

Another organizational tool included with Outlook is Notes. **Notes** provides you with a medium on which to record thoughts, ideas, questions, or anything else that you might write down on a sticky note or note pad. Notes can remain open while you perform other work on your computer. You can add to your notes, and your changes are saved automatically. Notes can be categorized per your personal specifications.

BTW

Meeting Workspace
Microsoft Outlook and SharePoint Services offer Meeting Workspace to help you plan your meeting more efficiently. A Meeting Workspace is a Web site for centralizing all the information required for one or more meetings. To learn more about Meeting Workspace, type `Meeting Workspace` in the Type a question for help box and then press the ENTER key to display a list of topics related to Meeting Workspace.

BTW

Meeting Times
If you use Windows SharePoint Services and have access to other attendees' calendars, use the AutoPick Next button in the Scheduling sheet of the Meeting window to find the next available free time for all attendees.

To Create and Edit a Note

The following steps create and edit a note that serves as a reminder for Marcus.

1

- Click the Notes button in the Navigation Pane.

- Click the New Note button on the Standard toolbar to open the Untitled – Notes window (Figure 2–64).

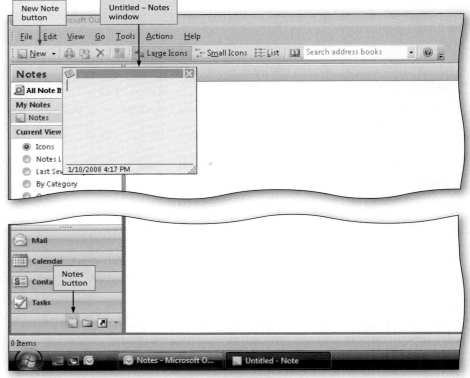

Figure 2–64

2

- Type `Talk to Coach about new equipment.` as the entry (Figure 2–65).

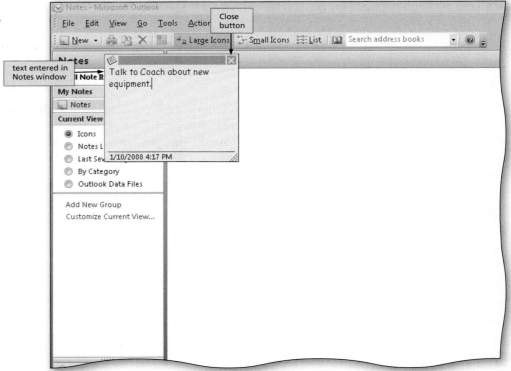

Figure 2–65

3

- Click the Close button to close the Notes window and place the note in the Notes folder (Figure 2–66).

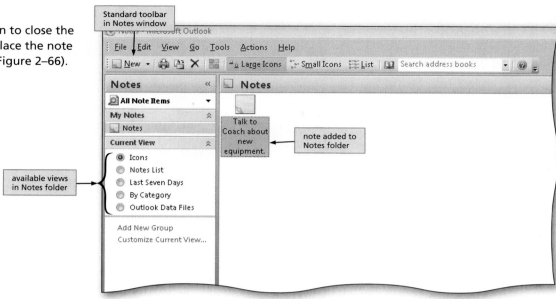

Figure 2–66

4

- Right-click the note and then point to Categorize on the shortcut menu (Figure 2–67).

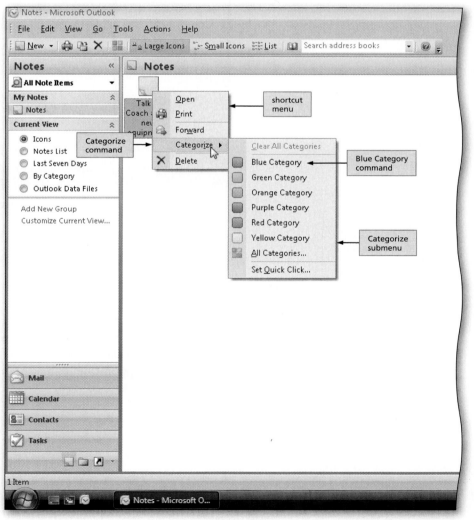

Figure 2–67

5

- Click Blue Category on the Categorize submenu to color the note blue (Figure 2–68). If the Rename Category dialog box is displayed, click the No button to close it.

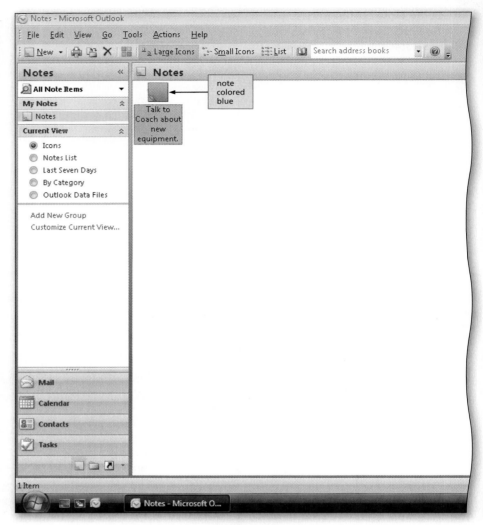

Figure 2–68

Customize Calendar Settings

Outlook provides you with several options to change the appearance of the Calendar window. You can customize your work week by selecting the days you work if they differ from the default Monday to Friday work week. You also can change the hours that appear as work hours in the appointment area. Additionally, you can categorize your appointments to make them easier to view.

To Set Work Week Options

Some people have schedules that differ from the standard Monday through Friday work week. Whether it is a six-days-per-week schedule, a four-days-per-week schedule, an alternating day schedule, or any other type of schedule, Outlook allows you to select the days that display in your calendar.

The following steps set work week options.

- Click Calendar in the Navigation Pane.

- With the Calendar window active, click Tools on the menu bar, and then click Options to open the Options dialog box (Figure 2–69).

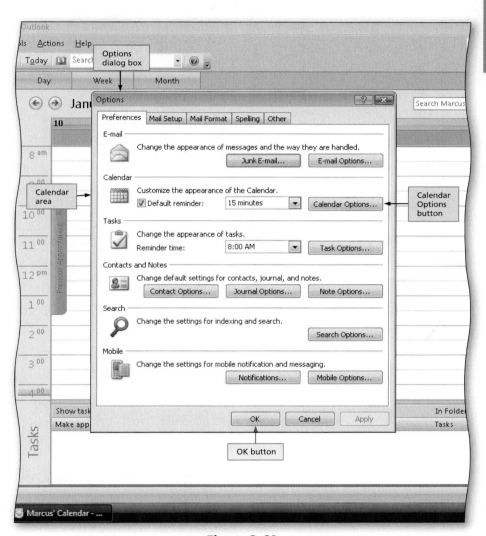

Figure 2–69

● Click the Calendar
Options button to
open the Calendar
Options dialog box
(Figure 2–70).

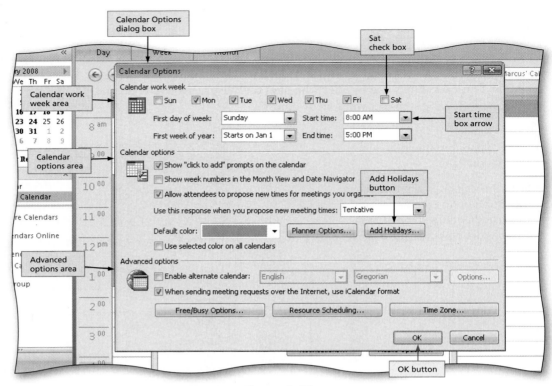

Figure 2–70

● In the Calendar work week area,
click the Sat check box to add
Saturday to your work week.

● Click the Start time box arrow and
then select 7:00 a.m. as the new
start time (Figure 2–71).

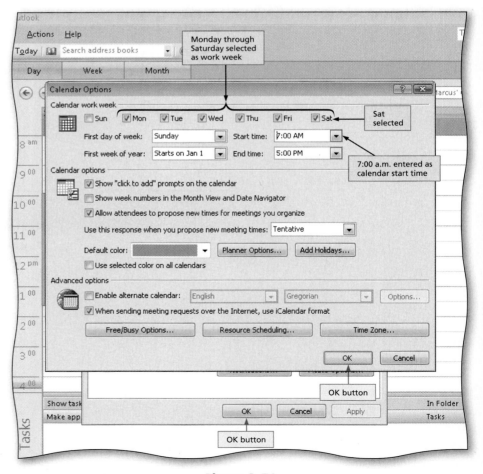

Figure 2–71

4

- Click the OK button in both open dialog boxes to close them.

- Scroll up in the Appointment area so that 6 a.m. shows as the first time slot (Figure 2–72).

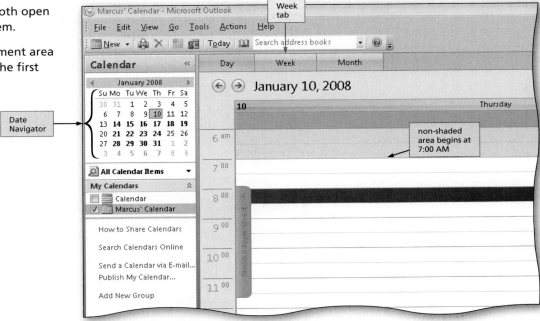

Figure 2–72

5

- Click January 14 in the Date Navigator.

- Click the Week tab in the Appointment area, and then, if necessary, click the Show work week option button to display the calendar in Work Week view (Figure 2–73).

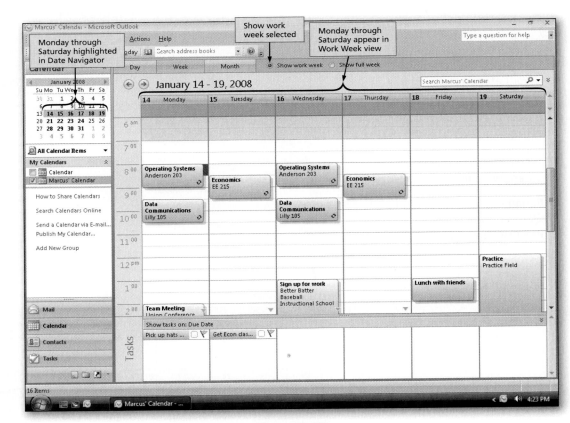

Figure 2–73

Other Ways

1. Press ALT+T, press O, press C

To Categorize the Calendar and Edit Category Labels

Outlook offers six default color categories from which to choose to categorize appointments and meetings. For example, you can categorize your class schedule, your work schedule, and your extracurricular activities. The categories can be renamed to fit your needs, or you can add your own categories.

The following steps categorize Marcus' calendar and edit the category labels.

1

- With the Calendar window active, click the Month tab in the Appointment area to display the calendar in Month view, and then click the Operating Systems appointment on January 14 to select it.

- Click the Categorize button on the Standard toolbar to display the Categorize menu (Figure 2–74).

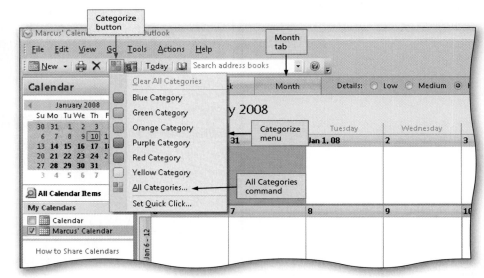

Figure 2–74

2

- Click All Categories on the Categorize menu to open the Color Categories dialog box.

- If necessary, click the Blue Category to select it, and then click the Rename button.

- Type `Work` as the new Category name.

- Rename the Green Category as Class, and the Orange Category as Practice (Figure 2–75)

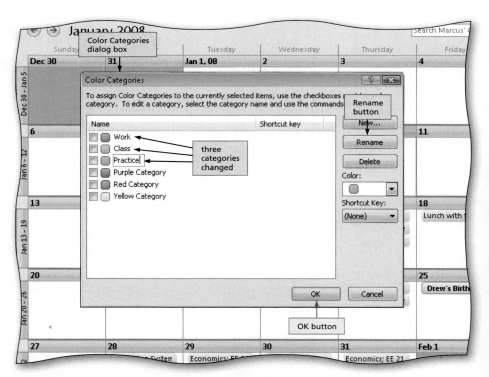

Figure 2–75

3

• Click the OK button to close the Color Categories dialog box and return to the Calendar window and select the Operating Systems appointment (Figure 2–76).

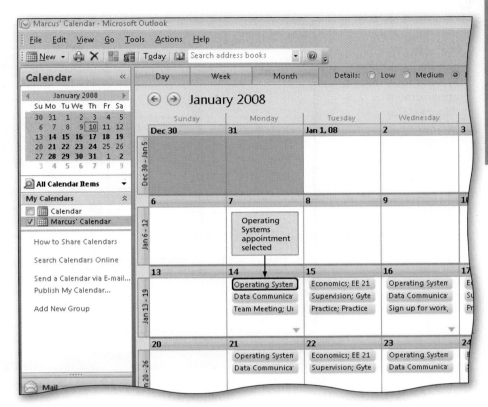

Figure 2–76

4

• Click the Categorize button on the Standard toolbar to display the Categorize menu (Figure 2–77).

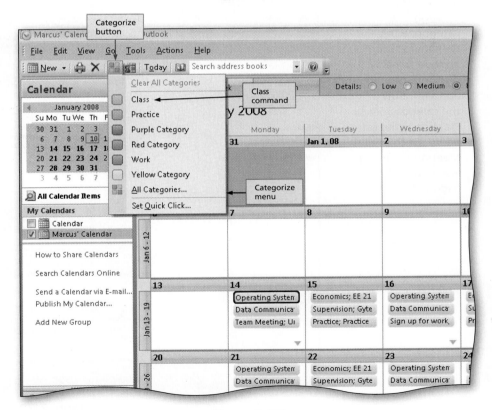

Figure 2–77

5

- Click Class on the Categorize menu to categorize the Operating Systems recurring appointment (Figure 2–78).

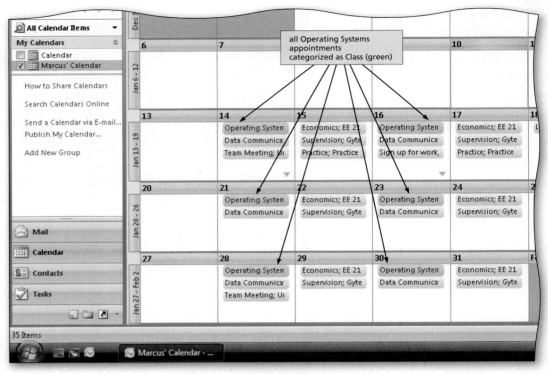

Figure 2–78

6

- Repeat Steps 3 through 5 to categorize the remaining recurring appointments and the work-related appointments in the calendar. Select Practice as the category for the Team Meeting recurring appointment (Figure 2–79).

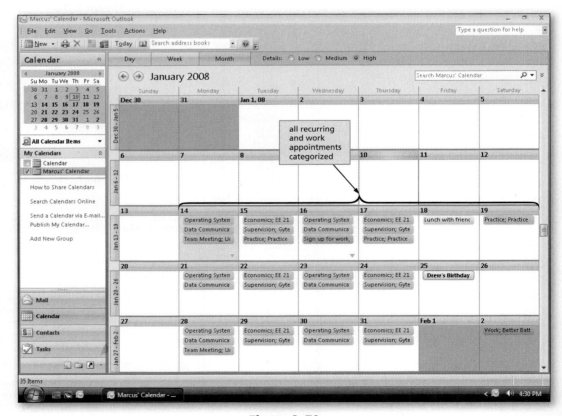

Figure 2–79

Printing a Calendar

All or part of a calendar can be printed in a number of different layouts, or **print styles**. The following section describes how to print the calendar in Daily, Weekly, and Monthly Styles.

To Print the Calendar in Daily Style

A printout of a single day of the calendar, called **Daily Style**, shows the day's appointments, tasks, and a two-month calendar. The following steps show how to print the calendar in Daily Style.

1
- Ready the printer.
- With the Calendar window active and January 14, 2008 selected in Day view, click the Print button on the Standard toolbar to display the Print dialog box (Figure 2–80).

2
- With the Daily Style selected in the Print Style list, click OK to close the dialog box and print the daily schedule of appointments for January 14, 2008 as shown in Figure 2–1d on page OUT 75.

Q&A

Is there a way to modify what is included on the printout?

Yes. The Page Setup button in the Print dialog box allows style modifications to include or omit various features, including the TaskPad and the Notes area. Specific time ranges also can be printed rather than the default 7:00 a.m. to 6:00 p.m.

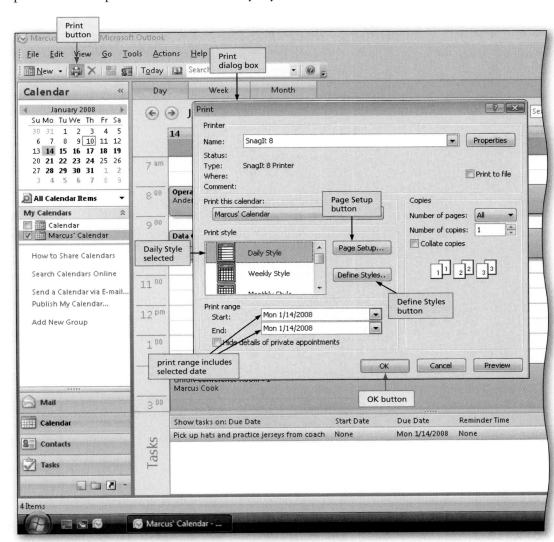

Figure 2–80

Other Ways
1. On File menu click Print
2. Press CTRL+P

To Print the Calendar in Weekly Style

Printing a calendar in Weekly Style can be accomplished through the Print button on the Standard toolbar while viewing the calendar in Week view, or by selecting the Weekly Style in the Print dialog box. The following step prints the calendar in Weekly Style.

1 Ready the printer. Click the Print button on the Standard toolbar. Click Weekly Style in the Print Style list and then click the OK button to print the document shown in Figure 2–1e on page OUT 75.

To Print the Calendar in Monthly Style

Printing
The margins, page orientation, or paper size can be changed in the Page Setup dialog box. To access the Page Setup dialog box, click the Page Setup button in the Print dialog box (Figure 2–80 on the previous page).

The following step prints the calendar in Monthly Style.

1 Ready the printer. Click the Print button on the Standard toolbar. Click Monthly Style in the Print Style list and then click the OK button to print the document shown in Figure 2–1f on page OUT 75.

To Print the Task List

To print only the task list, first open the Task folder. The following steps print the task list by itself.

1 Click the Tasks button in the Navigation Pane to display the task list.

2 Click the Print button on the Standard toolbar. When the Print dialog box is displayed, click the OK button to print the task list (Figure 2–81).

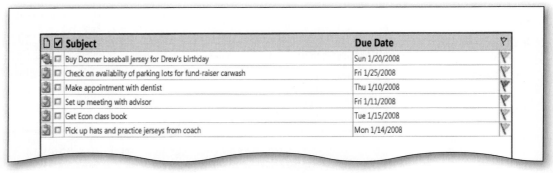

🗋 ☑ Subject	Due Date	🏴
Buy Donner baseball jersey for Drew's birthday	Sun 1/20/2008	
Check on availabilty of parking lots for fund-raiser carwash	Fri 1/25/2008	
Make appointment with dentist	Thu 1/10/2008	
Set up meeting with advisor	Fri 1/11/2008	
Get Econ class book	Tue 1/15/2008	
Pick up hats and practice jerseys from coach	Mon 1/14/2008	

Figure 2–81

Archiving Items

Outlook has a built-in feature called **AutoArchive** that helps manage Outlook folders. AutoArchive is on by default and can be scheduled to run automatically. AutoArchive searches Outlook folders for items that are used infrequently, and items of which the content is no longer valid (a completed task, an old meeting, etc.). AutoArchive can be set up either to delete expired items permanently, and/or move old items to a special archive file. When AutoArchive is run for the first time, Outlook automatically creates this archive file. Outlook also creates an Archive Folders folder in the Folder List. AutoArchive does not delete any folders even if they are empty. If you decide that you want to move archived items back to their original folders, you can use the Import Export wizard to move the items back to the original folder or any folder you specify.

Customizing AutoArchive

Outlook allows you to change how AutoArchive works. The default settings, or global settings, of AutoArchive are set to archive all folders except the Contacts folder. You also can specify **per-folder settings** that override the global settings. With per-folder settings, you can have different archive settings for different folders.

To Change the Default Settings for AutoArchive

The following steps show how to change the default settings for AutoArchive.

1
- Click Tools on the menu bar, and then click Options to display the Options dialog box.
- Click the Other tab to display the Other sheet (Figure 2–82).

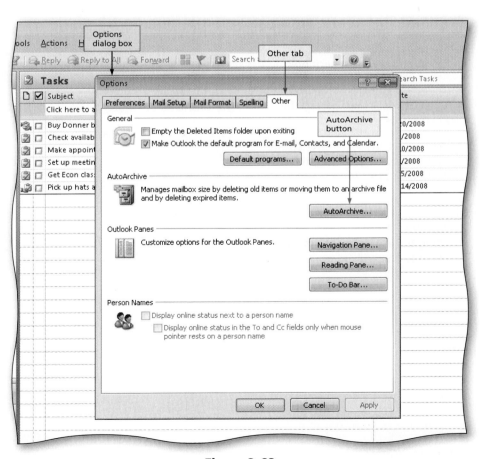

Figure 2–82

2

- Click the AutoArchive button to display the AutoArchive dialog box (Figure 2–83).

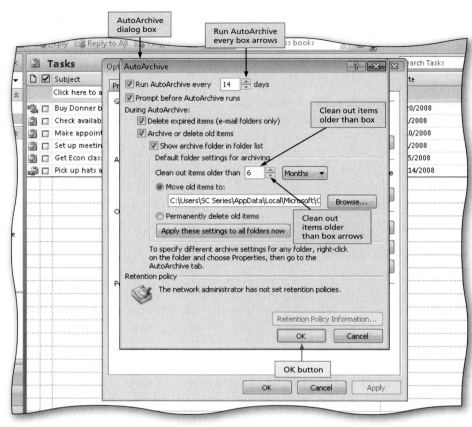

Figure 2–83

3

- If necessary, click the 'Run AutoArchive every' check box.

- Change the 'Run AutoArchive every' box to 10 by clicking the down arrow.

- Change the 'Clean out items older than' box to 8 by clicking the up arrow (Figure 2–84).

4

- Click the OK button on both open dialog boxes to close them and return to the Task window.

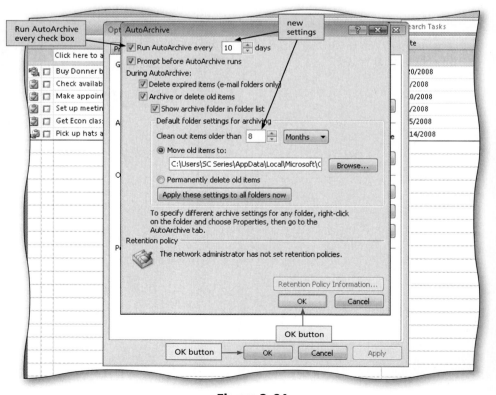

Figure 2–84

Other Ways

1. Press ALT+T, press O

Instant Messaging

One of the more useful communication tools available with Outlook is Windows Live Messenger. **Windows Live Messenger** allows you to communicate instantly with your online contacts using instant messaging. **Instant messaging (IM)** is real-time communication shown in a pop-up style application that occurs as a typed conversation between two or more participants. Windows Live Messenger is included with the Windows Vista operating system. The advantage of using Windows Live Messenger over e-mail is that the message you send appears immediately on the computer of the person with whom you are communicating, provided that person has signed in to Windows Live Messenger.

Before using Windows Live Messenger with Outlook, a contact first must have an MSN Hotmail account or a Windows Live ID and have Windows Live Messenger software installed and running on his or her computer. **MSN Hotmail** is a Microsoft service that provides free e-mail accounts to allow you to read your e-mail messages from any computer connected to the Internet. The **Windows Live ID** service is a secure way for you to sign in to multiple Web sites with a single user name and password. As an MSN Hotmail user, your MSN Hotmail sign-in name and password also are your Windows Live ID user name and password.

To Start and Sign In to Windows Live Messenger

Before using Windows Live Messenger with Outlook, you must enable instant messaging in Outlook, start Windows Messenger, and sign in to the .NET Messenger Service using your sign-in name and password. The following steps start Windows Live Messenger and sign in to the .NET Messenger Service using your sign-in name and password.

1

- Click the Minimize button on the Outlook window title bar to minimize the window to the Windows Vista taskbar.

- Click the Start button on the Windows Vista taskbar to display the Start menu.

- Click All Programs at the bottom of the left pane on the Start menu to display the All Programs list, and then click Windows Live Messenger in the All Programs list to open the Windows Live Messenger window (Figure 2–85)

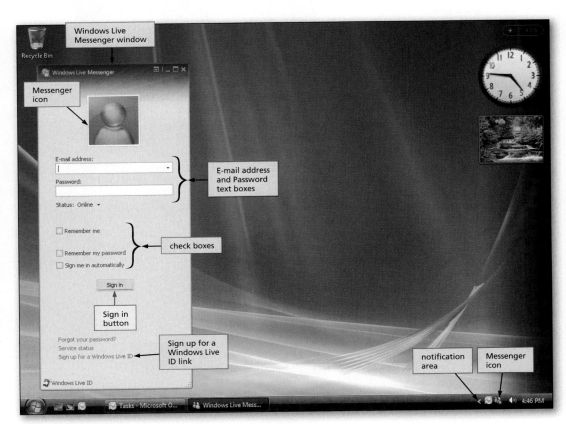

Figure 2–85

● Type your e-mail address and
password in the appropriate
text boxes in the Windows Live
Messenger window (Figure 2–86).

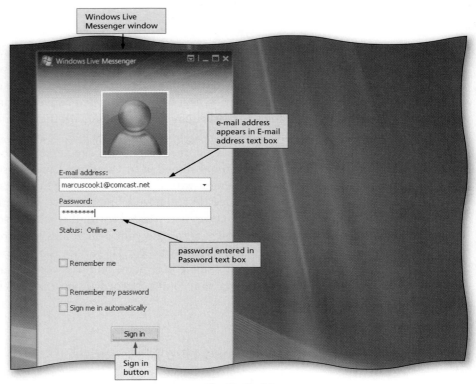

Windows Live
Messenger window

e-mail address
appears in E-mail
address text box

password entered in
Password text box

Sign in
button

Figure 2–86

● Click the Sign in button to sign in
to the Windows Live Messenger
Service (Figure 2–87).

Q&A

What happens if I click the Sign me
in automatically check box?

Clicking the Sign me in
automatically check box
allows Windows Live
Messenger to remember
your e-mail address and password
and sign-in automatically each
time you start Windows Live
Messenger.

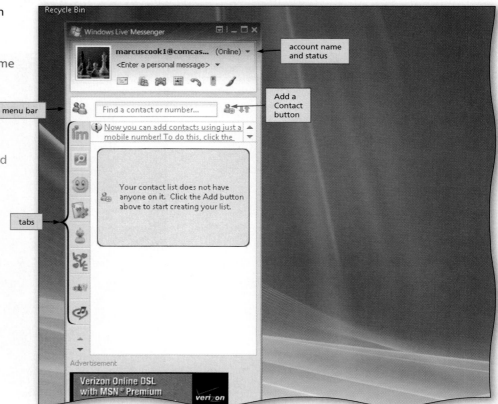

account name
and status

Add a
Contact
button

menu bar

tabs

Figure 2–87

To Enable Instant Messaging in Outlook

After signing into Windows Live Messenger, the next step is to enable instant messaging in Outlook. The following steps enable instant messaging in Outlook.

1

- Click the Tasks – Microsoft Outlook button on the Windows taskbar to display the Outlook window.

- With the Contacts window active, click Tools on the menu bar and then click Options to display the Options dialog box (Figure 2–88).

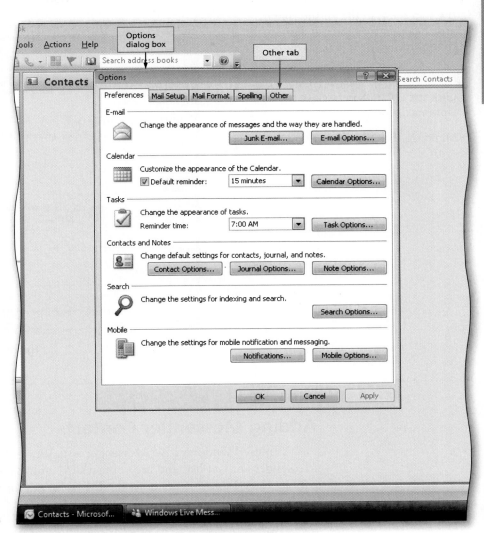

Figure 2–88

● Click the Other tab to display the Other sheet.

● In the Other sheet, confirm that the two boxes in the Person Names area have a check mark in each check box (Figure 2–89).

● Click the OK button to close the Options dialog box.

● Minimize the Outlook window.

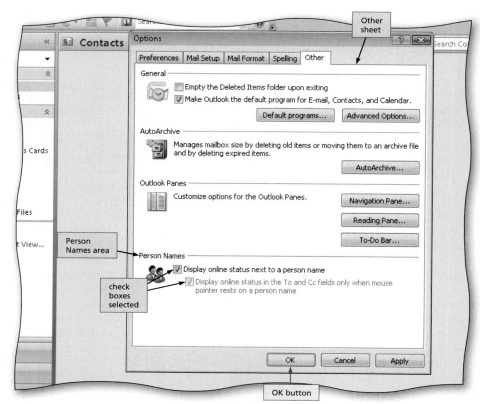

Figure 2–89

Adding Messenger Contacts

To use Windows Live Messenger with Outlook, contacts must be entered in the Messenger contact list, and the contact's IM address must be entered in the Outlook contacts list. Table 2–6 contains the IM addresses for the contacts in the Marcus' Contacts contact list.

Table 2–6 IM Addresses	
Contact Name	**IM Address**
Kevin Anderson	kevanderson123@hotmail.com
Kyle Baker	kylebaker101@hotmail.com
Luke Davis	lukedavis101@hotmail.com
Cale Freeman	calefreeman123@hotmail.com
Ryan Hunt	ryanhunt123@hotmail.com
Kenny Martin	kennymartin123@hotmail.com
Jake Nunan	jakenunan123@hotmail.com
Jim Osmont	josmont123@hotmail.com
Jose Quinteras	josequinteras123@hotmail.com
Kelly Shurpa	kshurpa123@hotmail.com
Matt Tartan	mtartan123@hotmail.com
Trevor Walker	trevwalker123@hotmail.com

After starting Windows Live Messenger, you can add a contact to the contact list if you know the e-mail address or Windows Live Messenger sign-in of the contact. A contact must have an MSN Hotmail account or a Windows Live ID and have the Windows Live Messenger or MSN Messenger software installed on their computer. If you try to add a contact that does not meet these requirements, you are given the chance to send the contact an e-mail invitation that explains how to get a passport and download the Windows Live Messenger or MSN Messenger software.

To Add a Contact to the Messenger Contact List

Windows Live Messenger allows you to add contacts to the contact list. The following steps add a contact to the Messenger contact list using the IM addresses listed in Table 2–6.

1

- Click the Add a Contact icon in the Windows Live Messenger window to display the Windows Live Contacts - Add a Contact dialog box (Figure 2–90).

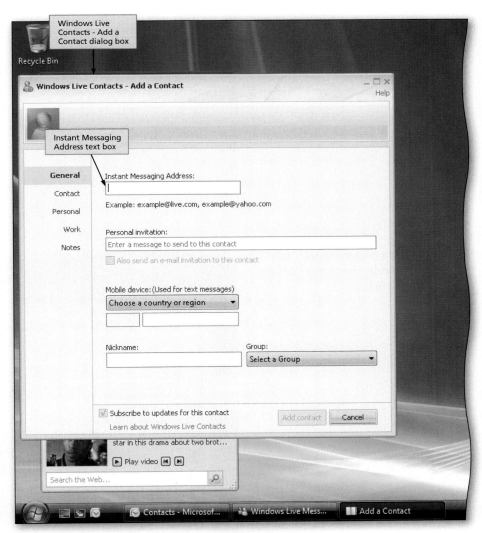

Figure 2–90

- Type kevanderson123@hotmail.
com in the Instant Messaging
Address text box (Figure 2–91).

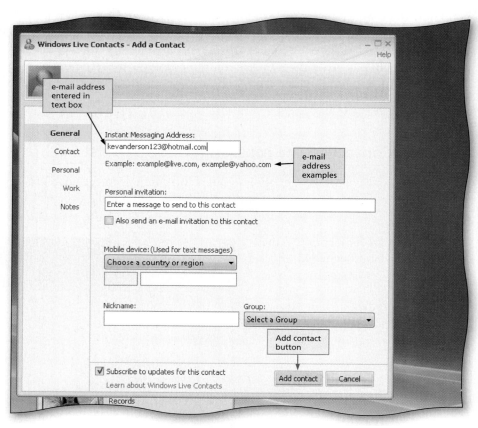

Figure 2–91

- Click the Add contact button to
add Kevin Anderson to the contact
list (Figure 2–92).

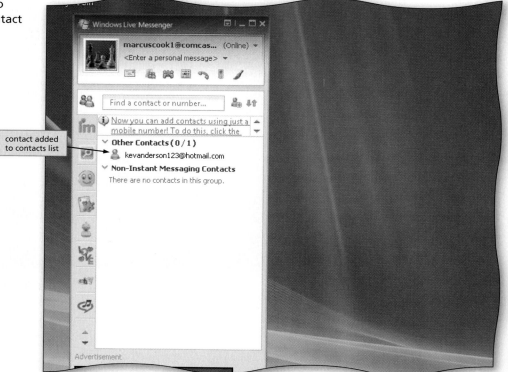

Figure 2–92

4

- Repeat Steps 1 through 3 to enter the remaining contacts in Table 2–6 and display the Windows Live Messenger window showing the added contacts (Figure 2–93).

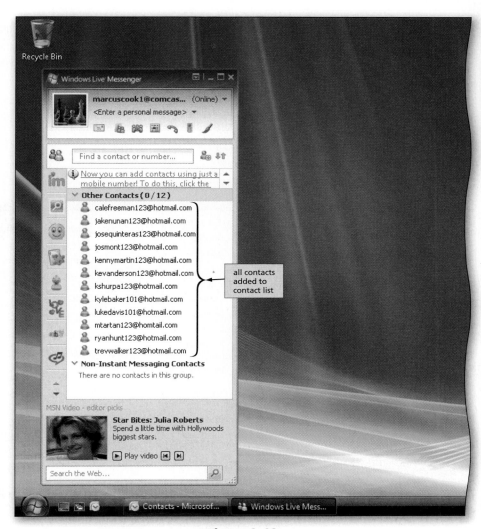

all contacts added to contact list

Figure 2–93

To Update the Outlook Contact List

To complete the process of setting up instant messaging with Outlook, the contact list must be updated with IM addresses of the contacts listed in Table 2–6.

The following steps show how to update the Marcus' Contacts contact list.

- If necessary, click the Contacts – Microsoft Outlook button on the Windows taskbar to display the Marcus' Contacts – Microsoft Outlook window.

- Double-click the Anderson, Kevin entry to open the Kevin Anderson – Contact window (Figure 2–94).

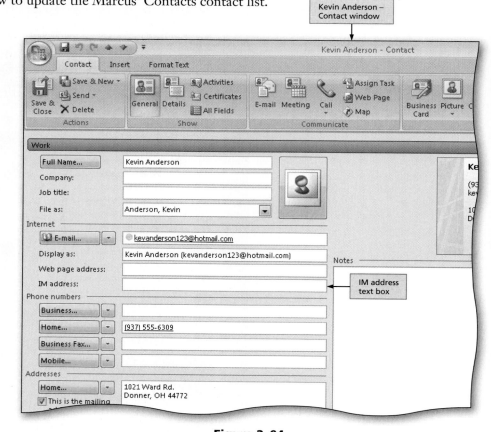

Figure 2–94

- Click the IM address text box.

- Type kevanderson123@hotmail. com as the IM address (Figure 2–95).

- Click the Save & Close button on the Ribbon to close the Contact window.

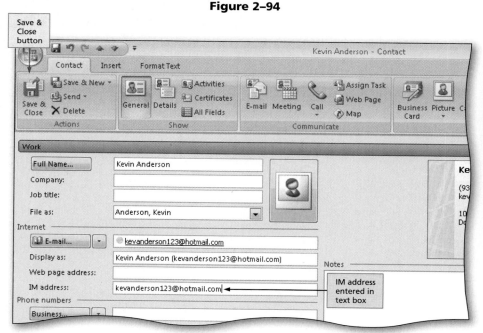

- Repeat Steps 1 through 3 to add the remaining IM addresses from Table 2–6 to the Marcus' Contacts contact list.

Figure 2–95

Communicating Using Instant Messaging

To use Windows Live Messenger with Outlook, the person with whom you want to communicate must be online, and, for this project, must have an e-mail message in an Outlook folder. Using Outlook, when you open an e-mail message from an individual or view the message in the Reading pane, the Person Names Smart Tag is shown next to the sender's name. Placing the mouse pointer over the Person Names Smart Tag will show a ScreenTip indicating the person's online status.

BTW

The Person Names Smart Tag
The Person Names Smart Tag can indicate online status for any person whose instant messaging e-mail address you have added to your instant messaging contact list. The Person Names Smart Tag also shows online status for individuals using the Exchange Instant Messaging Service or SIP Communications Service, even if they are not in your contact list.

Note: The following steps are for demonstration purposes only. Thus, if you are stepping through this project on a computer, you must have someone with an Instant Messenger address send you an e-mail so an ID appears in the Inbox, as shown in Figure 2–96.

To Send an Instant Message

The following steps show how to send an instant message to someone you know is online.

1

- With the Inbox window active, click the Kenny Martin e-mail message.

- Click the Person Names Smart Tag in the Reading pane to display the Smart Tag menu (Figure 2–96).

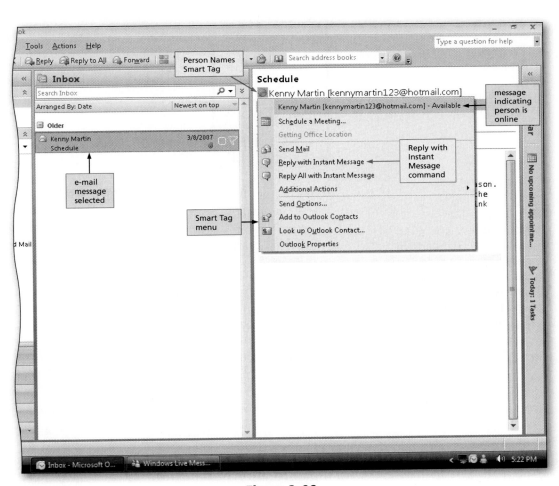

Figure 2–96

● Click Reply with Instant
Message on the
Smart Tag menu to
open the Kenny
window (Figure 2–97).

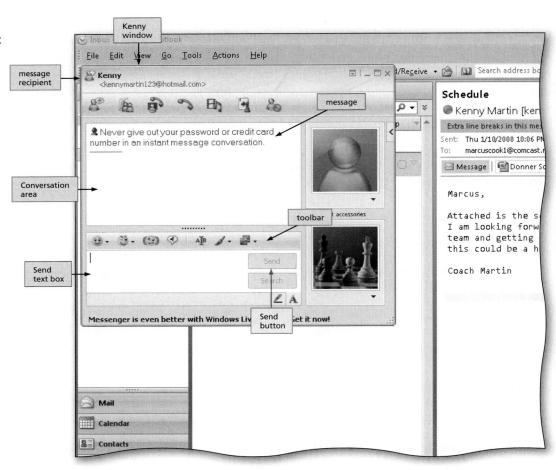

Figure 2–97

● **Type** Coach, I'm glad you're
online. I wanted to talk
about getting facemasks on
the batting helmets. in the
Send text box, and then click the
Send button to send the message
(Figure 2–98).

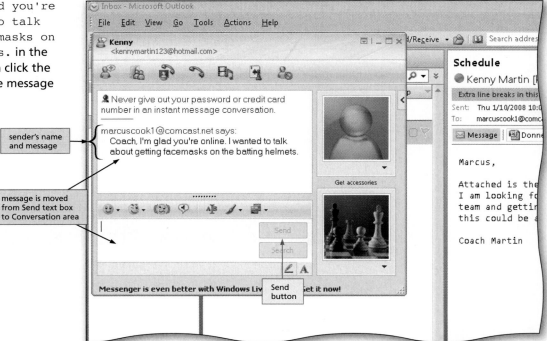

Figure 2–98

- The receiver of the message (Kenny Martin) types and sends a response (Figure 2–99).

Q&A

What can I do with the message toolbar above the Send text box?

The Emoticons, Wink, and Nudge buttons allow you to insert icons in a message that convey an emotion or a feeling. Icons are available that can convey happiness, surprise, confusion, and disappointment. The record a Voice Clip button allows you to insert a voice recording to your message. The Font button allows you to select a font, font style, font size, and apply special effects to the text in a message. The Change color scheme button allows you to change the appearance of the message window. The Background button allows you to select a background for your conversation window.

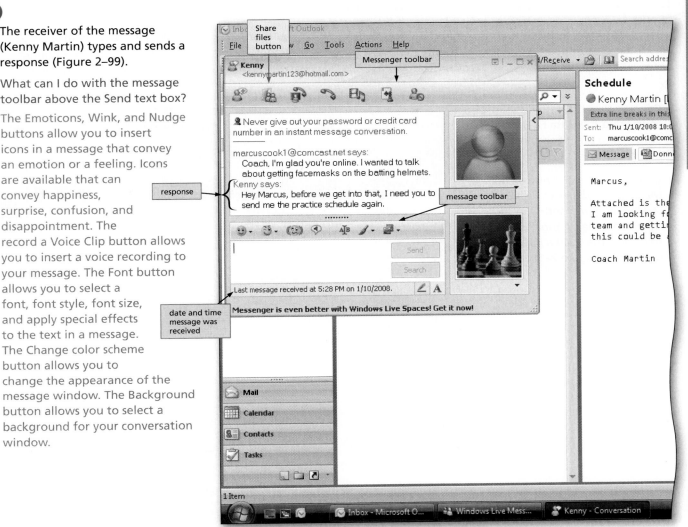

Figure 2–99

BTW

Certification
The Microsoft Certified Application Specialist (MCAS) program provides an opportunity for you to obtain a valuable industry credential – proof that you have the Outlook 2007 skills required by employers. For more information see Appendix G or visit the Outlook 2007 Certification Web page (scsite.com/out2007/cert).

To Attach and Send a File with Instant Messaging

The items in the Messenger toolbar in Figure 2–97 allow you to invite another person to the conversation, send a file or photo, start a Video Call, call a contact, see a list of activities, see a list of games, or block a contact from seeing or contacting you. The following steps show how to attach and send a file with instant messaging.

1

- Connect the USB flash drive containing the Data Files for Students to one of the computer's USB ports.

- Click the Share files button on the Messenger toolbar to display the Share files menu and then click the Send a file or photo command to display the Send a File to Kenny dialog box (Figure 2–100).

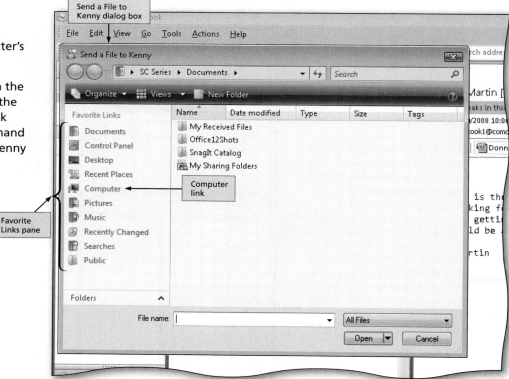

Figure 2–100

2

- Click Computer in the Favorite Links pane and then double-click UDISK 2.0 (E:) (Your drive name and letter may be different).

- Click Draft Practice Schedule in the Send a File to Kenny dialog box to select the file (Figure 2–101).

Figure 2–101

3

• Click the Open button to close the dialog box and display the Kenny window (Figure 2–102).

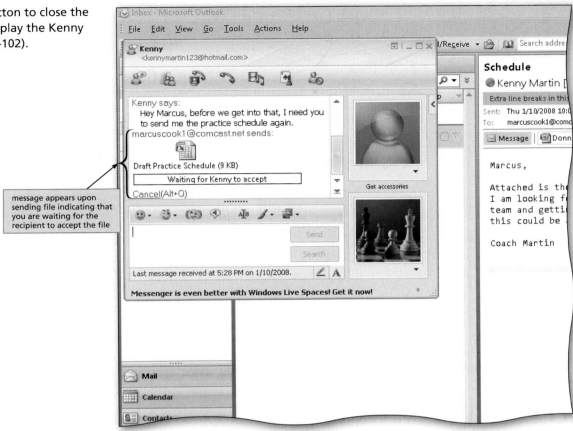

message appears upon sending file indicating that you are waiting for the recipient to accept the file

Figure 2–102

4

• The message in the window indicates the receiver (Kenny Martin) has accepted the file (Figure 2–103).

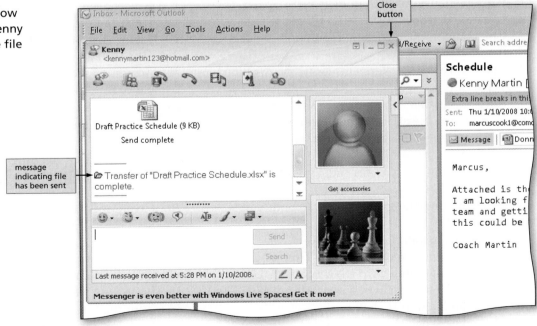

Close button

message indicating file has been sent

Figure 2–103

BTW

Quick Reference
For a table that lists how to complete the tasks covered in this book using the mouse, Ribbon, shortcut menu, and keyboard, see the Quick Reference Summary at the back of this book, or visit the Outlook 2007 Quick Reference Web page (scsite.com/out2007/qr).

To Close the Conversation Window

Participants can continue conversing in this manner, reading each other's messages and then typing their responses. When the conversation is complete, the Conversation window should be closed to end the conversation. The following step closes the Conversation window.

 Click the Close button in the Conversation window.

To Quit Outlook

With the project complete, the final step is to quit the Outlook program and return to the Windows desktop. The following step quits Outlook.

 Click the Close button on the right side of the title bar to quit Outlook.

Chapter Summary

In this chapter you have learned how to use Outlook to create a personal schedule, organize meetings, and create a task list, enter appointments, create recurring appointments, move appointments to new dates, schedule events, and view and print your calendar in different views and print styles, create a task list, assign tasks, and accept a task assignment; invite attendees to a meeting, accept a meeting request, and propose and change the time of a meeting; categorize your calendar to make it easier to view; create and edit notes; export your personal folder to an external storage device and import subfolders for further updating; use AutoArchive; enable and sign into Windows Live Messenger through Outlook; add contacts to the contact list, and send an instant message including sending a file through instant messaging. The following list includes all the new Outlook skills you have learned in this chapter.

1. Start and Customize Outlook (OUT 77)
2. Create a Personal Folder (OUT 79)
3. Enter Appointments Using the Appointment Area (OUT 81)
4. Enter and Save Appointments Using the Appointment Window (OUT 82)
5. Enter Recurring Appointments (OUT 84)
6. Move to the Next Day in the Appointment Area and Enter the Remaining Recurring Appointments (OUT 86)
7. Enter Appointment Dates and Times Using Natural Language Phrases (OUT 88)
8. Enter the Remaining One-Time Appointments (OUT 89)
9. Delete an Appointment (OUT 90)
10. Move an Appointment to a New Time (OUT 91)
11. Move an Appointment to a New Date (OUT 92)
12. Move an Appointment to a New Month (OUT 93)
13. Create an Event (OUT 95)
14. Change to Work Week View (OUT 96)
15. Change to Week View (OUT 97)
16. Change to Month View (OUT 98)
17. Create a Task List (OUT 99)
18. Export a Subfolder to a USB Flash Drive (OUT 101)
19. Delete a Personal Subfolder (OUT 103)
20. Import a Subfolder (OUT 104)
21. Assign a Task to Another Person (OUT 106)
22. Accept a Task Assignment (OUT 108)
23. Customize the Tasks Windows (OUT 110)
24. Move Tasks to a New Personal Folder (OUT 111)
25. Schedule Meetings (OUT 111)
26. Reply to Meeting Requests (OUT 114)
27. Propose a New Meeting Time (OUT 117)
28. Change the Time of a Meeting and Send an Update (OUT 117)
29. Create and Edit a Note (OUT 118)
30. Set Work Week Options (OUT 121)
31. Categorize the Calendar and Edit Category Labels (OUT 124)
32. Print the Calendar in Daily Style (OUT 127)
33. Print the Calendar in Weekly Style (OUT 128)
34. Print the Calendar in Monthly Style (OUT 128)
35. Print the Task List (OUT 128)
36. Change the Default Settings for AutoArchive (OUT 129)

37. Start and Sign In to Windows Live Messenger (OUT 131)
38. Enable Instant Messaging in Outlook (OUT 133)
39. Add a Contact to the Messenger Contact List (OUT 135)
40. Update the Outlook Contact List (OUT 138)
41. Send an Instant Message (OUT 139)
42. Attach and Send a File with Instant Messaging (OUT 142)
43. Close the Conversation Window (OUT 144)

If you have a SAM user profile, you may have access to hands-on instruction, practice, and assessment. Log in to your SAM account (http://sam2007.course.com) to launch any assigned training activities or exams that relate to the skills covered in this chapter.

Learn It Online

Test your knowledge of chapter content and key terms.

Instructions: To complete the Learn It Online exercises, start your browser, click the Address bar, and then enter the Web address scsite.com/out2007/learn. When the Outlook 2007 Learn It Online page is displayed, click the link for the exercise you want to complete and then read the instructions.

Chapter Reinforcement TF, MC, and SA
A series of true/false, multiple choice, and short answer questions that test your knowledge of the chapter content.

Flash Cards
An interactive learning environment where you identify chapter key terms associated with displayed definitions.

Practice Test
A series of multiple choice questions that test your knowledge of chapter content and key terms.

Who Wants To Be a Computer Genius?
An interactive game that challenges your knowledge of chapter content in the style of a television quiz show.

Wheel of Terms
An interactive game that challenges your knowledge of chapter key terms in the style of the television show *Wheel of Fortune*.

Crossword Puzzle Challenge
A crossword puzzle that challenges your knowledge of key terms presented in the chapter.

Apply Your Knowledge

Reinforce the skills and apply the concepts you learned in this chapter.

Creating a Schedule
Instructions: Start Outlook. Create a Calendar folder using your name as the name of the new folder.

Perform the following tasks: Create a schedule using the information in Table 2–7. Categorize the schedule using the following categories: School, Work, and Personal. This calendar is for the spring semester that begins Monday, January 14, 2008, and ends Friday, May 16, 2008. When the calendar is complete, print the calendar in Month view and submit to your instructor.

Table 2–7 Appointment Information

Appointment	Category	Days	Time	Occurrences
Chemistry	School	M, W	7:30 a.m. – 9:00 a.m.	30
Technical Report Writing	School	M, W	11:30 a.m. – 1:00 p.m.	30
Marketing	School	T, Th	7:00 p.m. – 8:30 p.m.	30
Work	Work	T, Th, Sa	7:00 a.m. – 3:30 p.m.	January 15 January 17 January 19
Doctor Appointment	Personal	W	4:00 p.m. – 5:00 p.m.	January 16
Work	Work	T, Th, Sat	9:00 a.m. – 6:00 p.m.	January 29 January 31 February 2
Volunteer for Park cleanup	Personal	Su	8:30 a.m. – 12:00 p.m.	February 3
Chemistry Study Lab	School	W	5:00 p.m. – 7:00 p.m.	Every other Wednesday for 15 occurrences

Extend Your Knowledge

Extend the skills you learned in this chapter and experiment with new skills. You may need to use Help to complete the assignment.

Customizing the Calendar

Instructions: Start Outlook. Using the calendar created in Apply Your Knowledge, use the Options command on the Tools menu to set up the calendar for a six-day work week with hours from 7:00 a.m. to 6:00 p.m..

Perform the following tasks: Export your personal folder to a USB flash drive and then delete the folder from the computer's hard disk. If possible, have your instructor verify that the folder is deleted.

Make It Right

Analyze a document and correct all errors and/or improve the design.

Editing a Calendar

Instructions: Start Outlook. Import the MIR 2-1 Calendar folder into Outlook. See the inside back cover of this book for instructions for downloading the Data Files for Students, or see your instructor for information on accessing the files required in this book.

Perform the following tasks:

1. Change the system date to February 4, 2008.
2. Change Kelly's Birthday Party from the 16th to the 23rd for the same time slot.
3. Reschedule the work on the 23rd for the 16th from 12:00 p.m. to 4:00 p.m.
4. The Chemistry Lab has been rescheduled for Wednesday evenings from 5:00 p.m. to 7:00 p.m. in CHM 225.
5. Intramural Basketball has been changed to Tuesdays and Thursdays for the same time slot.
6. Print the revised calendar in Month view and submit to your instructor.
7. Export the MIR 2-1 Calendar folder to a USB flash drive and then delete the folder from the hard disk.
8. Quit Outlook.

STUDENT ASSIGNMENTS

In the Lab

Design, create, modify, and/or use a document using the guidelines, concepts, and skills presented in this chapter. Labs are listed in order of increasing difficulty.

Lab 1: Planning a Meeting

Problem: You are the project manager for a large government project. The project involves working with individuals from county, state, and federal offices. With the project start date approaching, you need to organize a meeting to get all the required signatures on your contract.

Instructions:

1. Import the Lab 2-1 Contacts folder into Outlook (Figure 2–104).

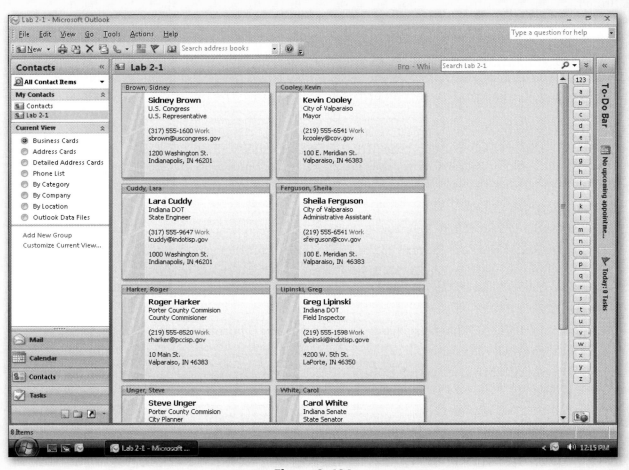

Figure 2–104

2. Organize a meeting for Wednesday, March 12, 2008 from 1:00 p.m. until 3:00 p.m., inviting only those contacts that hold a county, state, or federal office.

3. Submit a printout of the meeting to your instructor.

4. Change the date and time of the meeting from March 12, 2008 to March 14, 2008 from 9:00 a.m. to 11:00 a.m.

5. Send an updated meeting invitation.

6. Submit a printout of the updated meeting to your instructor.

7. You have just found out that your presence is required elsewhere on the meeting date. Cancel the meeting using the Cancel Meeting command on the Ribbon.

In the Lab

Lab 2: Using Windows Live Messenger with Outlook

Problem: You are preparing for an important meeting and need to have a file updated by a coworker in another department. You do not have that individual's information in your contact list, however. You leave a message on her voice mail about the file and she e-mails you a message requesting that you send the file to her. Because you have only a short time before the meeting begins, you decide to use Windows Live Messenger with Outlook to communicate and send the file to your coworker for her to revise. *Note:* To use instant messaging, you should complete this exercise with a classmate.

Instructions: Perform the following tasks:
1. Sign in to Windows Live Messenger using your own user name and password.
2. Send an e-mail message similar to the one shown in Figure 2–105 to your classmate.

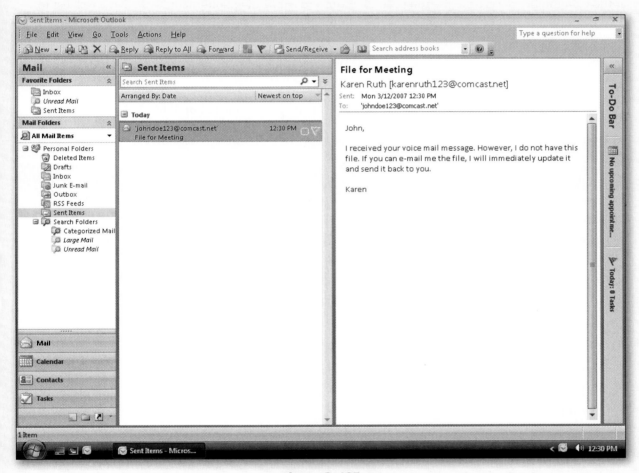

Figure 2–105

3. Add the sender to your Windows Live Messenger and Outlook contact list. Be sure to include his or her instant message address in Outlook.
4. Connect the USB flash drive containing the Data Files for Students to one of the computer's USB ports.
5. Send an instant message indicating that you will send the file using Windows Live Messenger.
6. Send the Quarterly Report file from the Data Files for Students to the sender.

Continued >

In the Lab *continued*

7. When you receive the file, open the file and submit a printout with your name and the name of the person you completed the exercise with to your instructor.

8. Sign out of Windows Live Messenger and close all the open windows.

In the Lab

Lab 3: Creating a Calendar and Task List

Problem: You are the owner of a small hardware store. Your company has experienced rapid growth during the last several months, and with spring approaching, you need to change to regular from seasonal stock. As the owner, you also have administrative duties to perform, such as staff meetings, payroll, advertising, and sales campaigns. To make your schedule even more hectic, you coach your child's spring soccer team on Wednesday nights from 5:30 p.m. to 7:00 p.m., and Saturdays from 1:00 p.m. to 3:00 p.m. at the Community Soccer Fields. You need to create a schedule of appointments as well as a task list to help you keep track of your various jobs and responsibilities each day.

Instructions Part 1: Perform the following tasks:

1. Create a personal Calendar subfolder named A-1 Hardware.

2. Change the start time of the calendar to 7:00 a.m.

3. Enter the appointments in the calendar, using the information listed in Table 2–8.

Table 2–8 Appointment Information

Desctiption	Date	Time
Staff meeting	Every Monday from March 10, 2008 – April 28, 2008	7:00 a.m. – 8:00 a.m.
Meeting to prepare Winter Closeout Sale	March 3, 2008	8:30 a.m. – 10:30 a.m.
Enter payroll	Every Thursday	4:00 p.m. – 5:00 p.m.
Eric's birthday	March 27, 2008	
Conference call with Liz & Greg	March 20, 2008	9:00 a.m. – 10:00 a.m.
Meet with lawn care supplier	March 21, 2008	1:00 p.m. – 2:00 p.m.
Lunch with Beth	March 31, 2008	12:00 p.m. – 1:00 p.m.

4. Create a task list containing the following tasks:

   a. Call Alex to confirm lawn care supplier's visit.

   b. Schedule meeting to discuss spring and summer sales goals.

   c. Call to check plumbing supplies delivery.

   d. Clear out snow blowers to make room for lawn mowers.

   e. Replace snow shovels with lawn and garden tools.

5. Print the calendar for the month of March and submit to your instructor.

Instructions Part 2: This part of the exercise requires that you work as a team with two classmates. With the growth of your hardware store, you have been able to hire a manager and assistant manager. Perform the following tasks:

1. Add the due dates in Table 2–9 to the tasks created in Part 1.

2. Using the tasks created in Part 1, assign the tasks per Table 2–9. Obtain and use the e-mail addresses of the two classmates for Manager and Assistant Manager.

3. Have the classmate representing the Manager accept one task and decline one task, and the classmate representing the Assistant Manager accept one task and decline one task.

4. Modify the current view of the task list to include the Owner field using the Customize Current View command accessed by pointing to Current View on the View menu.

5. Print the modified task list and submit to your instructor.

6. Create a personal Tasks subfolder called A-1 Tasks and move the task list you created to the new subfolder.

7. Export both the personal subfolders created in this exercise to a USB flash drive, archive the folders, and then delete them from the hard disk.

8. Close all open windows.

Table 2–9 Task Information		
Tasks From Part 1	**Assignment**	**Due Date**
Call Alex to confirm lawn care supplier's visit	Manager	March 14, 2008
Call to check plumbing supplies delivery	Manager	March 10, 2008
Clear out snow blowers to make room for lawn mowers	Assistant Manager	March 28, 2008
Replace snow shovels with lawn and garden tools	Assistant Manager	March 17, 2008

Cases and Places

Apply your creative thinking and problem solving skills to design and implement a solution.

• EASIER   •• MORE DIFFICULT

• 1: Create a Personal Schedule

Create a personal schedule for the next month. Include any work and class time, together with study time. You also can include any extracurricular activities in which you participate. Use recurring appointments when possible. All day activities should be scheduled as events. Categorize the calendar as necessary. Print the calendar in Monthly Style and submit to your instructor.

•• 2: Create a Work Schedule for Employees

At work, you are in charge of scheduling for the month of May. Create a schedule of work times for four employees. Dan works Mondays, Wednesdays, and Fridays from 9:00 a.m. to 5:00 p.m. Sally works Tuesdays, Thursdays, and Saturdays from 9:00 a.m. to 5:00 p.m. Juan works from 12:00 p.m. until 9:00 p.m. on Mondays, Wednesdays, and Fridays. Bridgette completes the schedule working from 12:00 p.m. until 9:00 p.m. on Tuesdays, Thursdays, and Saturdays. Set the calendar to reflect a six-day work week with hours ranging from 9:00 a.m. to 9:00 p.m. Print the calendar in Monthly Style and submit to your instructor.

•• 3: Create a Journal

Create journal entries from your personal schedule for the past week. Comment on activities in which you participated and tasks that you accomplished. Write when the activity started and ended. Note the problems (if any) associated with the activity. When commenting on completed tasks, include notes about results of having completed it. Specify what would have happened had the task not been completed when it was. Write a brief summary of your journal and submit to your instructor.

•• 4: Create a Calendar of Events

Make It Personal

Use the natural language phrase option in the Start time date box to create a list of events for the year. Create a calendar that contains the following holidays: New Year's Day, Valentine's Day, St. Patrick's Day, Independence Day, Halloween, Veteran's Day, Thanksgiving Day, Christmas Eve, Christmas Day, and New Year's Eve. For the last four holidays, indicate that you will be out of the office all day. Also, add events for several family or friend birthdays or anniversaries, using the natural language phrase option. For instance, schedule these events by utilizing the phrase "two weeks from today" (or something similar) as a start date. Try at least three different phrase options to schedule these events. Categorize the events to separate birthdays from anniversaries, and so on. Select two months to print in Monthly Style and submit them to your instructor.

•• 5: Create Meeting Invitations

Working Together

Choose a member of your team to act as meeting organizer. The organizer will use Outlook to send out a meeting invitation to each group member. Each member either should accept the meeting time or decline the meeting time and propose a new meeting time based on their individual schedules using Outlook. Use a combination of e-mail and Windows Live Messenger with Outlook to discuss proposed meeting times with the organizer. Each team member should print out the appointment and hand it in to the instructor.

Appendix A
Project Planning Guidelines

Using Project Planning Guidelines

The process of communicating specific information to others is a learned, rational skill. Computers and software, especially Microsoft Office 2007, can help you develop ideas and present detailed information to a particular audience.

Using Microsoft Office 2007, you can create projects such as Word documents, Excel spreadsheets, Access databases, and PowerPoint presentations. Computer hardware and productivity software such as Microsoft Office 2007 minimizes much of the laborious work of drafting and revising projects. Some communicators handwrite ideas in notebooks, others compose directly on the computer, and others have developed unique strategies that work for their own particular thinking and writing styles.

No matter what method you use to plan a project, follow specific guidelines to arrive at a final product that presents information correctly and effectively (Figure A–1). Use some aspects of these guidelines every time you undertake a project, and others as needed in specific instances. For example, in determining content for a project, you may decide that a bar chart communicates trends more effectively than a paragraph of text. If so, you would create this graphical element and insert it in an Excel spreadsheet, a Word document, or a PowerPoint slide.

Determine the Project's Purpose

Begin by clearly defining why you are undertaking this assignment. For example, you may want to track monetary donations collected for your club's fundraising drive. Alternatively, you may be urging students to vote for a particular candidate in the next election. Once you clearly understand the purpose of your task, begin to draft ideas of how best to communicate this information.

Analyze your Audience

Learn about the people who will read, analyze, or view your work. Where are they employed? What are their educational backgrounds? What are their expectations? What questions do they have?

PROJECT PLANNING GUIDELINES

1. DETERMINE THE PROJECT'S PURPOSE
Why are you undertaking the project?

2. ANALYZE YOUR AUDIENCE
Who are the people who will use your work?

3. GATHER POSSIBLE CONTENT
What information exists, and in what forms?

4. DETERMINE WHAT CONTENT TO PRESENT TO YOUR AUDIENCE
What information will best communicate the project's purpose to your audience?

Figure A–1

Design experts suggest drawing a mental picture of these people or finding photographs of people who fit this profile so that you can develop a project with the audience in mind.

By knowing your audience members, you can tailor a project to meet their interests and needs. You will not present them with information they already possess, and you will not omit the information they need to know.

Example: Your assignment is to raise the profile of your college's nursing program in the community. How much do they know about your college and the nursing curriculum? What are the admission requirements? How many of the applicants admitted complete the program? What percent pass the state Boards?

Gather Possible Content

Rarely are you in a position to develop all the material for a project. Typically, you would begin by gathering existing information that may reside in spreadsheets or databases. Web sites, pamphlets, magazine and newspaper articles, and books could provide insights of how others have approached your topic. Personal interviews often provide perspectives not available by any other means. Consider video and audio clips as potential sources for material that might complement or support the factual data you uncover.

Determine What Content to Present to your Audience

Experienced designers recommend writing three or four major ideas you want an audience member to remember after reading or viewing your project. It also is helpful to envision your project's endpoint, the key fact you wish to emphasize. All project elements should lead to this ending point.

As you make content decisions, you also need to think about other factors. Presentation of the project content is an important consideration. For example, will your brochure be printed on thick, colored paper or transparencies? Will your PowerPoint presentation be viewed in a classroom with excellent lighting and a bright projector, or will it be viewed on a notebook computer monitor? Determine relevant time factors, such as the length of time to develop the project, how long readers will spend reviewing your project, or the amount of time allocated for your speaking engagement. Your project will need to accommodate all of these constraints.

Decide whether a graph, photograph, or artistic element can express or emphasize a particular concept. The right hemisphere of the brain processes images by attaching an emotion to them, so audience members are more apt to recall these graphics long term rather than just reading text.

As you select content, be mindful of the order in which you plan to present information. Readers and audience members generally remember the first and last pieces of information they see and hear, so you should put the most important information at the top or bottom of the page.

Summary

When creating a project, it is beneficial to follow some basic guidelines from the outset. By taking some time at the beginning of the process to determine the project's purpose, analyze the audience, gather possible content, and determine what content to present to the audience, you can produce a project that is informative, relevant, and effective.

Appendix B

Introduction to Microsoft Office 2007

What Is Microsoft Office 2007?

Microsoft Office 2007 is a collection of the more popular Microsoft application software. It is available in Basic, Home and Student, Standard, Small Business, Professional, Ultimate, Professional Plus, and Enterprise editions. Each edition consists of a group of programs, collectively called a suite. Table B-1 lists the suites and their components. **Microsoft Office Professional Edition 2007** includes these six programs: Microsoft Office Word 2007, Microsoft Office Excel 2007, Microsoft Office Access 2007, Microsoft Office PowerPoint 2007, Microsoft Office Publisher 2007, and Microsoft Office Outlook 2007. The programs in the Office suite allow you to work efficiently, communicate effectively, and improve the appearance of the projects you create.

Table B–1

	Microsoft Office Basic 2007	Microsoft Office Home & Student 2007	Microsoft Office Standard 2007	Microsoft Office Small Business 2007	Microsoft Office Professional 2007	Microsoft Office Ultimate 2007	Microsoft Office Professional Plus 2007	Microsoft Office Enterprise 2007
Microsoft Office Word 2007	✓	✓	✓	✓	✓	✓	✓	✓
Microsoft Office Excel 2007	✓	✓	✓	✓	✓	✓	✓	✓
Microsoft Office Access 2007					✓	✓	✓	✓
Microsoft Office PowerPoint 2007		✓	✓	✓	✓	✓	✓	✓
Microsoft Office Publisher 2007				✓	✓	✓	✓	✓
Microsoft Office Outlook 2007	✓		✓				✓	✓
Microsoft Office OneNote 2007		✓				✓		
Microsoft Office Outlook 2007 with Business Contact Manager				✓	✓	✓		
Microsoft Office InfoPath 2007						✓	✓	✓
Integrated Enterprise Content Management						✓	✓	✓
Electronic Forms						✓	✓	✓
Advanced Information Rights Management and Policy Capabilities						✓	✓	✓
Microsoft Office Communicator 2007							✓	✓
Microsoft Office Groove 2007						✓		✓

Microsoft has bundled additional programs in some versions of Office 2007, in addition to the main group of Office programs. Table B–1 on the previous page lists the components of the various Office suites.

In addition to the Office 2007 programs noted previously, Office 2007 suites can contain other programs. Microsoft Office OneNote 2007 is a digital notebook program that allows you to gather and share various types of media, such as text, graphics, video, audio, and digital handwriting. Microsoft Office InfoPath 2007 is a program that allows you to create and use electronic forms to gather information. Microsoft Office Groove 2007 provides collaborative workspaces in real time. Additional services that are oriented toward the enterprise solution also are available.

Office 2007 and the Internet, World Wide Web, and Intranets

Office 2007 allows you to take advantage of the Internet, the World Wide Web, and intranets. The Microsoft Windows operating system includes a **browser**, which is a program that allows you to locate and view a Web page. The Windows browser is called Internet Explorer.

One method of viewing a Web page is to use the browser to enter the Web address for the Web page. Another method of viewing a Web page is clicking a hyperlink. A **hyperlink** is colored or underlined text or a graphic that, when clicked, connects to another Web page. Hyperlinks placed in Office 2007 documents allow for direct access to a Web site of interest.

An **intranet** is a private network, such as a network used within a company or organization for internal communication. Like the Internet, hyperlinks are used within an intranet to access documents, pages, and other destinations on the intranet. Unlike the Internet, the materials on the network are available only for those who are part of the private network.

Online Collaboration Using Office

Organizations that, in the past, were able to make important information available only to a select few, now can make their information accessible to a wider range of individuals who use programs such as Office 2007 and Internet Explorer. Office 2007 allows colleagues to use the Internet or an intranet as a central location to view documents, manage files, and work together.

Each of the Office 2007 programs makes publishing documents on a Web server as simple as saving a file on a hard disk. Once placed on the Web server, users can view and edit the documents and conduct Web discussions and live online meetings.

Using Microsoft Office 2007

The various Microsoft Office 2007 programs each specialize in a particular task. This section describes the general functions of the more widely used Office 2007 programs, along with how they are used to access the Internet or an intranet.

Microsoft Office Word 2007

Microsoft Office Word 2007 is a full-featured word processing program that allows you to create many types of personal and business documents, including flyers, letters, resumes, business documents, and academic reports.

Word's AutoCorrect, spelling, and grammar features help you proofread documents for errors in spelling and grammar by identifying the errors and offering suggestions for corrections as you type. The live word count feature provides you with a constantly updating word count as you enter and edit text. To assist with creating specific documents, such as a business letter or resume, Word provides templates, which provide a formatted document before you type the text of the document. Quick Styles provide a live preview of styles from the Style gallery, allowing you to preview styles in the document before actually applying them.

Word automates many often-used tasks and provides you with powerful desktop publishing tools to use as you create professional looking brochures, advertisements, and newsletters. SmartArt allows you to insert interpretive graphics based on document content.

Word makes it easier for you to share documents for collaboration. The Send feature opens an e-mail window with the active document attached. The Compare Documents feature allows you easily to identify changes when comparing different document versions.

Word 2007 and the Internet   Word makes it possible to design and publish Web pages on the Internet or an intranet, insert a hyperlink to a Web page in a word processing document, as well as access and search the content of other Web pages.

Microsoft Office Excel 2007

Microsoft Office Excel 2007 is a spreadsheet program that allows you to organize data, complete calculations, graph data, develop professional looking reports, publish organized data to the Web, and access real-time data from Web sites.

In addition to its mathematical functionality, Excel 2007 provides tools for visually comparing data. For instance, when comparing a group of values in cells, you can set cell backgrounds with bars proportional to the value of the data in the cell. You can also set cell backgrounds with full-color backgrounds, or use a color scale to facilitate interpretation of data values.

Excel 2007 provides strong formatting support for tables with the new Style Preview gallery.

Excel 2007 and the Internet   Using Excel 2007, you can create hyperlinks within a worksheet to access other Office documents on the network or on the Internet. Worksheets saved as static, or unchanging Web pages can be viewed using a browser. The person viewing static Web pages cannot change them.

In addition, you can create and run queries that retrieve information from a Web page and insert the information directly into a worksheet.

Microsoft Office Access 2007

Microsoft Office Access 2007 is a comprehensive database management system (DBMS). A **database** is a collection of data organized in a manner that allows access, retrieval, and use of that data. Access 2007 allows you to create a database; add, change, and delete data in the database; sort data in the database; retrieve data from the database; and create forms and reports using the data in the database.

Access 2007 and the Internet   Access 2007 lets you generate reports, which are summaries that show only certain data from the database, based on user requirements.

Microsoft Office PowerPoint 2007

Microsoft Office PowerPoint 2007 is a complete presentation graphics program that allows you to produce professional looking presentations. With PowerPoint 2007, you can create informal presentations using overhead transparencies, electronic presentations using a projection device attached to a personal computer, formal presentations using 35mm slides or a CD, or you can run virtual presentations on the Internet.

PowerPoint 2007 and the Internet   PowerPoint 2007 allows you to publish presentations on the Internet or other networks.

Microsoft Office Publisher 2007

Microsoft Office Publisher 2007 is a desktop publishing program (DTP) that allows you to design and produce professional quality documents (newsletters, flyers, brochures, business cards, Web sites, and so on) that combine text, graphics, and photographs. Desktop publishing software provides a variety of tools, including design templates, graphic manipulation tools, color schemes or libraries, and various page wizards and templates. For large jobs, businesses use desktop publishing software to design publications that are **camera ready**, which means the files are suitable for production by outside commercial printers. Publisher 2007 also allows you to locate commercial printers, service bureaus, and copy shops willing to accept customer files created in Publisher.

Publisher 2007 allows you to design a unique image, or logo, using one of more than 45 master design sets. This, in turn, permits you to use the same design for all your printed documents (letters, business cards, brochures, and advertisements) and Web pages. Publisher includes 70 coordinated color schemes; 30 font schemes; more than 10,000 high-quality clip art images; 1,500 photographs; 1,000 Web-art graphics; 340 animated graphics; and hundreds of unique Design Gallery elements (quotations, sidebars, and so on). If you wish, you also can download additional images from the Microsoft Office Online Web page on the Microsoft Web site.

Publisher 2007 and the Internet   Publisher 2007 allows you easily to create a multipage Web site with custom color schemes, photographic images, animated images, and sounds.

Microsoft Office Outlook 2007

Microsoft Office Outlook 2007 is a powerful communications and scheduling program that helps you communicate with others, keep track of your contacts, and organize your schedule. Outlook 2007 allows you to view a To-Do bar containing tasks and appointments from your Outlook calendar. Outlook 2007 allows you to send and receive electronic mail (e-mail) and permits you to engage in real-time communication with family, friends, or coworkers using instant messaging. Outlook 2007 also provides you with the means to organize your contacts, and you can track e-mail messages, meetings, and notes with a particular contact. Outlook's Calendar, Contacts, Tasks, and Notes components aid in this organization. Contact information is available from the Outlook Calendar, Mail, Contacts, and Task components by accessing the Find a Contact feature. **Personal information management** (**PIM**) programs such as Outlook provide a way for individuals and workgroups to organize, find, view, and share information easily.

Microsoft Office 2007 Help

At any time while you are using one of the Office programs, you can interact with **Microsoft Office 2007 Help** for that program and display information about any topic associated with the program. Several categories of help are available. In all programs, you can access Help by pressing the F1 key on the keyboard. In Publisher 2007 and Outlook 2007, the Help window can be opened by clicking the Help menu and then selecting Microsoft Office Publisher or Outlook Help command, or by entering search text in the 'Type a question for help' text box in the upper-right corner of the program window. In the other Office programs, clicking the Microsoft Office Help button near the upper-right corner of the program window opens the program Help window.

The Help window in all programs provides several methods for accessing help about a particular topic, and has tools for navigating around Help. Appendix C contains detailed instructions for using Help.

Collaboration and SharePoint

While not part of the Microsoft Office 2007 suites, SharePoint is a Microsoft tool that allows Office 2007 users to share data using collaborative tools that are integrated into the main Office programs. SharePoint consists of Windows SharePoint Services, Office SharePoint Server 2007, and, optionally, Office SharePoint Designer 2007.

Windows SharePoint Services provides the platform for collaboration programs and services. Office SharePoint Server 2007 is built on top of Windows SharePoint Services. The result of these two products is the ability to create SharePoint sites. A SharePoint site is a Web site that provides users with a virtual place for collaborating and communicating with their colleagues while working together on projects, documents, ideas, and information. Each member of a group with access to the SharePoint site has the ability to contribute to the material stored there. The basic building blocks of SharePoint sites are lists and libraries. Lists contain collections of information, such as calendar items, discussion points, contacts, and links. Lists can be edited to add or delete information. Libraries are similar to lists, but include both files and information about files. Types of libraries include document, picture, and forms libraries.

The most basic type of SharePoint site is called a Workspace, which is used primarily for collaboration. Different types of Workspaces can be created using SharePoint to suit different needs. SharePoint provides templates, or outlines of these Workspaces, that can be filled in to create the Workspace. Each of the different types of Workspace templates contain a different collection of lists and libraries, reflecting the purpose of the Workspace. You can create a Document Workspace to facilitate collaboration on documents. A Document Workspace contains a document library for documents and supporting files, a Links list that allows you to maintain relevant resource links for the document, a Tasks list for listing and assigning To-Do items to team members, and other links as needed. Meeting Workspaces allow users to plan and organize a meeting, with components such as Attendees, Agenda, and a Document Library. Social Meeting Workspaces provide a place to plan social events, with lists and libraries such as Attendees, Directions, Image/Logo, Things To Bring, Discussions, and Picture Library. A Decision Meeting Workspace is a Meeting Workspace with a focus on review and decision-making, with lists and libraries such as Objectives, Attendees, Agenda, Document Library, Tasks, and Decisions.

Users also can create a SharePoint site called a WebParts page, which is built from modules called WebParts. WebParts are modular units of information that contain a title bar and content that reflects the type of WebPart. For instance, an image WebPart would contain a title bar and an image. WebParts allow you quickly to create and modify a SharePoint site, and allow for the creation of a unique site that can allow users to access and make changes to information stored on the site.

Large SharePoint sites that include multiple pages can be created using templates as well. Groups needing more refined and targeted sharing options than those available with SharePoint Server 2007 and Windows SharePoint Services can add SharePoint Designer 2007 to create a site that meets their specific needs.

Depending on which components have been selected for inclusion on the site, users can view a team calendar, view links, read announcements, and view and edit group documents and projects. SharePoint sites can be set up so that documents are checked in and out, much like a library, to prevent multiple users from making changes simultaneously. Once a SharePoint site is set up, Office programs are used to perform maintenance of the site. For example, changes in the team calendar are updated using Outlook 2007, and changes that users make in Outlook 2007 are reflected on the SharePoint site. Office 2007 programs include a Publish feature that allows users easily to save file updates to a SharePoint site. Team members can be notified about changes made to material on the site either by e-mail or by a news feed, meaning that users do not have to go to the site to check to see if anything has been updated since they last viewed or worked on it. The search feature in SharePoint allows users quickly to find information on a large site.

Appendix C
Microsoft Office Outlook 2007 Help

Using Microsoft Office Outlook Help

This appendix shows how to use Microsoft Office Outlook Help. At any time while you are using Outlook, you can use Outlook Help to display information about all topics associated with Outlook.

In Outlook 2007, Help is presented in a window that has Web browser-style navigation buttons. Each Office 2007 program has its own Help home page, which is the starting Help page that is displayed in the Help window. If your computer is connected to the Internet, the contents of the Help page reflect both the local help files installed on the computer and material from Microsoft's Web site. As shown in Figure C–1, two methods for accessing Outlook's Help are available:

1. Microsoft Office Outlook Help button on the right side of the Standard toolbar.

2. Function key F1 on the keyboard

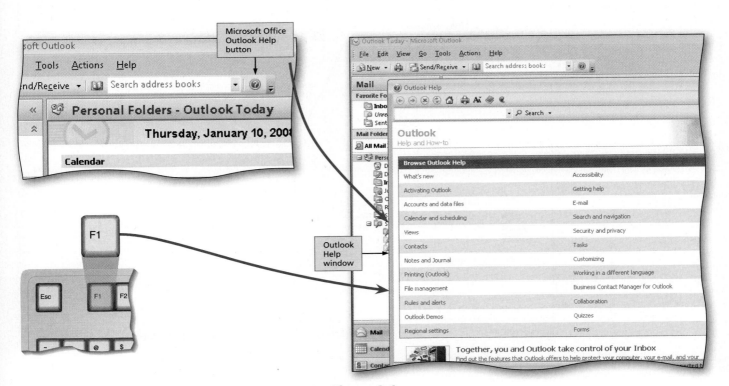

Figure C–1

To Open the Outlook Help Window

The following steps open the Outlook Help window and maximize the window.

1

• Start Microsoft Outlook, if necessary. Click the Microsoft Office Outlook Help button on the right side of the Standard toolbar to open the Outlook Help window (Figure C–2).

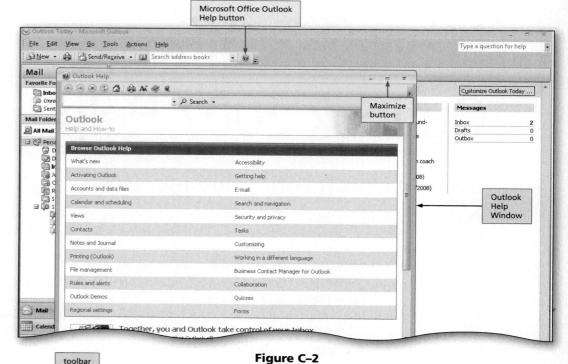

Figure C–2

2

• Click the Maximize button on the Help title bar to maximize the Help window (Figure C–3).

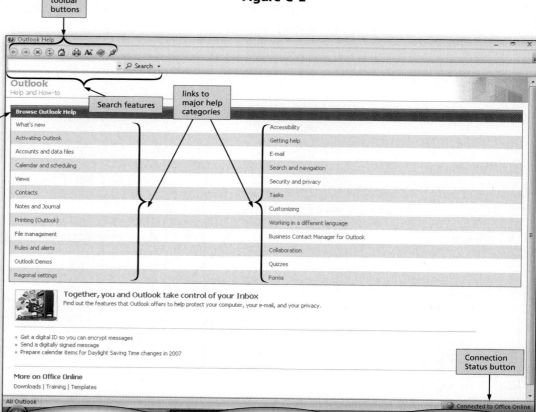

Figure C–3

The Outlook Help Window

The Outlook Help window provides several methods for accessing help about a particular topic, and also has tools for navigating around Help. Methods for accessing Help include searching the help content installed with Outlook, or searching the online Office content maintained by Microsoft.

Figure C–3 shows the main Outlook Help window. To navigate Help, the Outlook Help window includes search features that allow you to search on a word or phrase about which you want Help; the Connection Status button, which allows you to control where Outlook Help searches for content; toolbar buttons; and links to major Help categories.

Search Features

You can perform Help searches on words or phrases to find information about any Outlook feature using the 'Type words to search for' text box and the Search button (Figure C–4a). Click the 'Type words to search for' text box and then click the Search button or press the ENTER key to initiate a search of Outlook Help.

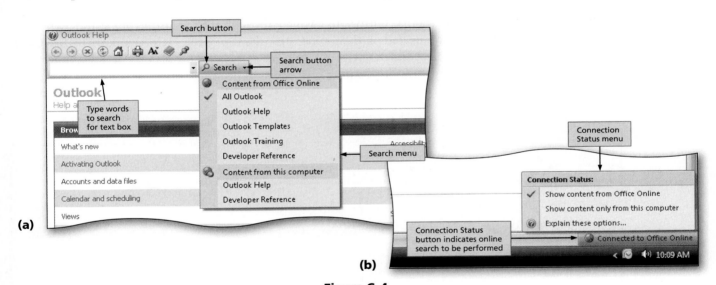

Figure C–4

Outlook Help offers the user the option of searching the online Help Web pages maintained by Microsoft or the offline Help files placed on your computer when you install Outlook. You can specify whether Outlook Help should search online or offline from two places: the Connection Status button on the status bar of the Outlook Help window, or the Search button arrow on the toolbar. The Connection Status button indicates whether Help currently is set up to work with online or offline information sources. Clicking the Connection Status button provides a menu with commands for selecting online or offline searches (Figure C–4b). The Connection Status menu allows the user to select whether help searches will return content only from the computer (offline), or content from the computer and from Office Online (online).

Clicking the Search button arrow also provides a menu with commands for an online or offline search (Figure C–4a). These commands determine the source of information that Help searches for during the current Help session only. For example, assume that your preferred search is an offline search because you often do not have Internet access. You would set Connection Status to 'Show content only from this computer'. When you have Internet access, you can select an online search from the Search menu to search Office Online for information for your current search session only. Your search will use the Office Online resources until you quit Help. The next time you start Help, the Connection Status once again will be offline. In addition to setting the source of information that Help searches for during the current Help session, you can use the Search menu to further target the current search to one of four subcategories of online Help: Outlook Help, Outlook Templates, Outlook Training, and Developer Reference. The local search further can target one subcategory, Developer Reference.

In addition to searching for a word or string of text, you can use the links provided on the Browse Word Help area (Figure C–3 on page APP 10) to search for help on a topic. These links direct you to major help categories. From each major category, subcategories are available to further refine your search.

Finally, you can use the Table of Contents for Outlook Help to search for a topic the same way you would in a hard copy book. The Table of Contents is accessed through a toolbar button.

Toolbar Buttons

You can use toolbar buttons to navigate through the results of your search. The toolbar buttons are located on the toolbar near the top of the Help Window (Figure C–5). The toolbar buttons contain navigation buttons as well as buttons that perform other useful and common tasks in Outlook Help, such as printing.

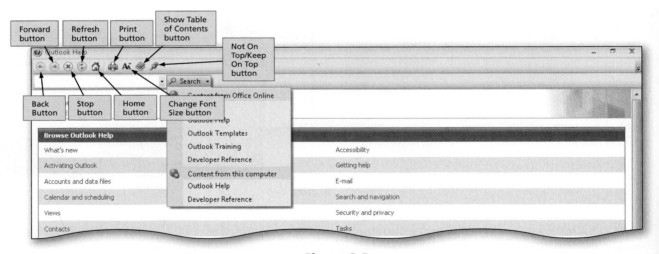

Figure C–5

The Outlook Help navigation buttons are the Back, Forward, Stop, Refresh, and Home. These five buttons behave like the navigation buttons in a Web browser window. You can use the Back button to go back one window, the Forward button to go forward one window, the Stop button to stop loading the current page, and the Home button to redisplay the Help home page in the Help window. Use the Refresh button to reload the information requested into the Help window from its original source. When getting Help information online, this button provides the most current information from the Microsoft Help Web site.

The buttons located to the right of the navigation buttons — Print, Change Font Size, Show Table of Contents, and Not on Top — provide you with access to useful and common commands. The Print button prints the contents of the open Help window. The Change Font Size button customizes the Help window by increasing or decreasing the size of its text. The Show Table of Contents button opens a pane on the left side of the Help window that shows the Table of Contents for Outlook Help. You can use the Table of Contents for Outlook Help to navigate through the contents of Outlook Help much as you would use the Table of Contents in a book to search for a topic. The Not On Top button is an example of a toggle button, which is a button that can be switched back and forth between two states. It determines how the Outlook Help window behaves relative to other windows. When clicked, the Not On Top button changes to Keep On Top. In this state, it does not allow other windows from Outlook or other programs to cover the Outlook Help window when those windows are the active windows. When in the Not On Top state, the button allows other windows to be opened or moved on top of the Outlook Help window.

You can customize the size and placement of the Help window. Resize the window using the Maximize and Restore buttons, or by dragging the window to a desired size. Relocate the Help window by dragging the title bar to a new location on the screen.

Searching Outlook Help

Once the Outlook Help window is open, several methods exist for navigating Outlook Help. You can search for help by using any of the three following methods from the Help window:

1. Enter search text in the 'Type words to search for' text box
2. Click the links in the Help window
3. Use the Table of Contents

To Obtain Help Using the Type Words to Search for Text Box

Assume for the following example that you want to know more about meetings. The following steps use the 'Type words to search for' text box to obtain useful information about meetings by entering the word, meetings, as search text. The steps also navigate in the Outlook Help window.

1

- Type meeting in the 'Type words to search for' text box at the top of the Outlook Help window.

- Click the Search button arrow to display the Search menu.

- If it is not selected already, click All Outlook on the Search menu to select the command. If All Outlook is already selected, click the Search button arrow again to close the Search menu.

Q&A

Why select All Outlook on the Search menu?

Selecting All Outlook on the Search menu ensures that Outlook Help will search all possible sources for information on your search term. It will produce the most complete search results.

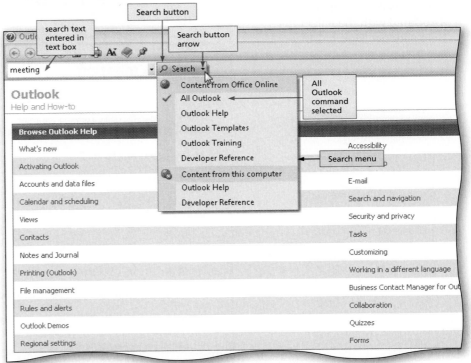

Figure C–6

- Click the Search button to display the search results (Figure C–7).

Q&A

Why do my results differ?

If you do not have an Internet connection, your results will reflect only the content of the Help files on your computer. When searching for help online, results also can change as material is added, deleted, and updated on the online Help Web pages maintained by Microsoft.

Q&A

Why were my search results not very helpful?

When initiating a search, keep in mind to check the spelling of the search text; and to keep your search very specific, with fewer than seven words, to return the most accurate results.

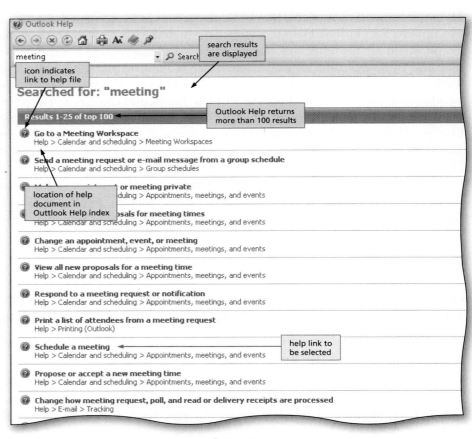

Figure C–7

- Click the 'Schedule a meeting' link to open the Help document associated with the link in the Help window (Figure C–8).

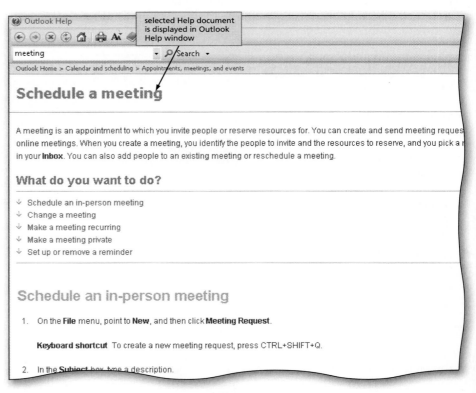

Figure C–8

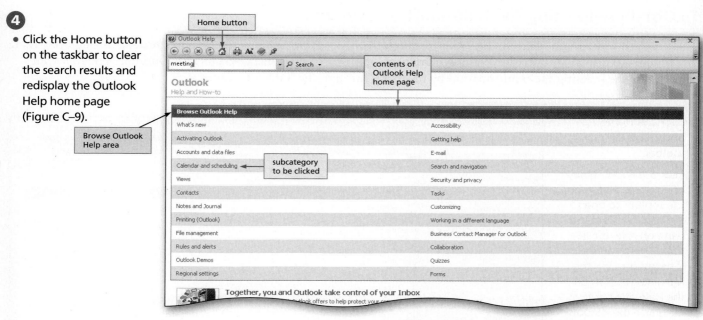

Figure C–9

To Obtain Help Using the Help Links

If your topic of interest is listed in the Browse Outlook Help area, you can click the link to begin browsing Outlook Help categories instead of entering search text. You browse Outlook Help just like you would browse a Web site. If you know in which category to find your Help information, you may wish to use these links. The following steps find the meeting Help information using the category links from the Outlook Help home page.

- Click the 'Calendar and scheduling' link to open the Calendar and scheduling subcategories page and then click the 'Appointments, meetings, and events' link to open the 'Appointments, meetings, and events' page.

- Click the 'Schedule a meeting' link to open the Help document associated with the link (Figure C–10).

Figure C–10

To Obtain Help Using the Help Table of Contents

A third way to find Help in Outlook is through the Help Table of Contents. You can browse through the Table of Contents to display information about a particular topic or to familiarize yourself with Outlook. The following steps access the meeting Help information by browsing through the Table of Contents.

1

- Click the Home button on the toolbar.

- Click the Show Table of Contents button on the toolbar to open the Table of Contents pane on the left side of the Help window. If necessary, click the Maximize button on the Help title bar to maximize the window (Figure C–11).

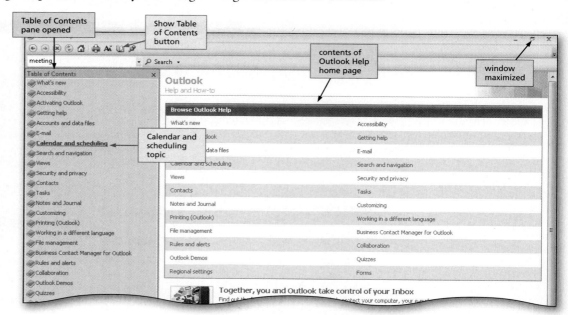

Figure C–11

2

- Click the 'Calendar and scheduling' link in the Table of Contents pane to view a list of Help subtopics.

- Click the 'Appointments, meetings, and events' link in the Table of Contents pane and then click the 'Schedule a meeting' link to view the selected Help document in the right pane (Figure C–12).

How do I remove the Table of Contents pane when I am finished with it?

The Show Table of Contents button acts as a toggle switch. When the Table of Contents pane is visible, the button changes to Hide Table of Contents. Clicking it hides the Table of Contents pane and changes the button to Show Table of Contents.

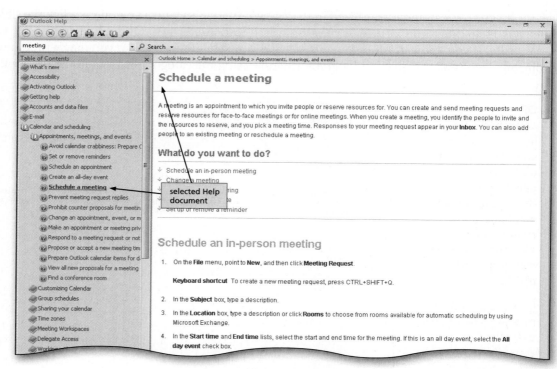

Figure C–12

Obtaining Help while Working in Outlook

Often you may need help while working on a document without already having the Help window open. For example, you may be unsure about how a particular command works, or you may be presented with a dialog box that you are not sure how to use. Rather than opening the Help window and initiating a search, Outlook Help provides you with the ability to search directly for help.

Figure C–13 shows one option for obtaining help while working in Outlook. If you want to learn more about a command, point to the command button and wait for the Enhanced ScreenTip to appear. If the Help icon appears in the Enhanced ScreenTip, press the F1 key while pointing to the command to open the Help window associated with that command.

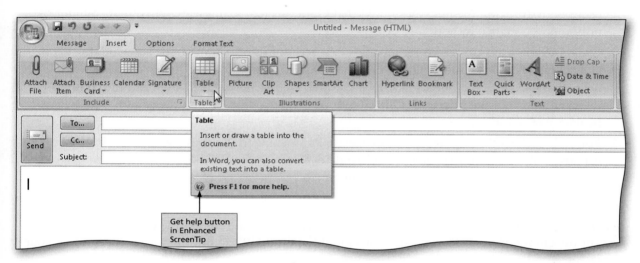

Figure C–13

Figure C–14 shows a dialog box with a Get help button in it. Pressing the F1 key while the dialog box is displayed opens a Help window. The Help window contains help about that dialog box, if available. If no help file is available for that particular dialog box, then the main Help window opens.

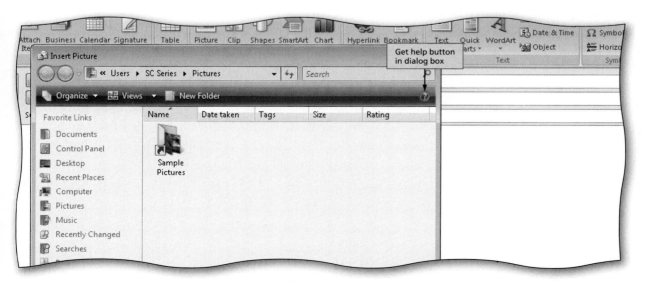

Figure C–14

Use Help

1 Obtaining Help Using Search Text

Instructions: Perform the following tasks using Outlook Help.

1. Use the 'Type words to search for' text box to obtain help about printing an e-mail message with an attachment. Use the Connection Status menu to search online help if you have an Internet connection.

2. Click Print an e-mail message and attachment in the list of links in the search results. Double-click the Microsoft Office Outlook Help window title bar to maximize it. Read and print the information. At the top of the printout, write down the number of links Outlook Help found.

3. Use the Search menu to search for help offline. Repeat the search from Step 1. At the top of the printout, write down the number of links that Outlook Help found searching offline. Submit the printouts as specified by your instructor.

4. Use the 'Type words to search for' text box to search for information online about adding a picture to a contact. Click the 'Add, change, or remove a picture for a contact' link in the search results. If necessary, maximize the Microsoft Office Outlook Help window. Read and print the contents of the window. Close the Microsoft Office Outlook Help window. Submit the printouts as specified by your instructor.

5. For each of the following words and phrases, click one link in the search results, click the Show All link, and then print the page: Day view; date; print preview; Ribbon; signatures; and flagging. Submit the printouts as specified by your instructor.

2 Expanding on Outlook Help Basics

Instructions: Use Outlook Help to better understand its features and answer the questions listed below. Answer the questions on your own paper, or submit the printed Help information as specified by your instructor.

1. Use Help to find out how to customize the Help window. Change the font size to the smallest option and then print the contents of the Microsoft Office Outlook Help window. Change the font size back to its original setting. Close the window.

2. Press the F1 key. Search for information about e-mail, restricting the search results to Outlook Templates. Print the first page of the Search results.

3. Search for information about e-mail, restricting the search results to Outlook Help files. Print the first page of the Search results.

4. Use Outlook Help to find out what happened to the Office Assistant, a feature in the previous version of Outlook. Print out the Help document that contains the answer.

Appendix D
Publishing Office 2007 Web Pages to a Web Server

With the Office 2007 programs, you use the Save As command on the Office Button menu to save a Web page to a Web server using one of two techniques: Web folders or File Transfer Protocol. A **Web folder** is an Office shortcut to a Web server. **File Transfer Protocol (FTP)** is an Internet standard that allows computers to exchange files with other computers on the Internet.

You should contact your network system administrator or technical support staff at your Internet access provider to determine if their Web server supports Web folders, FTP, or both, and to obtain necessary permissions to access the Web server. If you decide to publish Web pages using a Web folder, you must have the Office Server Extensions (OSE) installed on your computer.

Using Web Folders to Publish Office 2007 Web Pages

When publishing to a Web folder, someone first must create the Web folder before you can save to it. If you are granted permission to create a Web folder, you must obtain the Web address of the Web server, a user name, and possibly a password that allows you to access the Web server. You also must decide on a name for the Web folder. Table D–1 explains how to create a Web folder.

Office 2007 adds the name of the Web folder to the list of current Web folders. You can save to this folder, open files in the folder, rename the folder, or perform any operations you would to a folder on your hard disk. You can use your Office 2007 program or Windows Explorer to access this folder. Table D–2 explains how to save to a Web folder.

Table D–1 Creating a Web Folder
1. Click the Office Button and then click Save As or Open.
2. When the Save As dialog box (or Open dialog box) appears, click the Tools button arrow, and then click Map Network Drive... When the Map Network Drive dialog box is displayed, click the 'Connect to a Web site that you can use to store your documents and pictures' link.
3. When the Add Network Location Wizard dialog box appears, click the Next button. If necessary, click Choose a custom network location. Click the Next button. Click the View examples link, type the Internet or network address, and then click the Next button. Click 'Log on anonymously' to deselect the check box, type your user name in the User name text box, and then click the Next button. Enter the name you want to call this network place and then click the Next button. Click to deselect the 'Open this network location when I click Finish' check box, and then click the Finish button.

Table D–2 Saving to a Web Folder
1. Click the Office Button, click Save As.
2. When the Save As dialog box is displayed, type the Web page file name in the File name text box. Do not press the ENTER key.
3. Click the Save as type box arrow and then click Web Page to select the Web Page format.
4. Click Computer in the Navigation pane.
5. Double-click the Web folder name in the Network Location list.
6. If the Enter Network Password dialog box appears, type the user name and password in the respective text boxes and then click the OK button.
7. Click the Save button in the Save As dialog box.

Using FTP to Publish Office 2007 Web Pages

When publishing a Web page using FTP, you first must add the FTP location to your computer before you can save to it. An FTP location, also called an **FTP site**, is a collection of files that reside on an FTP server. In this case, the FTP server is the Web server.

To add an FTP location, you must obtain the name of the FTP site, which usually is the address (URL) of the FTP server, and a user name and a password that allows you to access the FTP server. You save and open the Web pages on the FTP server using the name of the FTP site. Table D–3 explains how to add an FTP site.

Office 2007 adds the name of the FTP site to the FTP locations list in the Save As and Open dialog boxes. You can open and save files using this list. Table D–4 explains how to save to an FTP location.

Table D–3 Adding an FTP Location
1. Click the Office Button and then click Save As or Open.
2. When the Save As dialog box (or Open dialog box) appears, click the Tools button arrow, and then click Map Network Drive... When the Map Network Drive dialog box is displayed, click the 'Connect to a Web site that you can use to store your documents and pictures' link.
3. When the Add Network Location Wizard dialog box appears, click the Next button. If necessary, click Choose a custom network location. Click the Next button. Click the View examples link, type the Internet or network address, and then click the Next button. If you have a user name for the site, click to deselect 'Log on anonymously' and type your user name in the User name text box, and then click Next. If the site allows anonymous logon, click Next. Type a name for the location, click Next, click to deselect the 'Open this network location when I click Finish' check box, and click Finish. Click the OK button.
4. Close the Save As or the Open dialog box.

Table D–4 Saving to an FTP Location
1. Click the Office Button and then click Save As.
2. When the Save As dialog box is displayed, type the Web page file name in the File name text box. Do not press the ENTER key.
3. Click the Save as type box arrow and then click Web Page to select the Web Page format.
4. Click Computer in the Navigation pane.
5. Double-click the name of the FTP site in the Network Location list.
6. When the FTP Log On dialog box appears, enter your user name and password and then click the OK button.
7. Click the Save button in the Save As dialog box.

Appendix E

Customizing Microsoft Office Outlook 2007

This appendix explains how to change the screen resolution in Windows Vista to the resolution used in this book. It also describes how to customize the Outlook window by changing the Ribbon, Quick Access Toolbar, and the color scheme.

Changing Screen Resolution

Screen resolution indicates the number of pixels (dots) that the computer uses to display the letters, numbers, graphics, and background you see on the screen. When you increase the screen resolution, Windows displays more information on the screen, but the information decreases in size. The reverse also is true: as you decrease the screen resolution, Windows displays less information on the screen, but the information increases in size.

The screen resolution usually is stated as the product of two numbers, such as 1024×768 (pronounced "ten twenty-four by seven sixty-eight"). A 1024×768 screen resolution results in a display of 1,024 distinct pixels on each of 768 lines, or about 786,432 pixels. The figures in this book were created using a screen resolution of 1024×768.

The screen resolutions most commonly used today are 800×600 and 1024×768, although some Office specialists set their computers at a much higher screen resolution, such as 2048×1536.

To Change the Screen Resolution

The following steps change the screen resolution from 1280×1024 to 1024×768. Your computer already may be set to 1024×768 or some other resolution.

1

- If necessary, minimize all programs so that the Windows Vista desktop appears.

- Right-click the Windows Vista desktop to display the Windows Vista desktop shortcut menu (Figure E–1).

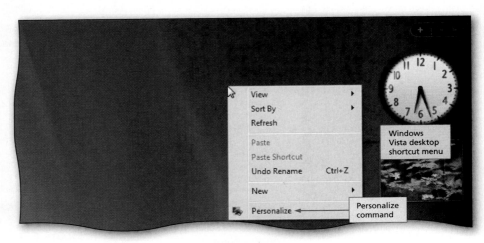

Figure E–1

- Click Personalize on the shortcut menu to open the Personalization window.

- Click Display Settings in the Personalization window to display the Display Settings dialog box (Figure E–2).

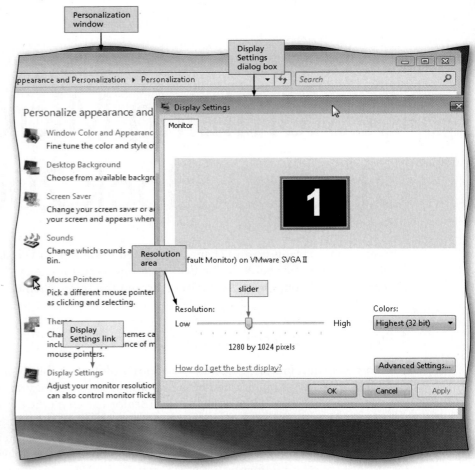

Figure E–2

- Drag the slider in the Resolution area so that the screen resolution changes to 1024 × 768 (Figure E–3).

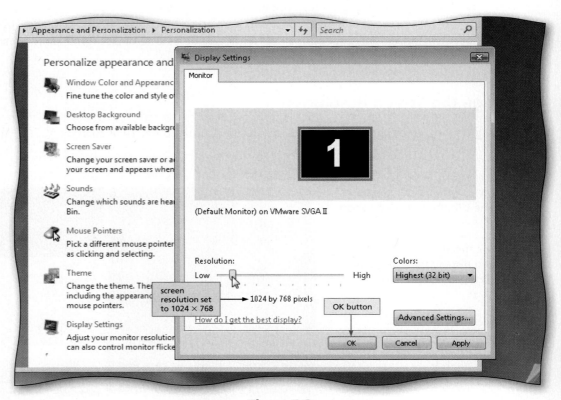

Figure E–3

4

- Click the OK button to change the screen resolution from 1280 × 1024 to 1024 × 768 (Figure E–4).

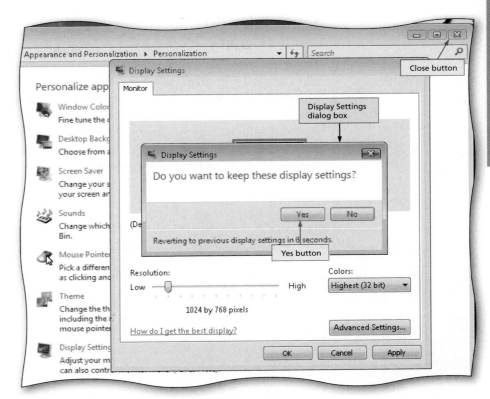

Figure E–4

5

- Click the Yes button in the Display Settings dialog box to accept the new screen resolution (Figure E–5).

 Q&A What if I do not want to change the screen resolution after seeing it applied after I click the OK button?

You either can click the No button in the inner Display Settings dialog box, or wait for the timer to run out, at which point Windows Vista will revert to the original screen resolution.

- Click the Close button to close the Personalization Window.

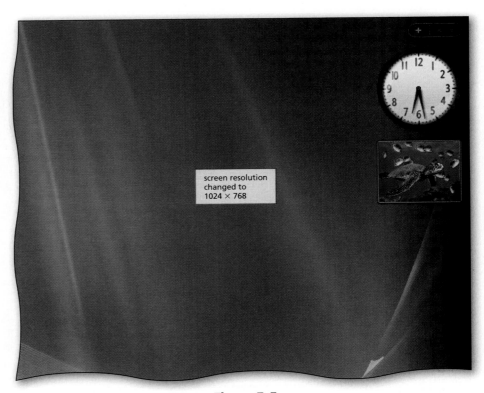

Figure E–5

Screen Resolution and the Appearance of the Ribbon in Outlook 2007

Changing the screen resolution affects how the Ribbon appears in Outlook 2007. Figure E–6 shows the Outlook Ribbon at the screen resolutions of 800×600, 1024×768, and 1280×1024. All of the same commands are available regardless of screen resolution. Outlook, however, makes changes to the groups and the buttons within the groups to accommodate the various screen resolutions. The result is that certain commands may need to be accessed differently depending on the resolution chosen. A command that is visible on the Ribbon and available by clicking a button at one resolution may not be visible and may need to be accessed using its group button at a different resolution.

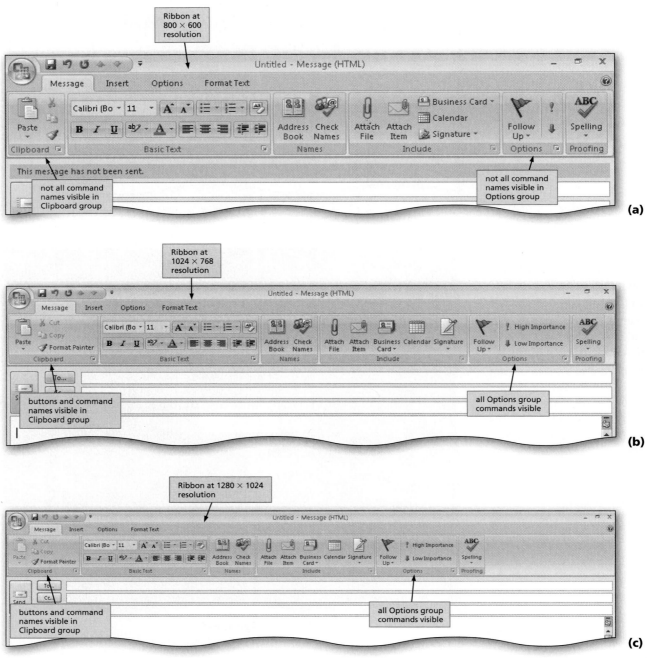

Figure E–6

Comparing the three Ribbons, notice changes in content and layout of the groups and galleries. In some cases, the content of a group is the same in each resolution, but the layout on the Quick Access Toolbar menu of the group differs. In some cases, the content and layout are the same across the resolution, but the level of detail differs with the resolution. In the Clipboard and Options group, when the resolution increases to 1024×768, the names of all the buttons in the group appear in addition to the buttons themselves. At the lower resolution, only the buttons appear.

Customizing the Outlook Message Window

When composing an e-mail message in Outlook, you may want to make your working area as large as possible. One option is to minimize the Ribbon. You also can modify the characteristics of the Quick Access Toolbar, customizing the toolbar's commands and location to better suit your needs.

To Minimize the Ribbon in Outlook

The following steps minimize the Ribbon.

1

- Start Outlook and then click the New Mail Message button to open the Untitled - Message window.

- Maximize the Message window, if necessary.

- Click the Customize Quick Access Toolbar button on the Quick Access Toolbar to display the Customize Quick Access Toolbar menu (Figure E–7).

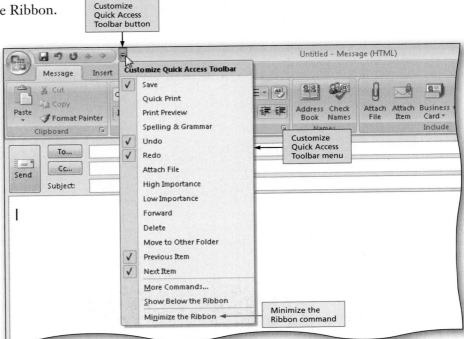

Figure E–7

2

● Click Minimize the Ribbon on the Quick Access Toolbar menu to reduce the Ribbon display to just the tabs (Figure E–8).

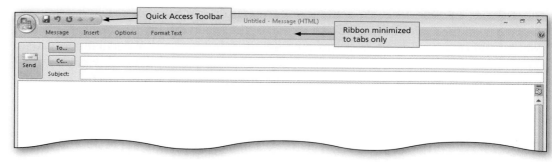

Figure E–8

Customizing and Resetting the Quick Access Toolbar

The Quick Access Toolbar, located to the right of the Microsoft Office Button by default, provides easy access to some of the more frequently used commands in Outlook (Figure E–7). By default, the Quick Access Toolbar contains buttons for the Save, Undo, Redo, Next Item, and Previous Item commands. Customize the Quick Access Toolbar by changing its location in the window and by adding additional buttons to reflect which commands you would like to be able to access easily.

To Change the Location of the Quick Access Toolbar

The following steps move the Quick Access Toolbar to below the Ribbon.

1

● Double-click the Message tab to redisplay the Ribbon.

● Click the Customize Quick Access Toolbar button on the Quick Access Toolbar to display the Customize Quick Access Toolbar menu (Figure E–9).

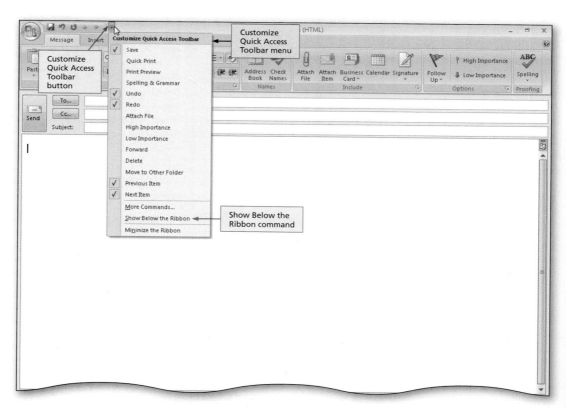

Figure E–9

2

● Click Show Below the Ribbon on the Quick Access Toolbar menu to move the Quick Access Toolbar below the Ribbon (Figure E–10).

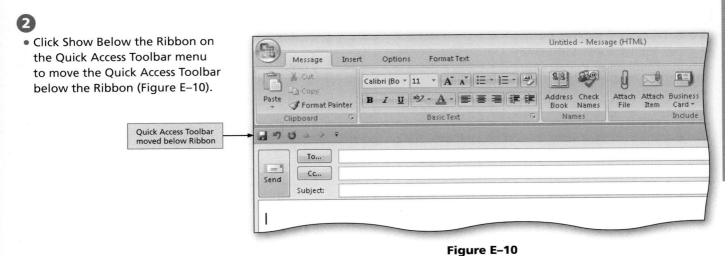

Figure E–10

To Add Commands to the Quick Access Toolbar Using the Customize Quick Access Toolbar Menu

Some of the more commonly added commands are available for selection from the Customize Quick Access Toolbar menu. The following steps add the Quick Print button to the Quick Access Toolbar.

1

● Click the Customize Quick Access Toolbar button to display the Customize Quick Access Toolbar menu (Figure E–11).

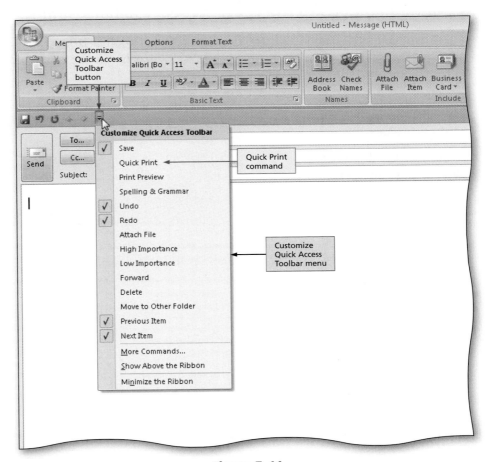

Figure E–11

2

- Click Quick Print on the Quick Access Toolbar menu to add the Quick Print button to the Quick Access Toolbar (Figure E–12).

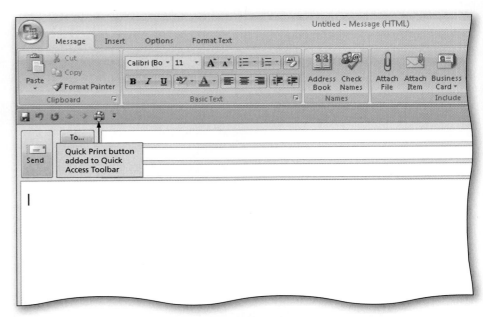

Figure E–12

To Add Commands to the Quick Access Toolbar Using the Shortcut Menu

Commands also can be added to the Quick Access Toolbar from the Ribbon. Adding an existing Ribbon command that you use often to the Quick Access Toolbar makes the command immediately available, regardless of which tab is active.

1

- Click the Format Text tab to make it the active tab.

- Right-click the Zoom button to display a shortcut menu (Figure E–13).

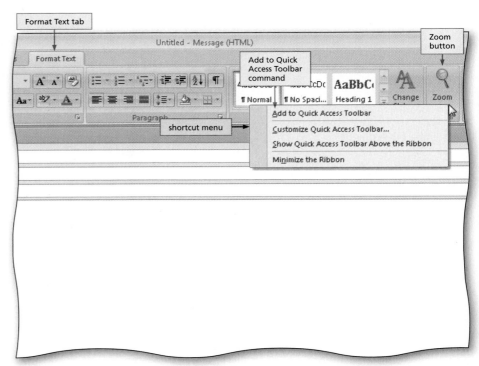

Figure E–13

2

• Click Add to Quick Access Toolbar on the shortcut menu to add the Zoom button to the Quick Access Toolbar (Figure E–14).

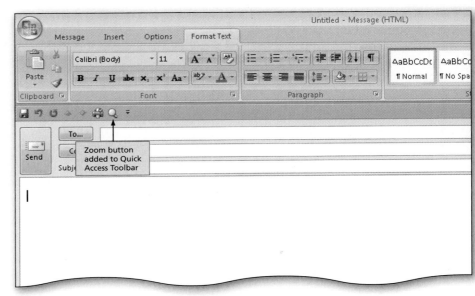

Figure E–14

To Add Commands to the Quick Access Toolbar Using Editor Options

Some commands do not appear on the Ribbon. They can be added to the Quick Access Toolbar using the Editor Options dialog box.

1

• Click the Office Button to display the Office Button menu (Figure E–15).

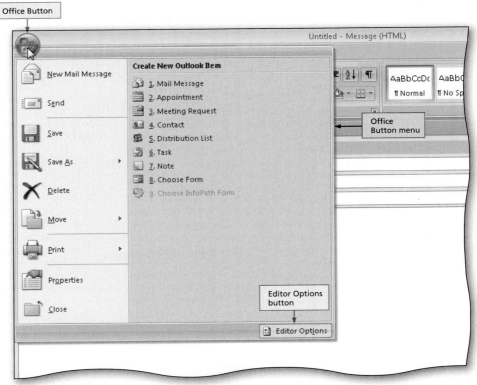

Figure E–15

● Click the Editor
Options button on
the Office Button
menu to display the
Editor Options dialog
box (Figure E–16).

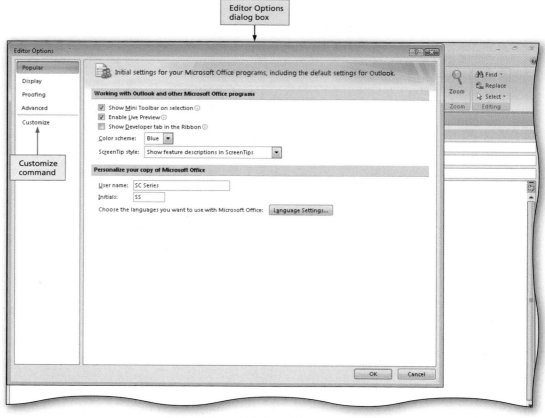

Figure E–16

● Click Customize in
the left pane.

● Click the 'Choose
commands from' box
arrow to display the
'Choose commands
from' list.

● Click Commands Not
in the Ribbon in the
'Choose commands
from' list.

● Scroll to display
the Task Request
command.

● Click Task Request
to select it
(Figure E–17).

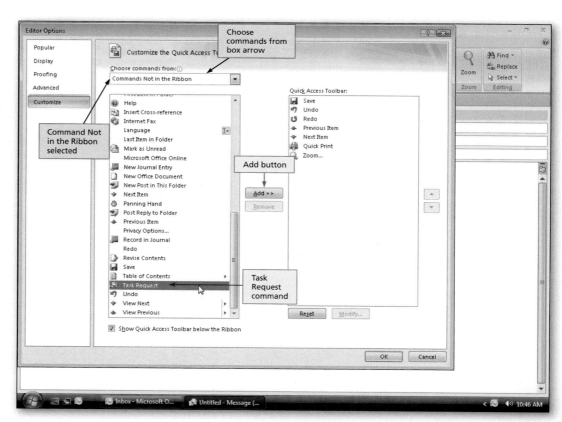

Figure E–17

● Click the Add
button to add the
Task Request button
to the list of buttons
on the Quick
Access Toolbar
(Figure E–18).

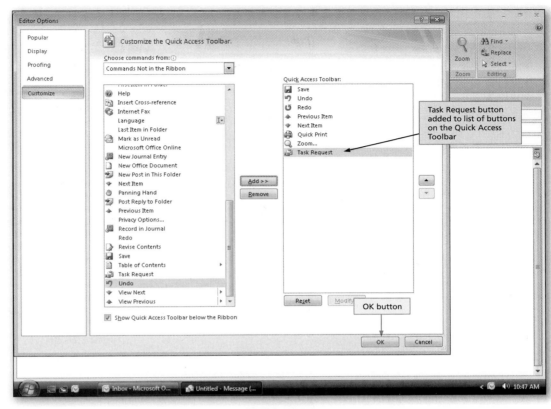

Figure E–18

● Click the OK button to add
the Task Request button
to the Quick Access Toolbar
(Figure E–19).

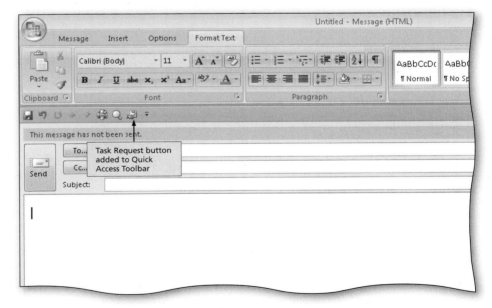

Figure E–19

To Remove a Command from the Quick Access Toolbar

1

• Right-click the Task Request button on the Quick Access Toolbar to display a shortcut menu (Figure E–20).

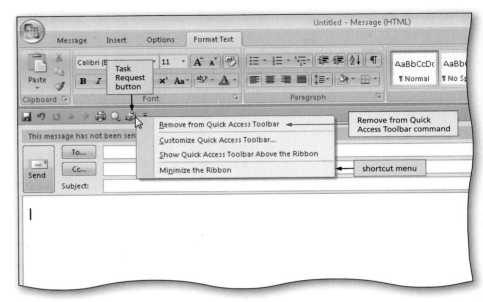

Figure E–20

2

• Click Remove from Quick Access Toolbar on the shortcut menu to remove the button from the Quick Access Toolbar (Figure E–21).

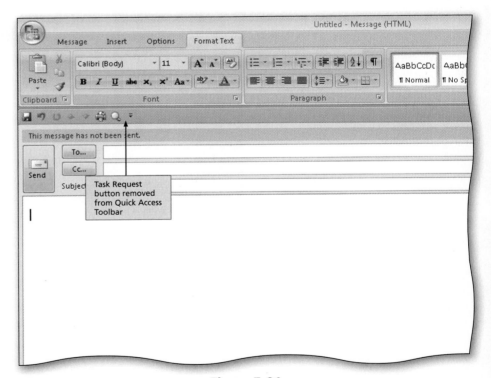

Figure E–21

Other Ways

1. Click Customize Quick Access Toolbar button, click More Commands, click the command you wish to remove in the Customize Quick Access Toolbar list, click Remove button, click OK button

2. If the command appears on the Customize Quick Access Toolbar menu, click the Customize Quick Access Toolbar button, click the command you wish to remove

To Reset the Quick Access Toolbar

1

- Click the Customize Quick Access Toolbar button on the Quick Access Toolbar.

- Click More Commands on the Quick Access Toolbar menu to display the Editor Options Dialog box.

- Click the Show Quick Access Toolbar below the Ribbon check box to deselect it (Figure E–22).

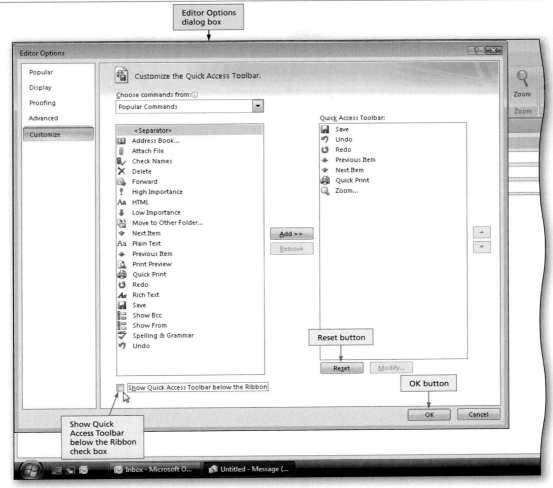

Figure E–22

- Click the Reset button, click the Yes button in the dialog box that appears, and then click the OK button in the Editor Options dialog box, to reset the Quick Access Toolbar to its original position to the right of the Office Button, with the original five buttons (Figure E–23).

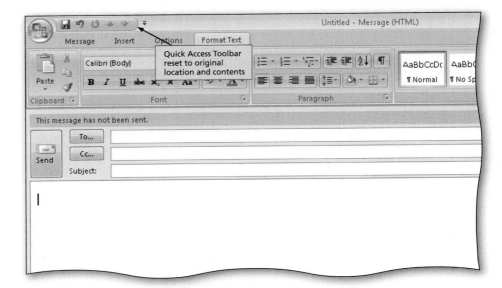

Figure E–23

Changing the Outlook Color Scheme

The Microsoft Outlook Message window can be customized by selecting a color scheme other than the default blue one. Three color schemes are available in Outlook.

To Change the Outlook Color Scheme

The following steps change the color scheme.

1

- Click the Office Button to display the Office Button menu.

- Click the Editor Options button on the Office Button menu to display the Editor Options dialog box.

- If necessary, click Popular in the left pane. Click the Color scheme box arrow to display a list of color schemes (Figure E–24).

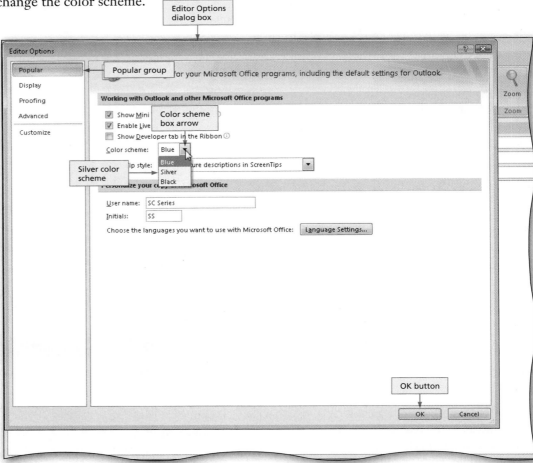

Figure E–24

2

- Click Silver in the list.

- Click the OK button to change the color scheme to silver (Figure E–25).

 How do I switch back to the default color scheme?

Follow the steps for changing the Outlook color scheme, and select Blue from the list of color schemes.

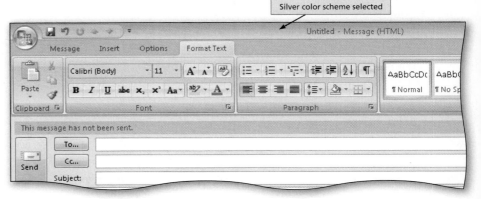

Figure E–25

Appendix F

Steps for the
Windows XP User

For the XP User of this Book

For most tasks, no differences exist between using Outlook under the Windows Vista operating system and using Word under the Windows XP operating system. With some tasks, however, you will see some differences, or need to complete the tasks using different steps. This appendix shows how to Start Outlook, Save a Contact List as a Text File and Display it in WordPad, and Import Subfolders while using Microsoft Office under Windows XP.

To Start and Customize Outlook

The following steps, which assume Windows is running, start Outlook based on a typical installation. You may need to ask your instructor how to start Outlook for your computer.

1

- Click the Start button on the Windows taskbar to display the Start menu.

- Point to All Programs on the Start menu to display the All Programs submenu.

- Point to Microsoft Office on the All Programs submenu to display the Microsoft Office submenu (Figure F–1).

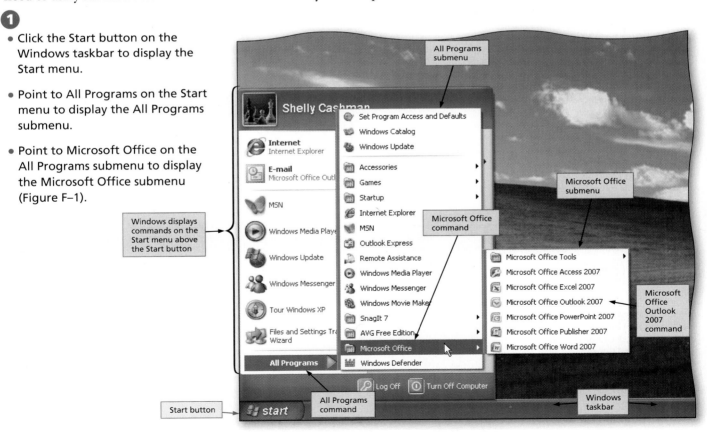

Figure F–1

2

- Click Microsoft Office Outlook 2007 to start Outlook. If necessary, click the Mail button in the Navigation Pane and then click the Inbox folder in the All Mail Folders pane to display the Inbox message pane (Figure F–2).

- If the Inbox – Microsoft Office Outlook window is not maximized, click the Maximize button next to the Close button on its title bar to maximize the window.

Q&A

What is a maximized window?

A maximized window fills the entire screen. When you maximize a window, the Maximize button changes to a Restore Down button.

3

- Drag the right border of the Inbox message pane to the right so that the Inbox message pane and the Reading pane have the same width.

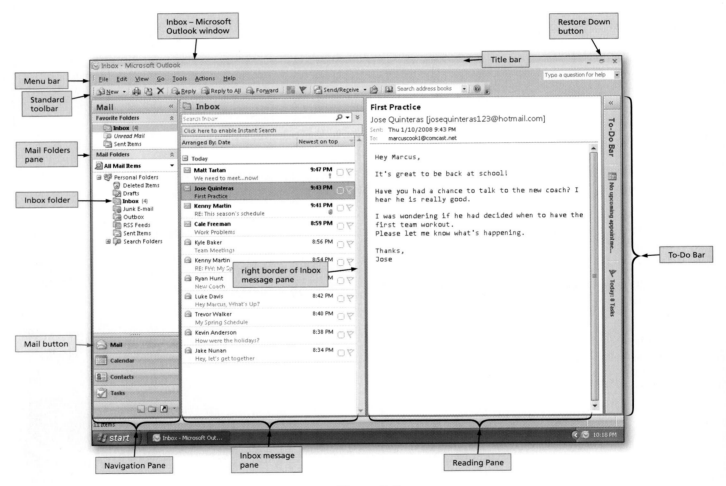

Figure F–2

Other Ways

1. Double-click Outlook icon on desktop, if one is present
2. Click Microsoft Office Outlook 2007 on Start menu

To Save a Contact List as a Text File and Display it in WordPad

The following steps save a contact list on a USB flash drive as a text file and display it in WordPad.

1

- Connect the USB flash drive containing the Data Files for Students to one of the computer's USB ports.

- With the Contacts window active, click the name bar of the first contact in the contact list.

- Press CTRL+A to select all the contacts.

- Click File on the menu bar to display the File menu (Figure F–3).

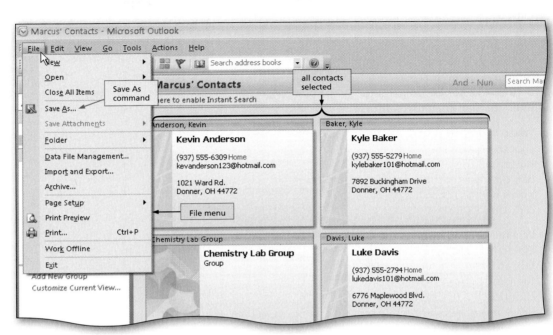

Figure F–3

2

- Click Save As on the File menu to display the Save As dialog box.

- Type Marcus' Contacts in the File name text box.

- If necessary, select Text Only in the Save as type box.

- Click the Save in box arrow and then select UDISK 2.0 (E:) (Figure F–4). (Your USB flash drive may have a different name and letter.)

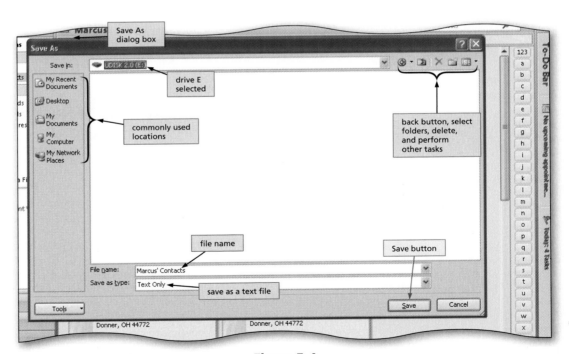

Figure F–4

- Click the Save button in the Save As dialog box.

- Click the Start button on the Windows taskbar, point to All Programs on the Start menu, point to Accessories on the All Programs submenu, and then click WordPad on the Accessories submenu to open the Wordpad text editor.

- When WordPad starts, click the Maximize button on the title bar, click File on the menu bar, and then click Open.

- When WordPad displays the Open dialog box, click the Files of type box arrow, select All Files, click the Look in box arrow, and then click UDISK 2.0 (E:) (your USB flash drive may have a different name and letter) in the Look in list.

- Double-click Marcus' Contacts to display Marcus' Contacts as a text file (Figure F–5).

- After viewing the text file, click the WordPad Close button.

contact list viewed as a text file

Figure F–5

To Import Subfolders

The following steps import subfolders.

1 Connect the USB flash drive containing the Data Files for Students to your computer.

2 Click File on the Outlook menu bar and then click Import and Export.

3 In the Import and Export Wizard dialog box, click Import from another program or file and then click the Next button.

4 In the Import a File dialog box, click Personal Folder File (.pst) and then click the Next button.

5 In the Import Personal Folders dialog box, click the Browse button to access drive E (your USB flash drive letter may be different), select the appropriate subfolder, click Open, and then click the Next button.

6 In the Import Personal Folders dialog box, select the appropriate folder from which to import and then click the Finish button.

Appendix G
Microsoft Business Certification Program

What Is the Microsoft Business Certification Program?

The Microsoft Business Certification Program enables candidates to show that they have something exceptional to offer – proved expertise in Microsoft Office 2007 programs. The two certification tracks allow candidates to choose how they want to exhibit their skills, either through validating skills within a specific Microsoft product or taking their knowledge to the next level and combining Microsoft programs to show that they can apply multiple skill sets to complete more complex office tasks. Recognized by businesses and schools around the world, more than 3 million certifications have been obtained in more than 100 different countries. The Microsoft Business Certification Program is the only Microsoft-approved certification program of its kind.

What Is the Microsoft Certified Application Specialist Certification?

The Microsoft Certified Application Specialist certification exams focus on validating specific skill sets within each of the Microsoft Office system programs. Candidates can choose which exam(s) they want to take according to which skills they want to validate. The available Application Specialist exams include:

- Using Microsoft® Windows Vista™
- Using Microsoft® Office Word 2007
- Using Microsoft® Office Excel® 2007
- Using Microsoft® Office PowerPoint® 2007
- Using Microsoft® Office Access 2007
- Using Microsoft® Office Outlook® 2007

> For more information and details on how Shelly Cashman Series textbooks map to Microsoft Certified Application Specialist certification, visit scsite.com/off2007/cert.

What Is the Microsoft Certified Application Professional Certification?

The Microsoft Certified Application Professional certification exams focus on a candidate's ability to use the 2007 Microsoft® Office system to accomplish industry-agnostic functions, for example Budget Analysis and Forecasting, or Content Management and Collaboration. The available Application Professional exams currently include:

- Organizational Support
- Creating and Managing Presentations
- Content Management and Collaboration
- Budget Analysis and Forecasting

Index

Quick Reference Summary

In the Microsoft Office Outlook 2007 program, you can accomplish a task in a number of ways. The following table provides a quick reference to each task presented in this textbook. The first column identifies the task. The second column indicates the page number on which the task is discussed in the book. The subsequent four columns list the different ways the task in column one can be carried out.

Microsoft Office Outlook 2007 Quick Reference Summary

Task	Page Number	Mouse	Ribbon	Shortcut Menu	Keyboard Shortcut
Accept Meeting	OUT 114		Open message | Accept button | send response | OK button		
Accept Task	OUT 108		Double-click Task Request | Accept		
Address E-Mail Message	OUT 27	Mail button in Inbox window	New Mail Message button on Message tab | To button		
Assign Task	OUT 106, 110		Assign Task button in Task window	Assign Task	
Attach File to E-Mail Message	OUT 31	Attach File button on Standard toolbar in Message window	Attach File button on Insert tab		
Categorize Calendar	OUT 124		Categorize button | All Categories *		
Change Appointment Date	OUT 92	Drag appointment to new date			
Change Appointment Month	OUT 93			Select appointment | Edit | Cut |scroll | click selected date | Paste	
Change Appointment Time	OUT 91	Drag appointment to new time or double-click appointment | edit Start time			
Change Meeting Time	OUT 117	Drag meeting to new time | Yes button | Send Update button			
Change Work Week	OUT 121	Open Calendar | Tools | Options | Calendar Options button | change dates in work week area			ALT+T, O, C

Microsoft Office Outlook 2007 Quick Reference Summary (continued)

Task	Page Number	Mouse	Ribbon	Shortcut Menu	Keyboard Shortcut
Close an E-Mail Message	OUT 15	Click Close button on title bar in Message window			ALT+F, C
Compose E-Mail Message	OUT 27	New button on Standard toolbar	New | Mail Message*		CTRL+N
Create Contact List	OUT 47	New button on Standard toolbar	Actions | New Contact*	New Contact	CTRL+SHIFT+C
Create Distribution List	OUT 58	New Contact button on Standard toolbar	New Contact button | Distribution List*		CTRL+SHIFT+L
Create E-Mail Signature	OUT 24		Tools | Options | Mail Format tab | Signatures button*		ALT+T, O
Create Event	OUT 95	Double-click appointment area day heading			
Create Personal Folder	OUT 44	Contacts button in Navigation pane	File | New | Folder*	New Contacts | New Folder	CTRL+SHIFT+E
Create Note	OUT 118		New Note button*		
Create View Filter	OUT 36		View | Arrange By*	Custom	
Delete Appointment	OUT 90		Select appointment | Delete button | OK*		
Delete E-Mail Message	OUT 21	Delete button on Standard toolbar	Select message | Delete*		CTRL+D or DELETE
Delete Subfolder	OUT 103			Right-click date banner | Delete | Yes	ALT+F, F, D
Display Contacts	OUT 52	Find a Contact box on Standard toolbar	Tools | Instant Search*		CTRL+E or ALT+T, I
Enter Appointment in Appointment Area	OUT 81	Select date in Date Navigator | select time | type appointment		File | Import and Export | Export to a file	
Enter Appointment in Appointment Window	OUT 82		Select date in Date Navigator | select time | click New Appointment button*	Actions menu | New Appointment	CTRL+N
Export Subfolder	OUT 101				
Find a Contact	OUT 50	Find a Contact box on Standard toolbar	Tools | Instant Search | Advanced Find*		CTRL+SHIFT+F
Flag E-Mail Messages	OUT 34	Follow Up button on Standard toolbar	Actions | Follow Up*	Follow Up	ALT+A, U
Forward E-Mail Message	OUT 20	Forward button on Standard toolbar		Forward	CTRL+F
Import Subfolder	OUT 104			File | Import and Export | Import from another program or file	
Month View	OUT 98	Month tab			
Move to Next Day	OUT 86		Go | Go to Date*	Go to Date	CTRL+G
Natural Language Phrasing	OUT 88			New Appointment button | enter time as natural language	
Open E-Mail Message	OUT 10	Double-click message	File | Open*	Open	CTRL+O

Microsoft Office Outlook 2007 Quick Reference Summary *(continued)*

Task	Page Number	Mouse	Ribbon	Shortcut Menu	Keyboard Shortcut
Print Calendar	OUT 127		Select calendar view | Print button | select style | OK*	File | Print	CTRL+P
Print Contact List	OUT 53	Print button on Standard toolbar	File | Print* or File | Print Preview | Print*		CTRL+P
Print E-Mail Message	OUT 15	Print button on Standard toolbar	File | Print | OK button*		CTRL+P, ENTER
Print Task List	OUT 127		Display task list | Print button | OK*		
Propose New Meeting Time	OUT 117		Propose New Time button in Meeting window	Propose New Time	ALT+A, S
Recurring Appointment	OUT 84		Recurrence button | Appointment Recurrence dialog box		
Reply to E-Mail Message	OUT 16	Reply button on Standard toolbar	Reply button on Message tab		CTRL+R
Save Contact List as Text File	OUT 60	Select name bar of contact | CTRL+A | File | Save As	File | Save As*		
Schedule Meeting	OUT 111		Open appointment | Scheduling button | Add Others button		
Send E-Mail Message	OUT 31	Send button in Message window	Send button on Insert tab		
Send Instant Message	OUT 139			Reply with Instant Message	
Send Meeting Update	OUT 117	Send Update button in Meeting window			
Set Message Importance, Sensitivity, and Delivery Options	OUT 38	New Mail Message button on Standard toolbar in Message window	Options dialog box launcher in the Options group on the Message tab		
Sort E-Mail Messages	OUT 35	Arrange By Command on View menu			ALT+V, A, E
Task List	OUT 99	Tasks button | New Task	New Task*	New | Task	CTRL+N
Work Week View	OUT 96	Week tab	Work Week on View menu*		ALT+V, R or CTRL+ALT+2

indicates a task handled by the Outlook Standard menu instead of the Ribbon